ABRAHAM ISAAC KOOK—

THE LIGHTS OF PENITENCE, THE MORAL PRINCIPLES, LIGHTS OF HOLINESS, ESSAYS, LETTERS, AND POEMS

TRANSLATION AND INTRODUCTION
BY
BEN ZION BOKSER

PREFACE
BY
JACOB AGUS
AND
RIVKA SCHATZ

PAULIST PRESS
NEW YORK • RAMSEY • TORONTO

Cover art:
The artist, RUTH ANAYA, is Canadian born and educated, and is a noted serigrapher and painter. She attended Montreal Museum of Fine Arts, McGill University, and Sir George Williams College. In 1952 she moved to New York City to continue her studies. Her prints and paintings are internationally represented in prominent private and public collections. She is a figurative expressionist, abstracting freely to convey mood.

RUTH ANAYA, in describing her feeling during the preparation of this book cover, explained, "As I put my pencil to the paper I could feel my right hand moving freely as though guided by the very image I was portraying. He was coming to life with little effort from me—the man, his aura, and his loves—Judaism, God, poetry, Zionism. I know this is how Abraham Isaac Kook wanted to be presented—a man bathed in spiritual light, his aura alive with hues of creativity and practicality and piety, all guarded by the Lions of Judah."

Design: Barbini Pesce & Noble, Inc.

Library of Congress
Catalog Card Number: 78-70465

ISBN: 0-8091-2159-X (Paper)
ISBN: 0-8091-0278-1 (Cloth)

Published by Paulist Press
Editorial Office: 1865 Broadway, New York, N.Y. 10023
Business Office: 545 Island Road, Ramsey, N.J. 07446

Printed and bound in the
United States of America

THE CLASSICS OF WESTERN SPIRITUALITY
A Library of the Great Spiritual Masters

CONTENTS

Editor of the Volume:

Ben Zion Bokser was born in Poland and he came to this country in 1920. He was ordained as rabbi at the Jewish Theological Seminary in 1931, and he received his Ph. D. degree at Columbia University in 1935. In 1964 the Jewish Theological Seminary awarded him the Doctor of Divinity degree *honoris causa*.

He has pursued a career in the active rabbinate, in the academic field, and as an author. Since 1934 he has held the pulpit of the Forest Hills Jewish Center, except for a two year period during the Second World War when he served as chaplain in the U.S. army. He has also taught at the Jewish Theological Seminary, and at the Hebrew University, and is presently serving as Adjunct Professor at Queens College.

He has authored twelve books including *Pharisaic Judaism in Transition, The Wisdom of the Talmud, From the World of the Cabbalah, The Legacy of Maimonides, Judaism and The Christian Predicament, Judaism – Profile of a Faith*, and *Jews, Judaism and the State of Israel*. His *Judaism — Profile of a Faith* was awarded a prize by the Jewish Book Council of America as a major contribution to Jewish thought. He also edited and translated into English the Daily, Sabbath and Festival Prayer Book and the High Holy Day Prayer Book.

Rabbi Bokser also serves as program editor of the Jewish Theological Seminary – NBC sponsored Eternal Light radio program. He was a contributing editor of the Encyclopedia of Religion, and his articles have appeared in the Encyclopedia Britannica, and the Encyclopedia Judaica, as well as in leading philosophical and scholarly journals. His writings have been translated into Hebrew, Italian, Spanish and Japanese.

Authors of the Preface

Rabbi Jacob B. Agus of Baltimore, Maryland, is Professor of Modern Jewish Thought at Dropsie University, and Visiting Professor of Religion at Temple University, was born in Poland and came to the United States in 1927. He was ordained by the Rabbi Isaac Elchanan Theological Seminary of Yeshiva University in New York City in 1935. The holder of a Ph.D. from Harvard University, Dr. Agus has enjoyed a distinguished career as an author, teacher and congregational rabbi. His books include *Modern Philosophies of Judaism*, *The Evolution of Jewish Thought*, *The Vision and the Way*, and *Banner of Jerusalem*, reissued as *Highpriest of Rebirth*, a study of the life and thought of Rabbi Kook.

Rivka Schatz-Uffenheimer was born in Rio de Janeiro, Brazil, and received her B.A., M.A., and Ph.D. at the Hebrew University in Jerusalem. She is presently Professor of Cabbalah and Hasidism at the Hebrew University in Jerusalem, where she teaches, among other subjects the philosophy of Rabbi Kook. Her published writings include *Hasidism as Mysticism: Quietistic Elements in 18th Century Hasidic Thought*, and a critical edition of *Maggid Devarov Le-Ya'akov* of the Maggid Dov Baer of Mezhirech, one of the classics in the early history of Hasidic thought. Her works are in Hebrew, with a synopsis in English added at the back of the book. Her preface to this work was written in Hebrew and translated into English by Rabbi Bokser.

Preface I

This book will be heartily welcomed by all students of religion and spirituality. The editor does not interpose himself between the reader and the fascinating personality of Rav Kook. Instead, Rabbi Bokser provides just enough guidance and background for the reader to confront at close range the rare genius of a titanic *homo religiosus*. Here are the private meditations as well as the public writings of a great religious leader, who was actively involved in all the facets of Jewish life.

Rav Kook was a mystic, a philosopher and a saint. He was a preeminent Talmudic scholar, respected for his vast erudition and for his bold legalistic innovations. He was also a Lurianic Cabbalist, engaged in cultivating the various grades of mystical ecstasy. At the same time, he responded graciously and at length to all who turned to him with questions relating to the philosophy of religion. However, his main concern was not the salvation of individuals, but the redemption of the Jewish people and of all mankind. As the leading prophet of religious Zionism, he labored and battled with impassioned fervor for the messianic redemption of the Jewish people, through the reclamation of the barren soil of the Holy Land and "the ingathering of the exiles."

His description of his ascent upon and descent from the mystical ladder are all the more significant because such documents are so rare in the entire range of Jewish literature. For various reasons, the experiences of great Jewish mystics were, if written down, kept out of the public domain and treasured only as part of "the hidden wisdom." Indeed, some historians have even assumed that the Jewish people lacked the capacity to feel the grandeur of the mystic's endeavor to sense the immediate presence of the Divine Being, either for ethnic reasons or because the Jewish religion stressed exclusively the transcendence and incomprehensibility of the Deity. Actually, the Biblical prophets and psalmists sought "the nearness of God" with all the passion of their souls. Philo was a Neo-platonic mystic, two centuries before Plotinus. During the Middle Ages, Jewish mysticism was so heavily overlaid with symbols by the various schools that the tortuous dialectic of the soul in its quest of "clinging to" God (*devekut*) can be discerned only uncertainly. Lurianic Cabbalah in the 16th century revived the mystical endeavor as a way of hastening the advent of the Messiah.

The Sabbataian-Frankist movement awakened the slumbering ghosts of Gnosticism within the Jewish mystical tradition. Then the Hasidic movement burst upon the scene and transformed Cabbalistic mysticism into a popular mass movement, with the various *zaddikim* teaching their trusted disciples to attain at least some levels (*madregot*) of the Holy Spirit (*Ruah ha-Kodesh*), which was conceived as a dynamic flow of grace from the divine Pleroma to the souls of men.

However, even among the *zaddikim* there were few attempts to describe the various psychological states of the mystic, as he rises to the point of total absorption within the highest Emanations and declines thereafter to the "dark night of the soul."

Rav Kook combined an exuberant and lyrical literary talent with the genius of mysticism. Furthermore, he represented with unequaled authority the main currents of Jewish thought. Though he was occasionally embroiled in controversy, he sought to embrace and to harmonize the rationalism of Maimonides with the ethnic romanticism of Judah Halevi and the personal romanticism of Ibn Gabirol, as well as the contributions of the Cabbalists and the Hasidim. Thus he lived and taught, not as a one-sided philosopher or as a maverick saint, but as an authentic exponent of the "sacred tradition" as a whole.

Hence, the great significance of his writings for the understanding of the entire spectrum of the Orthodox tradition—from the extreme end of naive transcendence in legalistic literature to that of vibrant immanence in the life and thought of mystical pietists.

Indeed, he reached out beyond the boundaries of Orthodoxy to the newly emerging socialists, secularists, spokesmen of liberal Judaism—above all, to the Zionist pioneers in the land of Israel. Determined to find "the holy sparks" in every ideology, he regarded the modern Zionist movement as a direct instrument of God in the furtherance of messianic redemption. Along with the medieval poet and philosopher Judah Halevi, he believed that only in the land of Israel would the genius of Hebraic prophecy be revived, with salutary benefits for all mankind. His closest disciple, Rav David Cohen, titled his own book *Kol Hanevuah* [The Voice of Prophecy].

Rav Kook's writings illustrate the principle of "intersubjective" potency—the deeper we probe into our own being, the closer we come to the understanding in depth of our fellowmen. For he drew his inspiration and his ideas almost entirely from the domain of the Jewish "sacred tradition," with only occasional glances at the intellectual scene of the Western world. Yet, his message is of peculiar relevance to the searching souls of our time, regardless of creedal and ethnic identifications. Briefly, he called for the integration and harmonization of the ideals deriving from all sources, in that all "lights of holiness" derive from God and lead back to Him. The entire range of creation is determined by two currents, which flow in opposite directions—the current of "expansion" (*hitpashtut*), whereby creative power flows from God down to the lowest levels of the material world, and the current of "unification" (*histalkut*), whereby "reflected light" (*hozer*) ascends back toward its source. The first flow enters into and vitalizes the various receptive creatures, diversifying as it descends; the second emerges out of a diverse, fragmented and even distorted existential reality and, in its quest of the divine source, harmonizes, unifies and redeems "the sparks of holiness," which are scattered throughout the world. In regard to the flow of power and grace from God, we need to render ourselves receptive and open to His love. All religious rituals are designed to serve this end. In regard to the return of the reflected "lights of holiness," we need to train ourselves to understand in love the ideologies and movements that stir mankind, separating the seeds of love from the shells of collective pride. Hence, the indispensability of training in the disciplines of religious humanism. It follows that religious faith and humanistic culture are not mutually contradictory, but rather are two aspects of the same dynamic, human-divine interaction.

Like Teilhard de Chardin, Kook regarded the process of cosmic evolution as the advance of nature toward divine perfection. Human history, too, moves toward "the Kingdom of the Almighty," when all forms of evil will be overcome. However, his 19th-century faith in progress was modified by the Cabbalistic doctrine of "shattering of the vessels" in this "world of separation." The emergence of a new ideal may cause a catastrophe because of the unreadiness of humanity to integrate fresh divine power within the established intellectual and social categories.

Evil is not a self-contained force, but a relative absence of the spirit of wholeness. The part seeks to usurp that which belongs to the whole. The lights of holiness are refracted, separated into their components and embodied in different institutions, which may be arrayed against one another. So the very incursion of divine power and grace into the structure of society may result in the fragmentation of ideals, with genuine idealists turning against one another; bifurcating society into hostile camps; threatening revolution, war and chaos—hence the crying need today for the spirit of harmonization and unification.

More than in any previous epoch, our age is tragically polarized. In religion, a deep abyss separates the believers of all traditional creeds from the camp of the secularists. The religious community itself is torn between the opposite trends of literalist orthodoxy and the liberal spirit of ecumenism.

Rav Kook addressed himself to this fundamental polarity between fragmentation and unification. He did not pretend to offer a super-plan for the solution of all problems, but his own religious experience led him to believe that the key to human advancement and peace lay in the hearts of people. They could reinforce the ascending, integrating, harmonizing trends in their own souls, thereby also strengthening the same forces in all men and in nature. For all mankind is mystically one body and one soul, and even physical nature is affected by the yearnings of mankind.

Within his own psyche, Kook experienced the dynamics of mystical life—the hunger for illumination by the presence of God and the anguish of the fall from His "nearness." In spite of his natural shyness, he described the rhythm of his soul in the hope that others would be inspired to follow his example and render themselves fitting "channels" for the flow of divine power and grace, reinforcing the trends toward unification as against those of fragmentation.

Readers of this volume should study it as a splendid hymn, celebrating the unity of God, the world and mankind. Beneath the overlay of beliefs and myths, characteristic of his milieu, they should discern the testimony of a prophetic soul, assuring us that it is in God that we live and move and find our true selves.

Jacob B. Agus
Baltimore, Maryland
June, 1978

Preface II

"And the people, returned to life, will head the wealth of life's secrets."
From a poem by Rabbi Kook

One cannot overestimate the significance of Rabbi Bokser's achievement in making available in this volume an English translation of the choicest writings of Rabbi Abraham Isaac Ha-Kohen Kook, his philosophical works and his poetry. Rabbi Bokser, moreover, presents to the reader Rabbi Kook's world view in a comprehensive, scholarly introduction that enables us to gain a profound understanding of his nature as a spiritual personality. I believe that Rabbi Kook was the best possible choice from the world of modern thought in Judaism to be included among the great masters of the spiritual life.

Rabbi Kook wrote at a time that marked a turbulent turning point not only for the Jewish people, but, in an ideological sense, for the entire world. This was the period of the Jewish renaissance that found its focus in the Zionist movement. This was also the time when historical materialism became an established force in European politics, the time of the Russian revolution and the formation of the communist regime. The materialistic philosophy of life posed a crisis not only in the world of Jewish thought, but in Christian culture as well. Rabbi Kook was of the opinion that Christian culture lacked the strength to withstand the challenge of historical materialism, which attacked it with full force.

In the ten years before the outbreak of the First World War, when he served as rabbi of Jaffa and the southern settlements in Eretz Yisrael, Rabbi Kook devoted his best thinking to the significance of the Jewish renaissance in the framework of the spiritual history of the nations of the world. It was his hope that the Jewish national rebirth would also be the historic occasion for the renewal of the promise of the spirit of Judaism and the spirit of humanity.

All Rabbi Kook's teaching oscillates between these two poles. One is the focus toward the inner world of Judaism, a reassessment of its value system and an attempt at an inner reinterpretation to liberate the creative energies of Judaism so as to function in a contemporary idiom. There is no effort here toward a new definition of Judaism, but rather an endeavor to enhance its will and vitality. If a spirit of rebellion is discernible in the style of his writing, it is the resistance of the tradition to being adapted toward new patterns of thought. The linkage of the broad horizons of the spirit of humanity with the element of the Jewish renaissance are most important here. The other is the clarification toward the outside world, a restatement of the significance of the religious experience as a knowledge of God. This "knowledge" was fed by the utopian spirit that informs all his writings and shaped the modern interpretation of his messianic philosophy.

The utopianism of Rabbi Kook seeks for itself new norms for human consciousness or, to be more exact, it believes in the expansion of that consciousness to a point of overcoming the phenomenological perception, which "fragments" and "confines" existence. Here comes to expression the anguish of the mystic who has discovered, through the trials of his own experience, the unity of existence. He knows the error of the different philosophies derived from following the side roads of the truth, the basic truth not having been revealed to them— the certainty of God's presence in existence. This certainty is the noblest utopian vision of Rabbi Kook, who believed that this was also the answer to the cultural confusions and the intellectual sorrow suffered by humanity. The logic of his argument maintained that this intuitive truth was given to the Jewish people as the singular bearer of the utopian ideal. They are the people who were tested by the sufferings of their history and by intellectual challenges that prepared them with the keenest vision for a confrontation with the truth.

He does not speak in the idiom of the Middle Ages about the chosenness of the Jewish people. He speaks rather in the widest possible terms of existentialism, in the categories rooted in experience. In his essay "The Culture of the Jewish People" (1909), Rabbi Kook states: "We began to say something of immense importance among ourselves and to the entire world, but we have not yet finished it. We are in the midst of our discourse, and we do not wish, and we are not able, to stop. We shall not abandon our distinctive way of life nor our universal aspirations. The truth is so rich that we stammer; our speech is still in exile. In the course of time we shall be able to express what we seek with our total being. Only a people that has completed what it started can leave the scene of history. To begin and not to finish—this is not in accordance with the pattern of existence."

The stress on Jewish existence as exemplifying "total being" is one of the more typical modes of expression of Rabbi Kook. The message of total being is also the promise of the Jewish people to humanity. Thus he also expresses himself in his important work whose publication began in 1914 but has not yet been completed to this day; that is, the book *Arple Tohar*: "People live with intellectual secondhands, with shadows of shadows from the original illuminations that act on their spirits. The original must be of the very purest.... But when the truth is neglected, everything is impoverished and people groan under the burden of the afflictions, the lusts, the sorrows, the declines, the wickedness, the deceptive loves and imaginings, and they are unable to come out of the confusion, either in this world or in the next. The noble spirits of humanity are therefore obligated to proclaim the name of God, the God of the universe, in His world. And if obstructions developed and individuals cannot summon the whole world to God, in all matters of thought and feeling, then a people must issue the call. The people must call out of its inner being, as an individual of great spiritual stature issues the call from his inner being. For a whole people to proclaim the name of God as an expression of its being—this is found only among the Jewish people" (p. 28).

Who is this "Jewish people" on whose shoulders Rabbi Kook had placed the messianic role at that time? The end of the 19th and the beginning of the 20th century was a time of the greatest crisis for the Jewish people. The crisis was not external. Pogroms, blood libels and religious persecutions were not a rare occurrence in the history of this people. The greater part of the Jewish people were concentrated in eastern Europe. They suffered the crisis of the *haskalah* [enlightenment] and the emancipation. The classic *yeshivot* that served for generations as centers of Jewish culture were abandoned as the enchantment of the outer world promising equality to the Jews swept away the best of the youth. The Lithuanian Yeshivah of Volozhin, too, gasped for breath in this particular moment of history, when people like the poet Bialik, the writer Berdichevsky and the thinker Rabbi Kook left it. Each one of them "left" in his own way; each one rebelled in his own way. Many of the rebels never returned to the world of Judaism, even after they became disillusioned with the emancipation. But in the very place where you find despair you also find hope—hope for physical survival and the search for a basis of a new spirit of religious faith. Zionism as a movement of liberation and rebirth pointed toward the normalization of Jewish existence in Eretz Yisrael, the land where came to birth the people as well as the idea of Judaism, where the Bible was written and where the prophets struggled for a just society. The dream of restoration was the domain embraced by Zionism, even of secular Zionism and of the pioneers of the early *aliyot* (migrations). Even when they interpreted this ideal in the spirit of the socialism of their generation, there still clung to it the pulsating presence of the romanticism of the distant past. The creative energy of the Jewish people found its fulfillment in converting the desert into a place of habitation and in the establishment of an egalitarian society. The thinkers of that generation translated the structure of Jewish values into the language of secularism.

This is what Rabbi Kook found when he set foot on the shores of Jaffa in 1904. The secular revolution fed the new Hebrew literature, and it was also a concomitant to the revival of the modern Hebrew language under the sponsorship of Ben Yehuda.

Whoever retained anything of the religious spirit was looked upon as belonging to the world of the Jewish "ghetto," and his esteem fell among the intellegiensia of the workers in Eretz Yisrael. The world of religion was looked upon as the closed, conservative world, whose time had passed. This was especially so in Eretz Yisrael, because this world was represented primarily by the Orthodox of the old *yishuv* in Jerusalem, which did not look favorably on the Zionist endeavor. Religious Zionism had not yet taken root in Eretz Yisrael in those days.

Who was this Jewish people about whom Rabbi Kook wrote as the bearer of the promise and of the light? Who among the circles described here could accept this ideology? I am reminded of a short story told to me by Rabbi Zevi Yehuda, the son of Rabbi Kook, of his recollections from the Jaffa period. Once the writer Brener—one of the literary leaders of the Labor movement, the writer of bereavement and defeatism, who was murdered some days later in Jaffa by the Arabs— came visiting Rabbi Kook, together with the writer A. Z. Rabinowitz. As he walked hither and thither he said to Rabbi Kook: "Tell me, your honor, how am I to understand this, that you write about 'light, light, light,' [most of Rabbi Kook's writings are indeed so designated], while I feel the dark in every part of my soul!" This short and sarcastic statement underscores the gap between reality and anticipation, between famished days, and nights for dreaming about life on a new level of greatness as Rabbi Kook hoped for it, a break with the life of confinement in time, and a sweep toward the eternal truth in the bright light of the new promise to the human spirit.

And though the pronouncements of Rabbi Kook appear to stand outside the historic horizon of his generation—and there may perhaps have been some of that character also—all the issues from which they grew were the issues of his generation.

The perspective of his vision is not a continuation of the Jewish mystical writing he had read. He is not the continuation of the Zohar or the Cabbalah of the Ari [Rabbi Isaac Luria] or of any other Cabbalistic work. His mysticism is not only new in its answers but also in its questions. If I have stated that his thought was inspired by realism, I have also stated that the reality was seen from the perspective of secularity. There is therefore the necessity to find an answer to this problem, for this is a paradox difficult to understand, how to explain in a manner reflecting the teachings immanent in the Jewish tradition that an "offending generation" was the generation worthy of seeing the beginning of the redemption and that it was destined to be the bearer of the great spiritual promise that is so tied up with the revitalization of the religious consciousness. However, Rabbi Kook believed that the Jewish people in its totality is the bearer of the promise, and not solely Orthodox Judaism! On the contrary, that Judaism which has narrowed itself to the issues of "tref and kosher" [ritually forbidden and permitted food], the "allowed and disallowed," cannot serve as the source from which will emerge the new song that "the mouth of the Lord shall pronounce" (Isa. 62:2).

The new demands of life brought him to contemplate the sources of human energy, where he hoped to find his answer.

The creative energy was centered in those days in the secular world of the pioneers who wrought the revolution in his time. Those heretics represented for him the wellsprings of renewal, and he was ready to offer a religious interpretation to their heresy. Those who denied with such ardor the sovereignty of God will be ready in one of these historic hours to battle for the great redemption he defined as "a firm will and great force to bring redemption to the world, to purge away all the obscurantism in life, and to overcome all its weaknesses. Everything depends on our will to rise to the heights of the higher holiness, in a continuing and original probing, in a firm hallowing of the flesh and the spirit by imitating God through walking in His ways" (*Arple Tohar*, p. 35).

Rabbi Kook did not believe that there exists an independent zone of the secular. It may be that his perception was influenced by the philosophy of Hasidism, which originally sought to find its way by closing the gap between the secular and the sacred. Perhaps we have here a new incarnation of that position as it came to new life in Eretz Yisrael under new historic and sociological circumstances.

But as to the substance of the matter—he grasped the concept of holiness as the most luminous perspective in which to see the possibility of defining the secular, the possibility of perceiving the transparent nature of existence, or, in his own words, "how the general light that abounds with life and engenders life in the world penetrates all particulars." The "darkness" in which all particulars are set—or if we translate this as existence in time—this brings about the denial of eternity. It is difficult for the human spirit to grasp the link between the fragmentary and the whole, the temporal and the timeless, between matter and spirit, for the "particulars are not [fully] illumined." In the realm of history also it is difficult for a person to grasp the "totality," and therefore he claims that it does not exist. He becomes an "unbeliever."

Rabbi Kook's mysticism claims to have broken this "darkness." The advantage unbelievers have is that they sounded the cry "We do not see, we do not understand!" But in the potency of the cry there is also the potency for breaking out of it, and thus the crisis serves the force of the transformation. This is how Rabbi Kook defines his belief in this process: "Our temporal existence is only one spark of an eternal existence of the most endless beauty, and it is impossible to bring to fruition the treasure of the good hidden in the domain of the temporal except to the extent of its harmonization with the life of eternity. This inner perception is immanent in the spirit of all existence, and all the spiritual conflicts will be unable to swerve it from this position, but only to clear the path for it; and even that which appears to contradict serves in a deeper grasp of the truth as supportive of it" (*Arple Tohar*, p. 36).

The mysticism of the transparency of existence, which removes the darkness from human consciousness, became the crowning perception in the philosophy of Rabbi Kook at a time when the Jewish people was destined to experience the beginning of redemption, fulfilling a substantive role of utopian messianism in the broadest sense of the term.

The messianic concept in Judaism had for hundreds of years been filled with a utopian content concerning the cosmic order as a whole. But here we have an additional element embracing the ideological issues of Rabbi Kook's time. Not only did the subject matter of mysticism change by including the natural life in this order, but it also served as a stimulus to daily life in Eretz Yisrael.

We must not assume that Rabbi Kook was an odd exception in concerning himself with utopian questions. On the contrary, in the secular camp of the pioneers, too, there was a preoccupation with a socio-national utopianism, especially among the members of the *kibbutzim*, particularly the Gordonia movement established by A. D. Gordon. This man, called "the sage of Degania" [the name of the kibbutz where he lived], was the proud advocate of the "religion of labor" and he spoke about the "people of man." The latter is undoubtedly a utopian concept, though it is also a profanation of the classic concept of Judaism that recognizes such corporate terms, as in referring to the "people of Israel." The utopian focus shifted here to the social ethos, in a reassessment of its values.

Despite all this, Rabbi Kook remained a lonely figure as a mystic. His many writings were published only in part and after the passage of many years. Perhaps his metaphysical "hastening of the coming of the end" had in it something to frighten even his closest intimates among his followers.

His vision was altogether one of grandeur and richness, and the heart found it difficult to convey to the lips all that he thought. There was here a kind of fear because of the imbalance between the poor historic situation and the mighty daring of the spiritual claim. The call to break out of the spiritual confinement in which the person finds himself, the testimony to the riches of the spiritual life, and the faith that all existence, of itself, is in a process that by necessity carries it to revelation— these are landmark proclamations of his teaching: "Once the concept of the grandeur of existence has been grasped by the imagination it cannot be voided. It must necessarily endure, and it is endowed with the vitality to battle for its survival; whoever would assault it injures only himself. If a multitude of thoughts are conjured up contradicting it, they are bound to make their peace with it; they will be reconciled to it, it will not be reconciled to them. Everything ascends and does not descend, everything develops and does not become impoverished and retreat" (*Arple Tohar*, p. 41).

Indeed, this is the call of immense significance that is well known to the great mystics.

Rivka Schatz Uffenheimer
Hebrew University
Jerusalem, June 1978

Foreword

I feel privileged to present the major writings of Rabbi Kook in a form that makes them accessible to the English reader. Rabbi Kook belongs among the truly great masters of spirituality in the history of Judaism. The well-springs of illumination were open generously to him, and he drew from them in great profusion. One is astonished at the profundity of his insights, at the far-reaching vision reflected in his writings. They represent a renewal of Judaism in its classic authenticity and its message speaks with remarkable cogency to Jews, as well as to all sensitive spirits in every faith community.

The present study begins with an introductory essay, which presents the basic outline of Rabbi Kook's biography as well as an assessment of his religious philosophy. Then follow in translation his basic writings, each prefaced with a brief prefatory statement indicating the literary and ideological context in which it appeared. These include *The Lights of Penitence* (Orot Hateshuvah); selected essays from his three volume work *The Lights of Holiness* (Orot Hakodesh); *The Moral Principles* (Midot Harayah); ten of his philosophical essays which appeared in different publications; selected letters from his three volumes of correspondence (Igrot Harayah); and his poems. All the translations are original, including the translation of Biblical verses quoted by Rabbi Kook. The reader is forewarned that these may diverge from the translations in the standard English version of the Bible with which he may be familiar.

I acknowledge with gratitude the assistance I received in preparing this work from colleagues and friends, and from members of my family. I am especially thankful to Rabbi Salaman Faber who reviewed the English version against the Hebrew original and offered some helpful criticism. Professor Arthur Green read the manuscript and was helpful not only in his comments on the translation, but also in suggesting the arrangement and structure of the work. I am grateful to my wife who assisted me with her critical comments and suggestions, as she has done with all my writings, to my son, Professor Baruch Bokser, for his many stimulating suggestions while this work was in progress, and to my daughter and son-in-law, Miriam and Dov Caravella, whose spiritual sensitivity stimulated my own openess to the spiritual life. My secretary, Mrs. Shirley Tendler, typed the manuscript in the various stages of its development and offered me other technical assistance in bringing this work to completion. I am also grateful to the Mosad Harav Kook and its director, Dr. Yitzhak Rafael, for granting me permission to translate the texts published by the Mosad. Richard Payne, my editor at the Paulist Press, and his assistant, Marianne Papaj, extended to me many courtesies for which I am deeply appreciative.

As I contemplate the unparalleled richness of Rabbi Kook's thought I am moved to offer the prayer enjoined in Jewish tradition on one who is in the presence of a sage in the wisdom of the Torah: "Be praised, O Lord, Sovereign of the universe, who imparts of Your wisdom on those who revere You."

May this work help bring Rabbi Kook's thought to the attention of a larger public that they, too, may be enriched by it, and that by his light they may see light.

ABRAHAM ISAAC KOOK
1865 - 1935

Introduction

The Religious Philosophy of Rabbi Kook

The following lines appear in a poem by Rabbi Abraham Isaac Kook:

Expanses divine my soul craves.
Confine me not in cages,
Of substance or of spirit.
I am love-sick—
I thirst, I thirst for God,
As a deer for water brooks.
Alas, who can describe my pain,
Who will be a violin to express the songs of my grief,
I am bound to the world,
All creatures, all people are my friends,
Many parts of my soul
Are intertwined with them,
But how can I share with them my light?

These lines express a mood that is characteristic of all Rabbi Kook's writings. The theme to which he returned again and again in his poetry as in his prose, is an unsatiable longing for God, an almost ecstatic affirmation of life, of the world, as suffused with the wonder of God's creation, and a struggle to find the word or deed that would illumine other minds with the light that shone so brightly in his.

1

He was born to a deeply pious and learned Jewish family in 1865, in Grieve, Latvia, the restricted world of the Jewish ghetto in Eastern Europe, but he was in constant rebellion against all that restricts and narrows the human spirit. He was a prolific writer, but he was also a man of action. He served as rabbi in the Lithuanian towns of Zoimel (1888-1895) and Boisk (1895-1904) and as chief rabbi of Jaffa, Palestine (1904-1919). While stranded by the First World War during a visit to Europe, he served as rabbi of a congregation in London, England (1917-1918). His career was climaxed by his election to the most august rabbinic office in world Jewry, the chief rabbinate of Jerusalem, and of the whole Jewish community in Palestine. He served in this post during sixteen stormy years till his death in 1935. His voluminous writings still await exploration and assessment but it is clear from even a brief acquaintance with his ideas that he belongs among the immortals of thought in the history of Judaism.

Rabbi Kook's thought differs sharply from that of classic Jewish theologians such as Philo, Judah Halevi and Maimonides. The classicists sought primarily to defend their faith against the challenge of various ideologies current in their time: Philo against Greek philosophy; Halevi against philosophic rationalism and against the rival faiths of Christianity and Islam, as well as against the Jewish heresy known as Karaism; Maimonides against Aristotelian naturalism which had a revival in the early Middle Ages and which taught the heretical doctrine of the eternity of the universe. Rabbi Kook's writings are almost wholly devoid of religious polemics. He was essentially an existentialist thinker to whom theological issues as such were of secondary importance. The essence of religion for him was in its existential implications, its concern to bring all life under the discipline of divine ideals. The test of religion at its highest was in the passion it inspires to bend life toward ethical and moral perfection.

The attempts to prove God's existence by dialectical arguments as an inference from the existing world was for him ultimately a nonsequitur. Every effort to probe God's nature, as He is in Himself, is a sterile endeavor, a presumption, and represents a kind of "spiritual idolatry" (*Orot*, Mosad Harav Kook, Jerusalem 1963, p. 124). We know God primarily through faith, in response to the prompting of the heart. It is only on the level of primitivism that we focus on God as an essence, an entity, apart from the world. As we rise toward maturity our focus shifts from a preoccupation with God as a spearate entity to divine ideals, which emanate from God and seek embodiment in the structure of life. These ideals become man's moral imperatives under whose impulse he is forever seeking to refashion his life and that of the world toward truth, justice, freedom and peace.

Rabbi Kook is an example of the Jewish mystical tradition in its pure form. He was inspired by Rabbi Judah Loew of Prague, a Cabbalist who freed the Cabbalah from superstitious admixtures, seeing in it largely a way to the immediacy of God. The immediacy of God shines through all of Rabbi Kook's writings. All things, for Rabbi Kook, were a crust with an inner essence, a divine dimension; seen aright all things have the capacity to reveal the light of holiness.

Rabbi Kook's writings are the direct outpourings of the soul as it contemplates the mystery of being, as it feels the stirring of God. His most significant writings were left in the form of a journal, in notebooks that constitute a kind of spiritual diary. The entries in this diary read like poems or prose-poems, and they are independent meditations, each born in the newness of the experience that continued to unfold day by day. The editor of these works, Rabbi David Cohen of Jerusalem, has attempted to arrange these meditations in systematic categories, but their essentially independent nature

persists and remains unobscured by the attempted sys-
tematization.

The thought of Rabbi Kook cannot be conveyed through
thematic interpretation. It is, like all poetry, like every art
form, to be experienced from within, by direct exposure. It is
only to gain some inkling into the kind of ideational world
Rabbi Kook inhabited that we offer a glimpse of what an
outsider looking in beholds, in purely thematic terms. It must
be deemed as no more than a prelude to the experience of
studying Rabbi Kook directly, in his own idiom.

The most revolutionary aspect of Rabbi Kook's thought
was his role as Cabbalist. He saw the whole universe stirred
by the pulsating energies emanating from the divine source of
all existence. But his interest in mysticism was not confined to
the scholarly and pietistic study of Cabbalistic texts. He saw
the divine illumination as an ongoing inpouring of divine light
upon those sensitive to receive it, and he portrayed the history
of Judaism in terms of an ongoing tension between the new
light evoking a constant regeneration of life, and a heritage
from earlier illuminations that had become crystallized in hallowed texts, a tension, in other words, between new creativity
and tradition. Tradition is a moment in the endless flow of
eternity, wrenched from the whole and given shape and form
that permits us to continually re-encounter it. But at the same
time it distracts us from new light pressing on us. Tradition is
precious as far as it goes, but it helps to keep us in the confinement of finitude.

The perception that the hallowed texts do not exhaust
the divine-human dialogue and that God is releasing new light
upon his world is responsible for his own inner anguish. Rabbi
Kook was torn between the traditional pietist and the harbinger
of new light. This comes vividly to expression in a short
meditation on the "holiness of silence." The summation of this
essay is in the final paragraph: "If a person who has risen to the

4

holiness of silence should lower himself to a particularized form of divine service, in prayer, study, the limited problems of morality, he will suffer and feel oppressed. He will feel that his soul, which embraces all existence, is being pressed as though with prongs, to surrender her to the lowland, where everything exists within a prescribed measure, to the narrowness of a particular path, when all paths are open to him, all abounding in light, all abounding in life's treasures" (*Orot Hakodesh*, Vol. II, Agudah Lehotzoat Sifre Harayan Kook, Jerusalem, 1938, p. 307).

This same tension is reflected in Rabbi Kook's attitude toward the *halakha*. He was a great halakhist and a staunch advocate of halakhic discipline in personal and group life. But he was sensitive to the divine rhythm that evoked the halakhic formulations but of which they are only imperfect expressions. He was a champion of the *halakha* but his heart was continually drawn to the higher reality that transcends it. In one passage he put it thus: "Great anguish is experienced by one who leaves the wide horizons of pure contemplation, suffered with feeling, with poetry of the most exquisite beauty, and enters the study of the confined world of halakhic enactments. ... A person who is stirred by a soul ennobled with the splendor of holiness suffers frightful anguish at the chains of confinement when he leaves the one branch of study for the other" (*Orot Hakodesh*, Vol. I, Agudah Lehotzoat Sifre Harayah Kook, Jerusalem, 1938, p. 28).

As halakhic authority charged with responsibility for rendering decisions that were to become the norm of law in the Jewish community, he revealed a flexibility that made him anathema to the zealots of the older type of traditionalism. Thus he sponsored a *takkana* that exempted Jewish agriculture from the restrictions of the sabbatical year. The zealots of the old order continue to ignore this *takkana* to this day, and are careful to avoid purchasing agricultural products from Jewish growers during the periods that their calculations tell them fall within the sabbatical year.

INTRODUCTION

Rabbi Kook's thought was dominated by two primary concepts, particularity and universality. All existence was for him an interdependent, organic, universal whole. Each particular individual is endowed with a unique identity, and feels called on to cultivate this identity and to assert it in interaction with other individuals. But particular individuals are not self-sufficient or autonomous. They exist within the pattern of the whole, they are nourished by the whole, and find their purposive fulfillment by contributing the fruits of their unique resources to the life of the whole. In the words of Rabbi Kook: "The more clearly one studies the character of individual human souls, the more baffled one becomes over the great difference between personalities. . . . It is, however, precisely through their differentiations that they are all united toward one objective, to contribute toward the perfection of the world, each person according to his special talent. Surely one must marvel at the higher wisdom wherein by an inner, mysterious power known only to God, these opposites are integrated and related one to the other, so that through the fusion of all the diverse minds and physiognomies, there emerges a unified structure of consummate harmony" (*Olat Rayah*, Mosad Harav Kook, and Agudah Lehotzoat Sifre Harayah Kook, Vol. I, Jerusalem, 1939, p. 388).

This vision of universality that filled Rabbi Kook's world with an aura of harmony and goodness was a discovery toward which one grows in the course of his odyssey in enlightenment. But life as it is generally obscures it, and what one encounters in the world is often hostility and open conflict between individuals and groups, between ideologies and life-styles. All such antagonism, according to Rabbi Kook, derives from an exaggerated isolationist individualism, from a loyalty of persons toward their private world, without realizing that their private world is only a partial, a fragmentary entity that needs to be complemented by the rest of life. It is born of the failure to orchestrate oneself with the rest of existence, in the universal ensemble toward which all particular beings are meant to contribute. "All the defects of the world, the material and the spiritual," wrote Rabbi Kook, "they all derive from the fact that every individual sees only the one aspect of existence that pleases him, and all other aspects that are uncomprehended by him seem to deserve purging from the world. And the thought leaves its imprint in individuals and groups, on generations and epochs, that whatever is outside one's own is destructive and disturbing. The result of this is a multiplication of conflict" (*Orot Hakodesh*, Vol. I, p. 121).

The individualism that places self-interest in opposition to a concern for others is, according to Rabbi Kook, a false individualism, which distorts life and begets pernicious consequences. It teaches men to see each other as competitors and even as enemies, instead of as what they truly are, sharers in a common adventure, who are meant to collaborate, and thereby lighten their respective burdens. In truth, self-interest merges with a concern for others, self-love expands to include the love of our fellowman. As Rabbi Kook put it: "In the light of the mighty idea of the unity of existence there is eliminated the problem of self-love, which some have made into the source of all sin, and others as the source of all morality. There is only the love for all things, which is in truth an enlightened, a nobler kind of self-love. The distorted love that loves only the puny spark seen in our myopic vision and hates the authentic love—this is a kind of blindness that is foolish as it is wicked" (*Orot Hakodesh*, Vol. II, p. 586).

The world of exaggerated and competing individualisms is a chaotic world, an unfinished world; it is waiting to find its completion through a disciplining by the spirit of harmony that will seek to effect reconciliation and unity. The goal of unity is to be realized not by suppressing any individual, but by moving all to contain their exaggerations and to find scope in the whole. Rabbi Kook put it thus: "A chaotic world stands before us as long as we have not attained to that degree of higher perfection of uniting all life-forces and all their diverse tendencies. As long as each one exalts himself, claiming, I am sovereign, I and none other—there cannot be peace in our midst. . . . All our endeavors must be directed toward disclosing the light of general harmony, which derives not from suppressing any power, any thought, any tendency, but by bringing each of them within the vast ocean of light infinite, where all things find their unity, where all is ennobled, all is exalted, all is hallowed" (*ibid.*, p., 588).

In Rabbi Kook's world of thought, the love of God carried with it a love for all God's creatures, an openness to all ideas and a continued passion to perfect life through reconciliation, harmony and peace. Said Rabbi Kook, "Whoever contemplates divine ideas in their purity cannot hate or be disdainful of any creature or any talent in the world, for through each does the Creator reveal Himself" (*Orot Hakodesh*, Vol. I, p. 327). But man's response to his fellowman must be more than the negative response of tolerance; it must reach the higher category of love. In the words of Rabbi Kook: "The higher holiness abounds with love, kindness and tolerance. . . . Hatred, sternness and severity are the result of forgetting God and the suppression of the light of holiness. The more the quest for God grows in a person's heart, the more does the love for all people grow in him, and he loves even wicked men and heretics, and he desires to perfect them, for he does indeed perfect them by his own great faith" (*ibid.*, p. 317).

Rabbi Kook called for a sympathetic hearing to all ideas, for in all ideas there is a core of valid truth that waits to be recognized and claimed from its frequent exaggerations in order to enter the process of intellectual and spiritual fermentation by which a larger truth is born. As Rabbi Kook put it: "Each body of thought has its own logic and all ideas are tied to each other by a systematic relatedness. . . . There is no such thing as a vain or useless thought . . . since each emanates from the same source in the divine wisdom. If there are thoughts that appear futile or empty, the futility and the emptiness are only in the outer garb in which these thoughts are enwrapped. But if we probe into all their inwardness, we shall find that they, too, offer us the sustenance of life. . . .And as man grows in the scale of perfection, he draws upon all ideas, his own and those of others, for the kernel of abiding truth. He is made more perfect through them, and they through him" (ibid., Vol. I, p. 17).

Man's response to the divine dimension in his being, Rabbi Kook generalized, is " a yearning to reveal the unity of the world, in man, among nations, and in the entire content of existence, without any dichotomy between action and theory, between reason and imagination, and even those dichotomies that are experienced are to be united through a higher enlightenment that recognizes the aspect of their unity and their interrelatedness. In the content of a person's life this constitutes the foundation of holiness" (ibid., Vol. II, p. 425).

Impelled by this philosophy, Rabbi Kook developed a remarkable openness toward all people and all ideas, even those toward whom we would normally expect him to be antagonistic. He saw merit even in atheism. Seen in terms of its own profession, atheism is, of course, a purely negative force that would rob life of its highest level of meaning. But when seen in a larger context we may discern here also positive elements. In the words of Rabbi Kook: "All the names and designations, whether in Hebrew or in any other language, give us no more than a tiny and dull spark of the hidden light toward which the soul aspires and calls it 'Elohim,' 'God.' Every definition in the divine *essence* evokes a reaction of atheism. Atheism is a kind of anguished cry to redeem man from this narrow and alien pit. . . . Atheism has a tempo-

9

rary legitimacy, because it is needed to purge the foulness that has attached itself to religion . . . to extirpate the dross that obscures from man the true light of godliness. . . . Through the clash of these contradictory forces [atheism and traditional religion] will mankind be aided greatly to approach an enlightened knowledge of God. . . . In place of sterile speculations, presuming to probe the divine *essence*, the heart will entertain the enlightened concern with morality and man's higher heroism, which radiate from the divine light and are at all times linked to its source. This will define man's path in life and place him within the sphere of the divine radiance" (*Orot*, pp. 126ff.).

Rabbi Kook felt in full rapport with the pioneering youth who were building the new Jewish settlements in Palestine. They were often hostile to religion, their Jewish self-affirmation was expressed in secular, nationalistic terms, and the general tendency among the pietists who made up the old Jewish settlement was bitterly opposed to them. A fierce feud raged between the pietists and the secularists. The pietists accused the secularists of being the enemies of Jewish tradition who posed a threat to the survival of Judaism; the secularists retorted with the charge that the pietists were decadent and parasitic and blind to the vision of Jewish redemption. Rabbi Kook saw truth as well as falsification in each of these claims, and he sought to mediate one to the other, calling on each to shed its extremism and to embrace what was valid in the other (*Hazon ha-Geulah*, Agudah Lehotzoat Sifre Harayah Kook, Jerusalem, 1941, pp. 203f.; *Igrot Harayah*, Vol. II, Agudah Lehotzoat Sifre Harayah Kook, Jerusalem, 1946, Letter 349). Rabbi Kook's position brought him abuse from many noted rabbis who were shocked by his tolerance toward a youth that scoffed at traditional sanctities, that had arrogated to itself the role of bringing the redemption by the labor of their own hands, rather than waiting for the coming of the Messiah. One critic accused him of "becoming a Zionist in his old age and sacrificing his soul for the sake of upbuilding Eretz Yisrael." He replied that if being a Zionist is to struggle for the upbuilding of the land invested by God with holiness, where the gifts of the prophecy were bestowed on the Jewish people and divine providence made itself manifest, then it is honorable to be a Zionist. He invited his critic to try to earn the same honorable epithet for himself (*Igrot*, Letter 555).

At the same time Rabbi Kook was critical of the Zionist pioneers because they had reduced Jewish identity to the level of nationalism. What is the highest goal of Jewish nationalism? A Jewish state! "But," declared Rabbi Kook, "a state cannot yield the highest happiness to man. . . . The Jewish people is the base on which God's throne rests, its greatest yearning is for the time when God will be One and His name One...." Nationalist movements are temporary phenomena, which are due to be transcended as man responds to the more universal claims of his nature. A secularly oriented Zionism, he argued, "has sufficient potency to be a theme of propaganda and, to some extent, win adherents for a limited span of time, but secularity cannot offer us a permanent directive for life. Already, since the movement in its secular form has been in vogue for a relatively brief period of time, we feel a drying up of its vitality and a tendency to fragmentation, despite its physical expansion. . . . Those who think that the new nationalist movement can supersede our concern with holiness are in grievous error. . . . This is a mistaken conception that will never take root and will never be able to gain permanent acceptance, either in the thought world of the Jewish people, or among the great and sensitive spirits of the nations. The dimension of holiness must regain its scope in our national and Zionist movement, for only therein is the source of abiding life. This will then revitalize, by its power, the domain of the secular, which is meant to be

11

auxiliary to it. And this will serve us as the way of penitence, which will heal all of our afflictions and bring near the full redemption" (*Orot*, p. 160; *Hazon Hageulab*, pp. 169f.).

Rabbi Kook stressed often the classic doctrine that the Jewish people were the bearers of a heritage that proclaimed God's word with incomparable power, and that all mankind was meant to be nurtured by it, but he took sharp issue with those who disparaged other religions. In all religions there are authentic elements, "a seeking after God and His ways in the world." It is especially Jews, as the bearers of the universal vision, who should be the protagonists of this principle, but decadence obscured it for them. "At a time such as this," Rabbi Kook wrote, "we must clarify the common elements of all religion, according to the degree of their development, and not be afraid of the customary disdain and deep hostility that lurks in the soul against everything alien" (*Igrot Harayah*, Vol. I, Agudah Lehotzoat Sifre Harayah Kook, Jerusalem, 1943, Letter 194). In Jewish tradition, the feud between Judaism and Christianity and Judaism and Islam is sometimes projected back into the brotherly feud between Jacob and Esau, and Isaac and Ishmael. Rabbi Kook seized on this projection and transmuted it into positive terms, the recognition of the essential brotherhood among the three faiths. "The brotherly love of Esau and Jacob, of Isaac and Ishmael," he wrote, "will rise above the confusions fostered by the evil emanating from our creaturely character; it will rise above them and turn them to light and compassion without end" (*Igrot*, Vol. II, Letter 355).

Rabbi Kook was grieved because of the parochialism that had developed in the Jewish people and caused them to stray from their authentic self. They had often become a self-centered people, forgetting that their destiny was to live in a larger human context, to contribute to the whole and to be enriched by the whole. He attributed this growth of parochialism to two factors: "the prolonged persecution . . . encountered at the hands of the larger world . . . and because of the radical change in the spiritual and practical pattern of life that set us apart from all other nations under the sun" (*Orot Hakodesh*, Vol. II, p. 557).

This parochialism is, of course, an ironic distortion, for the goal of the Torah is the very opposite; it is to sensitize us to holiness, to the vision of universality as an imperative for the perfection of all life. The true self of the Jew, declared Rabbi Kook, is stirred by a longing that "the light of truth and equity, as deriving from our affirmation of God, be made manifest in the life of the world," and "all our *mitzvot* and customs are but vessels that contain sparks of this great light" (*Ikve Hatzon*, "Hamahshavot," in *Eder Hayakar*, Mosad Harav Kook, Jerusalem, 1967, p. 124).

Rabbi Kook criticized the religious leaders of his time because they had contributed to this decadence. They had spurned secular culture. Even the study of Judaism was reduced by them to a concentration on Talmudic dialectics, ignoring the ethical, philosophical and mystical branches of Jewish literature in which the Jewish soul found vivid expression. They were clinging to a conception of Judaism that was narrow, pedantic, indifferent to the world and hostile to all progressive life. The result is, Rabbi Kook pointed out, that when they encounter "the light of knowledge, of some pure and exalted idea, they feel that their spiritual world is slipping under their feet. . . . The reaching out for worldly knowledge to the extent possible is a necessity. If every student of the Torah cannot be expected to master all branches of knowledge, he can be expected to attain familiarity with the general state of culture in the world and its impact on life, so that he may discern the spirit of his generation and thus be enabled to nurture it and improve it" (*Ikve Hatzon*, "Derishat Hashem," in *Eder Hayakar*, pp. 128-9).

Rabbi Kook discussed this subject often, and sometimes with great pathos and evident pain. In a letter to a correspondent he lamented: "We have abandoned the soul of the Torah. . . . Whoever speaks of this to the shepherds of our people is deemed presumptuous and mad. The hour calls for a mighty act of penitence. . . . We must be radical. With minor compromises we shall correct nothing. . . . Religious faith has dwindled, and is continuing to wane, because its Torahitic foundation has been undermined. No one attends to it. Orthodoxy, in waging her battles with negations, contents itself with vain imaginings that life and reality destroy, destroying also those who propound them. . . . Whoever is strong of heart, who wields a vigorous pen, and his soul is touched by the divine spirit, must go forth to the battlefield and cry out, Give us light. We would see an altogether different picture in our generation if but a portion of our talented people who are knowledgeable in the Torah and gifted with good sense devoted themselves to cultivate the vineyard of the Lord in the area of inwardness, to concern themselves with clarifying the conceptual elements of religion, such as the nature of prophecy, the holy spirit, the redemption and the anticipation of redemption, the redemption of the Jewish people and the redemption of the world, the perfection of the individual and of the community" (*Igrot*, Vol. II, Letter 481). In another letter he wrote in the same vein: "As long as Orthodoxy maintains stubbornly, No, we shall concern ourselves only with the study of Talmud and the legal codes, but not *aggadah*, not ethics, not Cabbalah, not scientific research, not the knowledge of the world, and not Hasidism, it impoverishes itself, and against all this I shall continue to wage battle" (*ibid.*, Letter 602).

Rabbi Kook's program to raise the spiritual state of Jewish life was to encourage a third force as a living embodiment of his ideal. It may be instructive to quote Rabbi Kook's own words as to how he understood the ideological cleavage in Judaism and the role he envisioned for the so-called third force. In a letter to the Agudat Yisrael, as a message to its annual conference, he offered the following analysis of the situation:

> There are three fundamental forces here [in Eretz Yis-rael]. One is the old force...largely absorbed in its quest for inner holiness, which thrusts aside whatever bears anything new in any form, which excludes from its schools and yeshivot every foreign language, even the language of the government and country, and every secular study, even that which is most urgent for practical life, which . . . refuses to introduce any changes in response to the demands of new conditions created by the new immigration of great numbers of our brothers from the western countries and from every part of Europe. . . . The second force has emerged only recently and has come to the fore, thanks to recent events in Eretz Yisrael, gaining recognition especially since I have begun my activity in Eretz Yisrael. . . . This is the force that proclaims that it is our duty to revitalize the spirit of God in our people and to gain respect for the Torah and the commandments through the acquisition of all cultural resources active in the world. . . . We must take whatever is good from any source where we find it to adorn our spirit and our institutions. . . . After the study of our holy Torah we must teach our children and our students the practical disciplines that a person needs in life. We shall train them to be brave of heart and agreeable in manner. We shall get them used to Hebrew speech, which is a source of dignity and strength to us in Eretz Yisrael, in addition to the fact that the language is holy and we perform a divine commandment in studying it.

We shall establish vocational schools for youth especially suited for this, and here, too, we shall infuse the living, creative spirit that knows our generation and is capable of influencing it toward the love of all things holy and beloved of God.

The third force is the force of complete secularism, which has discarded everything holy to us, concerning itself solely with mundane needs. . . . It stands to reason that this rejection of everything holy does not remain a mental activity, but it tends to undermine and destroy the foundations of religion and alienates great numbers of our people now settling in Eretz Yisrael from the light of God and His holy Torah. Nevertheless, it cannot be denied that, with all this, we have here also a great positive force, a deep love for our people, a firm dedication to extend the practical work of rebuilding Eretz Yisrael, to direct the spirit of our generation to draw closer to the land and the nation, in keeping with the historic character of our people. We have here a force that, despite all estrangement, contains a vital spark of holiness, waiting to be fanned into fuller life, through faithful and loving hands. (*Igrot*, Vol. II, Letter 427)

Rabbi Kook's program to serve the cause of renewal in Judaism involved him in a number of practical steps. He undertook a personal ministry of reconciliation by cultivating both camps and by acknowledging the elements of validity in their positions. He travelled extensively among the colonies and befriended the pioneers with many tokens of personal friendship. He embraced what was embraceable in their programs. He extolled the sanctity of creative labor. He wrote a glowing letter of welcome to the national Hebrew poet, Hayim Nahman Bialik, when the latter arrived to settle in Palestine. He welcomed the establishment of the Bezalel School of fine arts, exulting in this development as promising

a much-needed aesthetic enrichment in Jewish life. He partic-
ipated in the ceremonies launching the Hebrew University in
Jerusalem. In many instances he cautioned those to whom he
spoke that the pursuits of the Hebrew cultural renaissance
must avoid the secularist falsifications of Jewish tradition, but
his tone was always positive, and he hailed each development
for the positive gains it brought to the cultural renaissance in
Judaism.

At the same time he remained a friend of the Old Settlement. He appealed for funds to maintain its schools. He de-
fended them, despite their extremism, as carrying a deep
commitment to holiness. Their appearance, their manner,
alientated, but beneath their exterior form there was a deep
love for the Jewish people and its heritage. He was very critical of Rabbi A. M. Fishman, who had voiced public attack
against one of the schools of the Old Settlement, the Yeshivah
Shaarei Torah. Our way, he maintained, must not be the
negative way of destroying the old or the new. His program
called for renewing the old, and hallowing the new (*Orot Yisrael*, 4:4, 8:8, 9:5 in *Orot*; *Ikve ha-Zon*, "ha-Dor" in *Eder
Hayakar*, pp. 107-116; *Orot Meofel*, "Orot ha-Tehiah," 9, 21,
23, 34, 46, in *Orot*, pp. 25-85; *Hazon ha-Geulah*, pp. 105, 108,
109, 139, 148-50, 179, 199-304, 232-33, 267, 275-76, 332-33;
Igrot, Vol. I, Letters 44, 88, 112, 140, 158, 191, 266, 279,
295, 334; *Igrot*, Vol. II, Letters 341, 392, 516, 522, 570, 672,
724).

The most important step he advocated was the creation
of a network of new schools whose spirit would reflect the
synthesis he advocated. He offered personal sponsorship to
the secondary school Tahkemoni launched by the Mizrahi, as
an alternative to the Tel Aviv gymnasia, but he was disap-
pointed that it never attained the academic standing of the
leftist institution. The goal on which he was especially set was
the establishment of a new Yeshivah where a broad conception of Judaism was to be taught. This Yeshivah was to be

established in Jaffa rather than in Jerusalem, in order to avoid a contest with the old pietists.

The new Yeshivah would train the kind of rabbis who would be acceptable to the younger generation, and be able to bring them back to God. The Yeshivah he projected would be quite different from the seminaries established in Western countries, although he hastened to add that many of the founders of these seminaries were great scholars and righteous men who rendered invaluable services to the cause of Judaism (*Hazon ha-Geulah*, pp. 297, 304; *Igrot*, Vol. I, Letters 98, 103, 110, 111, 112, 118, 137, 141, 144, 149, 240, 277, 279, 286, 295, 325, 328; *Igrot*, Vol. II, Letters 647, 650, 653).

Rabbi Kook found a number of kindred spirits who rallied to him. The younger generation, the pioneers who built the nationalist revival, responded to him warmly, but they were not quite ready to embrace his call to holiness. Their very adulation of him, moreover, made him all the more suspect in the camp of the pietists. He found many elements in the Mizrahi, the Religious Zionist party, close to his spirit, but he could not accept its avowed concession to the factionalism by agreeing to serve as a separate party within the Zionist coalition. He wanted to be bolder and more aggressive in challenging the official Zionist slogan, that Zionism as such has nothing to do with religion. He wanted to speak to the entire Jewish people and the Mizrahi was content to be a fragment. At one time he attempted to launch a movement as a vehicle for his views, but nothing came of it (*Hazon ha-Geulah*, pp. 193, 196, 197, 209, 311-313, 314, 315, 332-333; *Igrot*, Vol. II, Letters 394, 497, 534, 555, 571).

He was the Chief Rabbi in Jaffa, and after the British Mandatory Power's recognition of an autonomous Jewish community, he became the Chief Rabbi of the entire Jewish community in Palestine. As such he was the spokesman of the official religiosity of the community, but his colleagues in the rabbinate remained aloof from his views. At one time it was suggested to him that he call a conference of rabbis to deal with the problems that were on his mind. He replied that such a conference would be futile. "The shepherds of our people are in a deep slumber," he replied. At such conferences these venerable men would bring forth sterile dialectics but they would not face life and its problems. "This is not the way," he continued. "We shall not seek conferences at this time, but we shall create a literature" (*Igrot*, Vol. I, Letter 184).

His gifted pen was the most formidable weapon at his disposal. In addition to his major works in mystical philosophy, which remain to be explored by our generation and by succeeding generations, he wrote poetry, and many occasional essays, and he carried on an extensive correspondence with kindred souls all over the world, offering advice as well as criticism. He wrote to Rabbi Meir Berlin, leader of the Mizrahi, protesting an anti-Arab article in the Mizrahi organ (*Igrot*, Vol. II, Letter 398). He wrote to another rabbi, praising him for a fine work he had published, but criticizing him for not correcting his Hebrew style, and for allowing himself to violate the rules of Hebrew grammar. To the editor of one magazine he wrote a sharp protest because the latter had allowed himself to use abusive language against an opponent. He encouraged one scholar to translate a work on Judaism and make it available among the Japanese, who were on the brink of a break with Shintoism and were likely to find Judaism an answer to their quest for a more vital faith. He wrote to another correspondent urging a respectful attitude toward other religions, asking that Judaism be affirmed in positive terms, for its own merits, without ridiculing the faith of other people (*Igrot*, Vol. I, Letters 112, 194: *Igrot*, Vol. II, Letters 344, 355, 398, 557, 669).

Rabbi Kook's role as an activist with a truly independent spirit that made him fearless when a righteous cause was at stake was shown especially in his reaction to the Stavsky case. A leader of the Labor Zionist movement, Chayim Arlosoroff, was killed by an unknown assassin in 1933. This was a period of intense feuding between the Labor Zionists and the Zionist Revisionists, an extreme rightist group. The general feeling in the Jewish community, where the Labor Zionists were the dominant group, was that Arlosoroff was a victim of this feuding and that the assassination was the act of a Revisionist by the name of Abraham Stavsky. After a trial by the British Mandatory authorities, Stavsky was found guilty of the murder and was sentenced to death. Rabbi Kook was convinced that political hysteria had created a climate that blurred the rational weighing of the evidence and he launched a campaign to save Stavsky from execution. His efforts were successful, the case was reviewed and Stavsky was finally freed.

The issues with which Rabbi Kook dealt in his extensive writings were varied, but he summed up his position in three basic categories. The Judaism that will rise to its historic authenticity and fulfill its liberating role in civilization will have to be a synthesis of Orthodoxy, nationalism and liberalism. By Orthodoxy he meant conventional religiosity based on the Torah and the commandments, by nationalism he meant the Zionist movement in its far-reaching expressions of Jewish creativity, and by liberalism he meant the general humanist tradition of the Enlightenment, with its characteristic expression in cultural and humanitarian ideals (*Orot Meofel*, "Orot ha-Tehiyah," 18, in *Orot*, pp. 70-72).

Rabbi Kook called for an integration of Orthodoxy, Zionism and liberalism. But this did not represent for him an introduction into Judaism of elements foreign to itself. It represented the very opposite — Judaism's claim to what was essentially its very own. Conventional religiosity had gone dry and reduced Judaism to the formal elements of the Torah and commandments, each pursued in narrow rather than broad terms. But the Torah and the commandments, seen in broader terms, implied the love for the Jewish people that was the heart of the Zionist movement and the humanist ideal that was the heart of the liberal movement. These three belonged together, to express the goal of holiness in all its manifestations.

Rabbi Kook offered us a noble view of what life ought to be. Why does life fall short of this ideal? Why is the vision of universality so difficult of realization? Why is man held in thrall by parochial loyalties, by a blind clinging to the self and an indifference and even hostility toward those beyond the self? In short, why did God so structure the world that there is so much folly, so much hostility and conflict in it? Rabbi Kook noted readily that God could indeed have created a world in which man, by nature, would be totally enlightened. But this would have robbed life of a precious dimension, the capacity for growth. "All striving presupposes some deficiency" (*Orot Hakodesh*, Vol. II, p. 481), stated Rabbi Kook, and only in a world of imperfection is there scope for ideals and for the striving toward perfection. Indeed, it is the fact that men must struggle against deficiency that authenticates and deepens for them life's values. The love for freedom is forged in part in the crucible of suffering under servitude (*Olat Rayah*, Mosad Harav Kook and Agudah Lehotzoat Sifre Harayah Kook, Jerusalem, 1949, Vol. II, pp. 262f.).

Light is steadily pitted against the dark, and light will increasingly overcome the dark. In Rabbi Kook's words: "Nothing remains the same; everything blooms, everything ascends, everything steadily increases in light and truth. The enlightened spirit does not become discouraged even when he discerns that the line of ascendence is circuitous, including both advance and decline, a forward movement but also fierce retreats, for even the retreats abound in the potential of future progress" (*Orot Hakodesh*, Vol. II, p. 484). This vision of development "gives us ground for optimism in the world" (*ibid.*, p. 555) in the face of all discouragements.

The world, in Rabbi Kook's thought, is a school for human enlightenment. Men now walk side by side in different states of light or of darkness. Many steps in the ladder of perfection must be climbed before the height of a truly universal man is reached. Rabbi Kook at times became lyrical as he wrote on this subject: "There is one who sings the song of his own life, and in himself he finds everything, his full spiritual sufficiency. There is another who sings the songs of his people. He leaves the circle of his private existence, for he does not find it broad enough. . . . He aspires for the heights and he attaches himself with tender love to the whole of Israel, he sings her songs, grieves in her afflictions, and delights in her hopes. He ponders lofty and pure thoughts concerning her past and her future, and probes lovingly and wisely the content of her inner essence. Then there is one whose spirit extends beyond the boundary of Israel, to sing the song of man. . . . He is drawn to man's universal vocation and he hopes for his highest perfection. And this is the life source from which he draws his thoughts and probings, his yearnings and his visions. But there is one who rises even higher, uniting himself with the whole existence, with all creatures, with all worlds. With all of them he sings his song. It is of one such as this that tradition has said that whoever sings a portion of song each day is assured of the life of the world to come" (*ibid.*, p. 458).

The universal man, as Rabbi Kook conceived of him, is one whose sympathies embrace all forms of life, not only the purely human. Rabbi Kook extended his concern to animals. The enlightened man of the future, he felt, was to shun the eating of meat as an act of compassion for animal life. The original man as God created him was to use as his food "every herb yielding seed, which is upon the face of all the earth, and every tree yielding fruit" (Gen. 1:29). The eating of meat was first sanctioned to Noah (Gen. 9:3). After Adam's disobedience, when man disclosed his pitifully low moral state, God compromised and allowed him to be a meat eater. But on reaching his true spiritual maturing he was to return to his original innocence.

In the words of Rabbi Kook: "The thrust of the idealism that continues to develop will not remain forever in its confinement. Just as the democratic aspiration will emerge into the world through the general intellectual and moral perfection, 'when man will no longer teach his brother to know the Lord, for they will all know Me, small and great alike' (Jer. 31:34), so will the hidden yearning to act justly toward animals emerge at the proper time" ("Talele Orot," *Tahkemoni*, vol. I, Bern, 1910, p. 21).

Rabbi Kook went so far as to project the abolition of animal sacrifices in a restored Temple in Jerusalem, which was to take place in the messianic age of the future. In those days the animals themselves will be changed in their psyche, losing their harshness and developing a morally higher sensitivity. "In the future the abundance of enlightenment will spread and penetrate even the animals. 'They will not hurt nor destroy on My holy mountain, for the earth will be full of the knowledge of the Lord' (Isa. 11:9). The gift offerings of vegetation that will then be brought as sacrifices will be as acceptable as the sacrifices of ancient days" (*Olat Rayah*, vol. II, p. 292).

The future, as Rabbi Kook envisioned it, favored the light. Man was destined to learn the truth about his nature, about his relatedness to all existence. This was the theme of the goals toward which history was ultimately directed. Jewish tradition expressed this by the conception of a messianic culmination to the process of history. "The illumination to be bestowed by the Messiah," according to Rabbi Kook, "is derived primarily from the philosophy of the unity of all existence" (*Orot Hakodesh*, vol. II, p. 474).

Life itself, in its natural drive for self-perfection, moves us toward this consummation. For we impoverish life and shrink its scope when we live by parochial loyalties. A sympathetic responsiveness to other people is a boon to them but also to ourselves for we thereby add dimensions to our own being. In Rabbi Kook's words: "The Holy One, praised be He, bestowed mercy on His world by not confining His endowments to one place, one person, one people, one land, one generation or one world, but His endowments are diffused, and the quest for perfection, which is the most idealistic striving of our nature, directs us to seek the higher unity that must finally come in the world. In that day — God will be one and His name one" (*Orot Yisrael*, 5:2, in *Orot* p. 152).

The fact that there is among men widespread ignorance of their true nature and destiny leaves room for those who are enlightened to share in the greatest of life's adventures — to work with God for the advancement of harmony and perfection. When such men see the world "full of feuds, hostilities, persecutions and conflicts, they at once yearn to participate with all their being in the quest that brings about the comprehensiveness of life and its unity, its welfare and its tranquility. When they encounter nations, religions, sects and movements in opposition to each other, they strive with all their strength to harmonize all, to mitigate the breach and to effect unity. . . .They desire that every particular be preserved and perfected, and the collective ensemble be united and at peace" (*Orot Hakodesh*, Vol. II, p. 457).

The yearning to effect unity and perfection in the world is part of the divine strategy to emancipate man from ignorance and parochialism. God has reinforced this with the additional attributes that He has invested in the structure of life. One is the dynamism of the enlightened life; the good that pervades a person draws others to itself. In the words of Rabbi Kook: "Whenever a person raises himself through good deeds, through a higher stirring of his yearning for godliness, for wisdom, justice, beauty and equity, he perfects thereby the spiritual disposition of all existence. All people become better in their inwardness through the ascendency of the good in any one of them. . . . Such virtue in any one person is due to spread among the general populace, to stir each one, according to his capacity, toward merit, and thus all existence thereby becomes ennobled and more exalted" (*ibid.*, vol. III, Agudah Lehotzoat Sifre Harayah Kook, Jerusalem, 1950, pp. 314f.).

Another attribute of life that aids man's quest for enlightenment is the phenomenon of penitence, which, for Rabbi Kook, has much deeper significance than the conventional notion of remorse and atonement for specific wrongdoings, in response to traditional admonitions. In truth penitence is a universal and an essentially positive phenomenon, acting on some levels as a natural process, and expressing a revolt against deficiency and the quest for perfection. We are not directed by the automatic workings of our nature to embrace divine ideals, but an affinity, a predisposition for those ideals, is part of us. The ideals that spell out the existential content of our affirmation of God "are inscribed on the human soul, and the deepest yearning hidden in the depths of the soul is to effect the transition of this hidden light from potentiality to actuality . . . in the forms of life itself, the personal and the collective, in deed, desire and thought" (*Ikve Hatzon*, "Avodat Elohim," in *Eder Hayakar*, p. 145). It is this yearning for perfection that sends man to seek a good greater than the good embodied in his present condition and makes him open to the testimony of dreamers who have glimpsed the larger vision. But this yearning is not confined to man. All existence is stirred by an inchoate longing to overcome its alienation from God and return to Him who is the source of its being. "Penitence," declared Rabbi Kook, derives from the yearning of all existence to be better, purer, firmer, nobler than it is" (*Orot Hateshuvah*, Yeshivat B'nei Akiba "Or Etzion," Merkaz Shapiro, Jerusalem, 1966, 6:1).

The act of penitence, whether as reaction to a specific

wrongdoing or to a general dissatisfaction with the state of one's life, is free of morbidity. It is, on the contrary, a liberation from morbidity. It is a therapy that cancels out the anguish of remorse and endows a person with a sense of elation for having ascended out of the mire and toward the heights. The penitent who has shed an old self and assumed a new and higher self has in effect been reborn as a new person. He has released by his act a divine song and a divine joy throughout the universe. All existence has been renewed through his renewal. For man is not self-sufficient, he does not live in detachment from the rest of existence. He is linked with all his griefs and all his joys with the whole, and all life grieves when he grieves and exults when he exults. Rabbi Kook summed up this phase of his subject by quoting the well-known Talmudic maxim (Yoma 66a): "Great is penitence for it brings healing to the world, and if but a single person repent, he—and the whole world—are granted forgiveness" (*Orot Hateshuvah*, 3, end).

Another factor in the enlightenment of man, according to Rabbi Kook, is the impact of Judaism's presence in the world. For Rabbi Kook the essence of Judaism, which flows from Jewish monotheism, is the passion to overcome separatism, the severance of man from God, of man from man, of man from nature. It is the passion to perfect the world through man's awareness of his links to all else in existence. It is the rejection of the alleged antagonism between the material and the spiritual. It is the rejection of nationalism as an ultimate center of moral values. It is the rejection of every parochialism that seeks to build man's spiritual home and his structure of values by taking to itself a fragment of life and ignoring the rest. "The Jewish outlook" said Rabbi Kook, " is the vision of the holiness of all existence" (*Orot Yisrael* 7:12, in *Orot*, p. 167f.).

Judaism has exerted an influence on the religious consciousness of the world, but, for the most part, this has been to the adoption of certain conceptual abstractions detached from the life context in which they appear in Judaism. They were drawn into a religious system that centers its concern on reverence for God as an exalted Being who exists in splendid transcendence from man's world. This tends to separate religion from the ethical goals by which the world may be transformed toward righteousness.

Judaism centers the religious concern not on the divine Being, but on divine ideals, on the goals that God has ever sought to realize in the world of His creation. It is in the very concern to effectuate those goals in the context of a people struggling with the worldly problems of a nation functioning in history that the characteristic of Judaism is disclosed, and its cogency for a larger world service indicated. At stake in the difference between the two approaches is "not the exalted metaphysical truth of the unity of God," declared Rabbi Kook, "but the divine aspect of the passion for equity and righteousness and the mighty aspiration to effectuate these divine ideals in all their strength" (*Ikve Hatzon*, "Avodat Elohim," in *Eder Hayakar*, p. 149f.).

The crisis in Jewish peoplehood as a result of centuries of exile and persecution and the resultant defensiveness it has fostered among Jews have created a distortion in Judaism and its authentic nature has been obscured. We have already noted Rabbi Kook's complaint about the decadence in the Judaism of his time. He was hopeful that the return to Eretz Yisrael and the Jewish renaissance to be engendered by it as a result of the Zionist endeavor would, in due time, also create a religious renewal enabling Judaism once more to be fully itself, and thus to assert a greater influence on world culture. In the words of Rabbi Kook: "A great people exerts an influence not primarily through a detached part of itself but through its total being. As long as the striving for divine ideals and their effectuation in the course of a continuous historical existence does not manifest itself in the nation, the divine Presence is in exile, and the life-force released by the service of God is in a state of weakness" (*Ikve Hatzon*, "Daat Elohim," in *Eder Hayakar*, pp. 130-141). The ultimate goal of the return to Zion is to enable the Jews once again "to bear the torch of holiness in all its purity before all the nations of the world" (*Hazon ha-Geulah*, p. 178); to enable Judaism to bear witness to Torah in the world, "both a political Torah that would foster peace and freedom . . . and a religious Torah enlightened by the knowledge of divine truth and the love of God's ways in the life of the individual and society" (*ibid.*, p. 202)

Rabbi Kook's vision of a reasserted Jewish service to the world did not mean that he expected Judaism to supplant the other religions of mankind. Rabbi Kook believed that the diversity of religion is a legitimate and permanent expression of the human spirit, that the different religions are not meant to compete but to collaborate. "Conventional theology," he declared, "assumes that the different religions must necessarily oppose each other. . . . But on reaching full maturity the human spirit aspires to rise above every manner of conflict and opposition, and a person then recognizes all expressions of the spiritual life as an organic whole." This does not erase the difference of levels between religions, between higher and lower, between the more holy and the less holy and between the holy and the common. But each has its place in the life of the whole. Each is a path through which God is seeking to raise man to Himself.

Religions can serve one another as a stimulus, as a model to challenge, and invite emulation. There are, too, some elements in religion that one faith may adopt from another. But in some fundamental respects every religion is integrally linked to a people's historical experience, and a faith superimposed upon a people from without will, in a vital sense, remain alien to its life. It is in the harmonious coexistence of the different religions and their free interaction that a ferment is released and native energies are evoked so that each is aided to make the ascent toward God in its own terms. Each religion is thus a permanent participant in the "ensemble of faiths, and this domain also, where the wrangling of the different faiths once raged, becomes filled with peace and light" (*Tahkemoni*, "Talele Orot," vol. I., pp. 17f.; *Ikve Hatzon*, "Hamahshavot," in *Eder Hayakar*, pp. 122-25).

It is in this perspective that Rabbi Kook viewed the anticipated reassertion of Judaism's service to the world. The goal of Judaism, Rabbi Kook wrote, "is not to absorb or destroy the other faiths . . . but to perfect them and to stimulate them toward a higher development, so that they may free themselves of their dross, and they will then automatically attach themselves to the root of Israel. . . . This applies even to pagan faiths, and certainly so to those faiths that are partly based on the light of Israel's Torah" (*Igrot*, vol. I, Letter 112). This conception of the legitimacy of religious diversity is itself, according to Rabbi Kook, a contribution of Jewish universalism that does not obliterate the particular but integrates it in the ensemble of the larger whole. As Rabbi Kook put it: "When the light of Israel shines in the world and vanquishes the darkness and the mist that has fallen on it through a failure to understand itself, there is at once disclosed in the world the grace of unity that links all forces into one comprehensive whole, while leaving intact the private essence of each one" (*Eder Hayakar, ibid.*, "Talele Orot," *ibid.*)

Rabbi Kook's teachings were more than a conceptual system rationally arrived at. They objectified the values that stirred deeply in his own life. In one of the most revealing testimonials about himself he declared: "I love everybody. It is impossible for me not to love all people, all nations. With all the depth of my being, I desire to see them grow toward beauty, toward perfection. My love for the Jewish people is with more ardor, more depth. But my inner desire reaches out with a mighty love toward all. There is veritably no need for me to force this feeling of love. It flows directly from the holy depth of wisdom, from the divine soul.

"It is no accident, but of the very essence of my being, that I find delight in the pursuit of the divine mysteries in unrestrained freedom. This is my primary purpose. All my other goals, the practical and the rational, are only peripheral to my real self. I must find my happiness within my inner self, unconcerned whether people agree with me, or by what is happening to my own career. The more I shall recognize my own identity, and the more I will permit myself to be original, and to stand on my own feet with an inner conviction which is based on knowledge, perception, feeling and song, the more will the light of God shine on me, and the more will my potentialities develop to serve as a blessing to myself and to the world.

"The refinements to which I subject myself, my thoughts, my imagination, my morals, and my emotions, will also serve as general refinements for the whole world. A person must say, 'The whole world was created for my sake'" (*Arple Tohar*, p. 22).

There were times when Rabbi Kook was discouraged by the storm and stresses of his public life and he longed for solitude and obscurity. It is this that created the tension characteristic of his life. The pathos of his predicament is well expressed in a letter to his son. "The burdensome necessity to involve myself with people impedes me greatly from concentrating on inner concerns. My soul yearns and is thirsty for inner reflection, while the stream of distractions drags it to endless conversations, discourses, sermonizing and thinking about finite matters, set in their narrow framework, to which the simple masses in their imitation-based piety are accustomed. . . . For Your help, O God, I hope and I shall always trust, to add to Your praise" (*Igrot*, vol. III, Mosad Harav Kook, Jerusalem, 1965, Letter 764).

We have a touching letter by him in which he asked to be recommended for an administrative post in a *kolel*, a residence for poor scholars in Jerusalem maintained by a charitable fund from diaspora communities. He complained that the rabbinic office was not in accord with his inclination or his strength. He thought himself qualified for this post that would, at the same time, enable him to live "in the holy city of Jerusalem without the yoke of the rabbinate" (*Igrot*, vol. I, Letter 84). In another letter he expressed the wish that he had the financial means to free himself from his rabbinic labors in order to pursue various literary projects to which he felt drawn (*Igrot*, vol. II, Letter 645). But nothing came of such dreams, and he submitted to life's necessities with all their pressures and distractions.

Rabbi Kook's life was often beset by conflict and controversy. But he himself was a person of unusual tenderness and pacific disposition. This is reflected clearly in the will he wrote in 1919 when he was stricken with a serious illness. Here are his words in this document:

By the grace of God, 21 Iyar, 5679 (1919), between the hours of 9 and 10 in the morning.

My hope is that God, in His mercy, will grant me a complete healing, among the other sick persons of His people Israel, and that in His abundant kindnesses He will enable me to return to Him in love. Especially do I pray that He enable me to mend whatever wrong I may have committed, whether in man's relationship to God or man's relationship to man, and that He grace me with the opportunity to repay my debts.

To my great regret I do not remember all my debts in detail. But I hope that God will bestir me and remind me of them all, and that He will help me to repay them. Some of those that have come to my mind I wrote down in a small notebook with a white cover, where there will also be found some poems. Some pages that were torn off from this notebook are with Zevi Yehuda* , may he be granted life, and some debts are also recorded there.

Most of the books in my apartment here do not belong to me. May God help me to return them to their owners. In my house in Jaffa, too, there are also many books that belong to others. May God enable me to clarify everything and to set everything in order.

May it be God's will to inspire whomever I may have pained or offended to forgive me with a full forgiveness. As for me, I surely forgive all. On the contrary I regard as a good every pain and humiliation to which I was subjected. May it be God's will that no one suffer retribution on account of me, and may God bestow on all members of the fellowship of Israel only good and mercy.

O Lord, help me and heal me in your abundant mercies, and strengthen me with Your help. Help Your holy people, and hasten the light of Your deliverance and establish Your holiness in all the worlds. Amen.

Resigned, yet anticipating Your help,

Abraham Isaac ha-Kohen Kook

My gold watch and chain is a gift of dear Shlesinger, may his memory be for a blessing, and I have some scruples about the gift. May God enable me to straighten it out properly, in accordance with the precepts of our holy Torah (Harayah, Mosad Harav Kook, Jerusalem, 1960, p. 6).

Rabbi Kook's published writings include four volumes in rabbinic law; a collection of poetry; a treatise on the mysti-

---

*[his son]

cism of the Hebrew alphabet, the cantillation and vowel signs; a treatise on penitence; a treatise on morals; two volumes of a commentary on the Prayer Book; three volumes of correspondence; three volumes of reflections on God and man (*Orot ha-Kodesh*); and various occasional essays on problems in contemporary Jewish life. But the greater part of his work still remains in manuscript. In 1937 a society was formed to publish the remaining works of Rabbi Kook; thirty volumes were projected. One is awed by the sheer labor involved in this prodigous creation, especially when one recalls that he was not a literary recluse but busily involved in life, that he held an office that was most onerous in its demands on his time and energy.

A definitive appraisal of Rabbi Kook's contributions as a religious philosopher must await the publication of all his writings. What has been published thus far, however, clearly reveals him as a seer of great stature who added a most remarkable chapter to the history of Judaism. He belongs among the great spirits of Western spirituality.

ABRAHAM ISAAC KOOK~

THE LIGHTS OF PENITENCE, THE MORAL PRINCIPLES,
LIGHTS OF HOLINESS, ESSAYS, LETTERS, AND POEMS

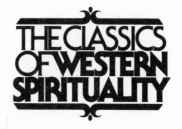

THE CLASSICS OF WESTERN SPIRITUALITY

The Lights of Penitence

A Note on the Text

The Lights of Penitence is Rabbi Kook's most popular work.
The first edition appeared in 1925 and several newer editions,
with a somewhat more amplified text, have appeared since
then. The first three chapters were written by Rabbi Kook
himself; the rest of the material consists of selections culled by
his son, who edited the work, from various other writings.
Rabbi Kook touched on the various aspects of penitence in
many of his writings.

The conventional conception of penitence sees it as an
effort to redress a particular transgression in the area of man's
relationship to God or to his fellowman. For Rabbi Kook
penitence is the surge of the soul for perfection, to rise above
the limitations imposed by the finitude of existence. It is a
reach for reunion with God from whom all existence has been
separated by the descent to particularity and finitude as inci-
dents of creation. Penitence in man is, in other words, only
one episode in the entire drama of cosmic life, which is forever
seeking higher levels of development. Penitence begins with
the will, but it slowly moves toward implementation in the
fabric of life. Its primary focus is the quest for self-perfection,
but it overflows into the endeavor to perfect society and the
world. The Jewish people is here treated as a link in the chain
of being, and the goals of penitence act on it as an autonomous
entity; this in turn interacts with the penitence of the individual, and that of the larger world.

Introduction

For a long time now an inner struggle goes on in me, and I feel prodded by a mighty force to speak about penitence, and all my thoughts are focused on this theme alone. Penitence holds a primary place in the teachings of the Torah and in life; all the hopes of the individual and of society depend on it. It embodies a divine commandment that is, on the one hand, the easiest to carry out, since a stirring of the heart toward penitence is a valid expression of penitence, and on the other hand, it is the most difficult to perform, since it has not yet been effectuated fully in the world and in life.

I find myself constantly tending to think and to speak on this subject. A good deal is written on this subject in the Torah, the prophets, and the writings of the sages. But for our generation this subject is still a closed book and is in need of clarification. Our literature, which explores every area where there is manifest the poetry of life, did not probe at all into this wonderful treasure of life, the treasure of penitence. Indeed, it has not even begun to take any interest in it, to discover its character and value, not even from its poetic side, which is a source of endless inspiration. It certainly has thus far failed to touch its practical aspect, especially insofar as it bears on the conditions of our modern life.

My inner being impels me to speak about penitence, but I recoil inwardly from my intention. Am I worthy to discuss the subject of penitence? The greatest spirits of past generations wrote on the subject of penitence, including the prophets, the noblest of the sages, the greatest of the saints, and how dare I place myself in their category? But no reticence can relieve me of this inner claim. I must speak about penitence,

41

particularly about its literary and practical aspects, to understand its significance for our generation, and the manner of its implementation in life, the life of the individual and the life of society.

Chapter One

Penitence According to Nature, Faith and Reason

We encounter the phenomenon of penitence on three levels: penitence according to nature, penitence according to faith and penitence according to reason. Penitence according to nature may be divided into two parts: the physical and the spiritual.

Physical penitence is related to all transgressions against the laws of nature, and such laws of morals and the Torah as are linked to the laws of nature. Every act of wrongdoing must in the end engender illness and pain, and the individual as well as society is exposed to much suffering as a result of this. After it becomes clear that the person himself, as a result of his misbehavior, is responsible for his distress, he necessarily gives thought to correcting his condition, to conforming to the laws of life, to becoming obedient to the laws of nature, of morality and of the Torah, that he may be renewed in life's vitality.

The science of medicine concerns itself a good deal with this, but this important phenomenon has not yet been fully clarified. We have not yet found the answer to all questions pertaining to physical penitence, to clarify how far it is possible within the delimitations of existence to restore to a person all the losses he sustained as a result of those offenses that damage the body and its functions. It appears that this phase of penitence is linked in a profound way with other forms of penitence—the spiritual phase of natural penitence, and penitence according to faith and penitence according to reason.

The spiritual dimenstion of natural penitence is more

inward. It embraces the role of what is called the "reprimand of the conscience." It is a requisite of human nature to pursue the righteous path, and when a person strays from the right course, when he lapses into sin, then, if he has not suffered a total spiritual degeneration, his sensitivity will cause him disquiet, and he will suffer pain. He will become zealous to repent, to redress his wrongdoing, until he can feel that his sin has been purged away. This dimension of penitence is very complicated. It is dependent on many subjective and objective conditions, and it is open to many possibilities of misjudgment that one must guard against. This is, however, one of the foundations on which the essence of penitence depends.

After the natural phase of penitence comes penitence inspired by religious faith. This phase of penitence is operative as a result of religious tradition, which frequently concerns itself with penitence. The Torah promises the penitent forgiveness. The sins of individuals and of the community are purged away through penitence. The prophets abound with exalted utterances on the subject of penitence. In a general way all the admonitions of the Torah deal with penitence from the perspective of religious faith. From its conceptual depth flow endless details. A clarification of their basic principles alone calls for considerable discussion and many explanations.

Penitence according to reason comes after penitence according to nature and religious faith have already taken place. It represents the peak of penitential expression. This level of penitence is inspired not only by a natural malaise, physical or spiritual, or by the influence of religious tradition, whether it has induced in the person a fear of retribution or conditioned him to the acceptance of some law or precept. It is also inspired by a comprehensive outlook on life that came to crystallization after the natural and religious phases of penitence had registered their influence. This phase of penitence, in which the previous are included, abounds in endless delight. It transforms all the past sins into spiritual assets. From every error it derives noble lessons, and from every lowly fall it derives the inspiration for the climb to splendid heights. This is the type of penitence toward which all aspire, which must come and which is bound to come.

Chapter Two

Sudden and Gradual Penitence

In terms of time, penitence may be divided into two parts: sudden penitence and gradual penitence.

Sudden penitence comes about as a result of a certain spiritual flash that enters the soul. At once the person senses all the evil and the ugliness of sin and he is converted into a new being; already he experiences inside himself a complete transformation for the better. This form of penitence dawns on a person through the grace of some inner spiritual force, whose traces point to the depths of the mysterious.

There is also a gradual form of penitence. No sudden flash of illumination dawns upon the person to make him change from the depth of evil to the good, but he feels that he must mend his way of life, his will, his pattern of thought. By heeding this impulse he gradually acquires the ways of equity, he corrects his morals, he improves his actions, and he conditions himself increasingly to becoming a good person, until he reaches a high level of purity and perfection.

The higher expression of penitence comes about as a result of a flash of illumination of the all-good, the divine, the light of Him who abides in eternity. The universal soul, the spiritual essence, is revealed to us in all its majesty and holiness, to the extent that the human heart can absorb it. Indeed, is not the all of existence so good and so noble, and is not the good and the nobility in ourselves but an expression of our relatedness to the all? How then can we allow ourselves to become severed from the all, a strange fragment, detached like tiny grains of sand that are of no value? As a result of this perception, which is truly a divinely inspired perception, comes about penitence out of love, in the life of the individual and in the life of society.

Chapter Three

Particularized Penitence and General Penitence

There is a form of penitence that addresses itself to a particular sin or to many particular sins. The person confronts his sin face to face, and feels remorseful that he fell into the trap of sin. Slowly he struggles to come out of it, until he is liberated from his sinful enslavement and he begins to experience a holy freedom that is most delightful to his weary self. His healing continues; rays of a benign sun, bearing divine mercy, reach out to him, and a feeling of happiness grows within him. He experiences this at the same time that his heart remains broken and his spirit bowed and melancholy. Indeed this lowly feeling itself, which suits him in his condition, adds to his spiritual satisfaction and his sense of true peace. He feels himself drawing closer to the source of life, to the living God, who but a short time before was so remote from him. His wistful spirit recalls with joyous relief its previous inner anguish, and is filled with a feeling of gratitude. It breaks into a hymn of thanksgiving: "Praise the Lord, O my soul, forget not all His kindnesses, He forgives all Your sins, He heals all your afflictions, He rescues your life from the pit, He adorns you with grace and compassions, He sates you with every good, He renews your youth like an eagle; the Lord performs merciful acts, He vindicates the cause of the oppressed" (Ps. 103: 2-6). How anguished the soul was when the burden of sin, its dark, vulgar and frightfully oppressive weight, lay upon her! How depressed she was, even if outer riches and honors fell to her lot! What good is there in all the wealth if the inner content of life is impoverished and dry? And how blissful she now is in the inner feeling that her sin has been forgiven, that the nearness of God is already alive and shining in her, that her inner burden has been made lighter, that she has already paid her debt and is no longer oppressed by inner confusion and distress. She is at rest, and filled with an innocent peace. "Return to your peace, O my soul, for the Lord has bestowed His kindness on you" (Ps. 116:7).

There is another kind of feeling of penitence, unspecified and general. A person does not conjure up the memory of a past sin or sins, but in a general way he feels terribly depressed. He feels himself pervaded by sin; that the divine light does not shine on him; that there is nothing noble in him; that his heart is unfeeling, his moral behavior does not follow the right course, worthy of sustaining a meaningful life for a wholesome human being; that his state of education is crude, his emotions stirred by dark and sinister passions that revolt him. He is ashamed of himself; he knows that God is not within him, and this is his greatest misfortune, his most oppressive sin. He is embittered against himself; he can find no escape from his oppressive thoughts, which do not focus on any particular misdeeds; his whole being is as though in a torture chamber. For this state of spiritual malaise penitence comes as the therapy from a master physician. The feeling of penitence, with an insight to its profound nature, its basis in the deepest levels of the soul, in the mysterious workings of nature, in all the dimensions of the Torah and our religious tradition comes with all its might and streams into his soul. A sense of assurance in the healing, the general renewal that penitence extends to all who embrace it, distills in him a spirit of grace and acceptance. He senses the fulfillment of the verse

"I will comfort you as the person who is comforted by his mother" (Isa. 66:13).

Day by day, inspired by this higher level of general penitence, his feeling becomes more firm, clearer, more illumined by reason and more authenticated by the principles of the Torah. His manner becomes increasingly brightened, his anger recedes, a kindly light shines on him, he is filled with vigor, his eyes sparkle with a holy fire, his heart is bathed in rivers of delight, holiness and purity hover over him. His spirit is filled with endless love, his soul thirsts for God, and this very thirst nourishes him like the choicest of foods [lit. "like marrow and fat" as in Ps. 63:6]. The holy spirit rings out before him like a bell, and he is given the good news that all his transgressions, the known and the unknown, have been erased, that he has been born anew as a new being, that the whole world, all realms of being, have been renewed with him, and that all things now join in a chorus of song, that the gladness of God fills all creation. "Great is penitence, for it brings healing to the world, and even one individual who repents is forgiven and the whole world is forgiven with him" (Yoma 86a).

Chapter Four

Private Penitence and Public Penitence –
in the World and in the Jewish People

1. The currents of particular and general penitence rush along. They are like the streams of flame on the surface of the sun, which in an unceasing struggle break out and ascend, and endow life to countless worlds and numberless creatures. One is powerless to absorb the multitiude of varying colors that emanate from this great sun that shines on all the worlds, the sun of penitence. They are so many, they come with such

mighty sweep, with such wondrous speed. They come from the source of life itself, for whom time is only a limited expression of His providential design. The individual and the collective soul, the world soul, the soul of all realms of being cries out like a fierce lioness in anguish for total perfection, for an ideal form of existence, and we feel the pain, and it purges us. Like salt that seasons the meat, it purges away all our bitterness. It is impossible to express this vastly profound concept. We will place all things in the context of the divine unity, we will invoke the mystical meanings of the names of God: a punctuation mark—a new heaven and a new earth, and all their fullness are contained in it; a letter—and worlds become revealed; words—and [we have before us] countless worlds and multitudes of creations, tranquil and joyous, abounding with a mighty gladness, full of peace and truth. And the soul grows toward perfection.

2. Through penitence all things are reunited with God; through the fact that penitence is operative in all worlds, all things are returned and reattached to the realm of divine perfection. Through the thoughts of penitence, its conceptual implications and the feelings it engenders, the basic character of all our thinking, our imagination and our knowledge, our will and our feeling, is transformed and placed again within the context of the holy order of the divine.

3. General penitence, which involves raising the world to perfection, and particularized penitence, which pertains to the personal life of each individual, including the smallest constituents of special penitential reforms that the holy spirit can itemize in tiniest details—they all constitute one essence. Similarly all the cultural reforms through which the world rises from decadence, the improvements in the social and economic order through this redress of every form of wrongdoing, from the most significant to the minutest ordinances of later sages and the most extreme demands of ethically sensitive spirits—all of them constitute an inseparable whole. "All of

them integrate to form one entity" [based on Zohar II 162b].

4. The nature of all existence and every particular creature, the whole of human history and the life of every individual person, must be seen from one comprehensive perspective, as one essence constituent of many particularities. Then will come readily the perception that will condition the emergence of penitence.

5. In truth one cannot rise to the spiritual level of seeking the reformation of society without a deep inner repentance of every sin and wrongdoing. An individual who has repented in this sense is forgiven and the whole world is forgiven with him. Similarly many may be raised to the ideal state hidden in the soul of the Jewish people through the penitence of one individual who is motivated by the goal of bringing to fruition his people's noblest aspiration for greatness.

6. The highest sensibility in the soul of the people of Israel is the quest for universality. The people aspire for this by the very essence of its being, and this affects all existence. The desire for penitence in its highest form is rooted in this hidden longing.

7. The soul of the people of Israel expresses itself in the striving for absolute justice, which, to be effectuated, must include the realization of all moral virtues. It is for this reason that any moral misdeed committed by an individual Jew weakens his link with the soul of the people. The basic step in penitence is to attach oneself again to the soul of the people. Together with this it is mandatory to mend one's ways and one's actions in conformity with the essential characteristic of the people's soul.

8. The highest form of penitence is penitence inspired by the ideal of honoring God. All other expressions of penitence are auxiliary to it. As our enlightenment progresses, our perceptions are raised to a higher level and the ideal of honoring God with all its comprehensiveness seems too narrow to include the entire sweep of all penitential strivings. Their sub-

stantive content appears too rich to be encompassed by wisdom or God's honor. But the concept of honoring God as the foundation of penitence will become clear at the inception of the enlightenment in the messianic age, and it will be seen as embracing the lower forms of penitence. The larger light of penitence appears initially as negating the lesser light, and rash spirits arise and attempt to formulate ideologies accordingly, but they will fail. The failure results from the claims of the lesser lights, which seemed to have been negated. The great light will continue to do its work and it will not cease until it will be recognized in its higher and lower manifestations. "Repair the breach with the son of Peretz [a metaphor for the Messiah] and pluck a rose from a thorn."[1]

9. Various forces will stimulate the emergence of penitence. A special factor in this process will be the anguish felt over the humiliation visited on the great spiritual treasure of our ancestral heritage, which is of incomparable vigor and nobility. This great spiritual treasure derives from the source of life, from the highest order of the divine, which has been transmitted from generation to generation. When one is attentive to it one can find everything in it, everything precious and beautiful, but a crude denial of our religion has led many to detach themselves from this "fruitful corner" and to stray in alien fields, which have no sustaining nourishment for us at all. This great anguish will erupt powerfully and with it will come discretion and moderation to know what positive elements may be garnered from the different paths of straying on which they stumbled. The free stirring of holiness inside the soul will emerge from its imprisonment, and every sensitive

---

1. The essence of penitence is the surge to perfect life on all levels, which thereby enhances the glory of God. The particularized expressions of this surge often take on purely secular forms and seem remote from the concept of honoring God but the messianic enlightenment will clarify this. Conventional pietists, the "rash spirits," detach God's glory from the various efforts to reform the world on an existential level, but they fail because the excluded values assert their claim. The result is that the reformers and the pietists clash and the glory of God remains in a low state, but this will be set right in the more enlightened state in the end of days.

spirit will begin to drink avidly from this exalted source of life. Then there will be engendered and become revealed, as one whole, knowledge and feeling, the enjoyment of life, a world outlook and a desire for national revival, the redress of spiritual defects and the revitalization of physical vigor, the ordering of the political system and the love for the improvement of the community in good manners and tolerance, together with a lively impatience with everything ugly and evil. To support these goals we need a conditioning of the human heart toward the true inner Torah, the mystical meanings in the Torah, whose influences on ill-prepared students have led so many to reject them and to mock them. It is, however, this very source of life-giving light whose influence on the ill-prepared engenders peril and trouble for the world that will prove to be a source of enduring deliverance. From this source will come the healing light by which to revitalize the community as well as the individual, to "raise the fallen tabernacle of David" (Amos 9:11) and to "remove the humiliation of the people of God from all the earth" (Isa. 25:8)

10. The impudence encountered prior to the coming of the Messiah derives from the fact that the world is ready for the concept that links all particulars within the universal, and any particularity not linked within the larger scope of the general cannot offer satisfaction. If people pursued the study of Torah in this spirit, to enlarge our spiritual perspective so as to recognize the proper connection between the particulars and the universal categories of the spiritual, then penitence and the resultant perfection of the world would arise and come to fruition. However, as a result of negligence, the light of the inner Torah whose pursuit needs a high state of holiness has not been properly established in the world. The result is that the call to regard the particulars as embraced within the general comes at a time that is not ripe for this concept. This has led to the frightful nihilism now rampant. We must make use of the higher therapy, to strengthen the

spiritual disposition so that the realization of the link between the teachings and the actions emanating from the Torah with the noblest of principles will be readily understood on the basis of common sensibilities. Then will the vigor of the spiritual life, in action and in thought, be reasserted in the world. General penitence will then begin to bear its fruit.

11. In the deep recesses of life there is always stirring a new illumination of higher penitence, even as a new light radiates in all the worlds, with all their fullness, to renew them. According to the degree of the light, and the wisdom and the holiness it embodies, do human souls become filled with the treasures of new life. The highest expression of ethical culture and its programmatic implementation is the fruit grown as a result of this illumination. It thus turns out that the light of the whole world and its renewal in its diverse forms depend at all times on penitence. Certainly the light of the Messiah, the deliverance of Israel, the rebirth of the people and the restoration of its land, language and literature—all stem from the source of penitence, and all lead out of the depths to the heights of penitence.

Chapter Five

The Inevitability of Penitence and its Effects in Man, in the World, and in the Jewish People

1. Penitence is the healthiest feeling of a person. A healthy soul in a healthy body must necessarily bring about the great happiness afforded by penitence, and the soul experiences therein the greatest natural delight. The elimination of damaging elements has beneficent and invigorating effects on the body when it is in a state of health. The purging away of every evil deed and its resultant evil effects, of every evil thought, of every obstruction that keeps us away from the

divine spiritual reality, is bound to arise when the organism is in a state of spiritual and physical health.

2. Over against every measure of ugliness that is withdrawn from a person through his inner conformity to the light of penitence, worlds resplendent with higher sensibility come to expression in his soul. Every removal of sin resembles the removal of an obstruction from the seeing eye, and a whole new horizon of vision is revealed, the light of vast expanses of heaven and earth and all that is in them.

3. The world must inevitably come to full penitence. The world is not static, but it continues to develop, and a truly full development must bring about the complete state of health, material and spiritual, and this will bring penitence along with it.

4. The spirit of penitence hovers over the world, and it is that which endows it with its basic character and the impetus to development. With the scent of its fragrance it refines it and endows it with the propensity to beauty and splendor.

5. The stubborn determination to remain with the same opinion and to invoke it in support of a sinful disposition to which one has become habituated whether in action or in opinion is a sickness resulting from a grievous enslavement that does not permit the light of penitence to shine in full strength. Penitence is the aspiration for the true original freedom, which is the divine freedom, wherein there is no enslavement of any kind.

6. Were it not for the thought of penitence, the peace and security it brings with it, a person would be unable to find rest, and the spiritual life would not be able to develop in the world. The moral sense demands of man justice and what is good, perfection—but how difficult it is for a person to realize moral perfection, and how weak he is to conform his behavior to the pure ideal of full justice! How then can he strive for that which is beyond his attainment? Therefore, penitence is natural for a person, and it is this that perfects

him. The fact that a person is always prone to stumble, to deviate from justice and morality, does not discredit his perfection, since the basis of his perfection is the constant striving and the desire for perfection. This desire is the foundation of penitence, which is constantly a directing influence on his way in life, and truly perfects him.

7. Penitence was planned before the creation of the world, and it is for this reason the foundation of the world. The quest for the perfection of life is a phase of its manifestation according to its nature. Since nature, by its own workings, is without probing and discrimination, sin thus becomes inevitable. "There is no man so righteous that he will [always] do good and not sin" (Kohelet 7:20). To nullify the basic nature of life that man shall become a non-sinner—this itself would be the greatest sin. "And one must make atonement for the sin committed against the self" (Num. 6:11).[2] Penitence redresses the defect and restores the world and life to their original character precisely by focusing on the basis of their highest attribute, the dimension of freedom. It is for this reason that God is called the God of life.

8. The future will disclose the remarkable power of penitence, and this revelation will prove of far greater interest to the world than all the wondrous phenomena that it is accustomed to behold in the vast areas of life and existence. The wonders of this new revelation will draw all hearts to it, exerting an influence on everyone. Then will the world rise to its true renewal and sin will come to an end. The spirit of impurity will be purged away, and all evil will vanish like smoke.

9. The people of Israel, because of their added spiritual sensitivity, will be the first with regard to penitence. They are the one sector of humanity in whom the special graces of penitence will become manifest. They experience a prodding

---

2. As interpreted in Nedarim 10a, that the nazirite vows of abstention were a sin that called for atonement.

to conform to the divine light radiant in the world, which is beyond sin and wrongdoing. Every deviation from this disposition damages the perfection that is characteristic of this people. In the end, the vigor of its life's rhythm will overcome the deviation, and they will attain full health, and they will assert it with great force. The light of penitence will be manifest first in Israel, and she will be the channel through which the life-giving force of the yearning for penitence will reach the whole world, to illuminate it and to raise its stature.

Chapter Six

The Prevalence and Inner Action of Penitence in the Hidden Depths of Man, the World and the Jewish People

1. Penitence emerges from the depths of being, from such great depths in which the individual stands not as a separate entity, but rather as a continuation of the vastness of universal existence. The desire for penitence is related to the universal will, to its highest source. From the moment the mighty stream for the universal will for life turns toward the good, many forces within the whole of existence are stirred to disclose the good and to bestow good to all. "Great is penitence for it brings healing to the world, and an individual who repents is forgiven and the whole world is forgiven with him" (Yoma 86a). In the great channel in which the life-sustaining force flows, there is revealed the unitary source of all existence, and in the hovering life-serving spirit of penitence all things are renewed to a higher level of the good, the radiant and the pure.

Penitence is inspired by the yearning of all existence to be better, purer, more vigorous and on a higher plane than it is. Within this yearning is a hidden life-force for overcoming every factor that limits and weakens existence. The particular penitence of the individual and certainly of the group draws its strength from this source of life, which is always active with never-ending vigor.

2. Penitence is always present in the heart. At the very time of sin penitence is hidden in the soul, and it releases its impulses, which become manifest when remorse comes summoning to repent. Penitence is present in the depths of existence because it was projected before the creation of the world, and before sin had occurred there had already been readied the repentance for it. Therefore, nothing is more certain than penitence, and in the end everything will be redressed and perfected. Certainly the people of Israel are bound to repent, to draw closer to their original goal to activate in life the nature of their soul, despite all the obstructions that impede the manifestation of this mighty force.

3. The natural fear of sin, in the general area of morals, is the healthiest expression of human nature. It is the singular characteristic of the nature of the Jew in reacting to every form of wrongdoing that violates the Torah and the commandments, the heritage of the community of Jacob. This disposition will not return to the Jewish people except through a program of popular education in Torah, to raise scholarly individuals and to establish fixed periods of study for the general populace. It will not be possible to restore the Jewish people to natural health without a full restoration of its spiritual characteristic, one aspect of which—the most vital one—is the fear of sin, a recoiling from it, and a turning to prescribed penitence if they, God forbid, lapse into any sin. As the people's vitality is strengthened in all its aspects, there will come an end to the maddening restlessness, and our national institutions will resume their concern with reasserting the unique, natural interest in morality among the Jewish people which is so exacting in differentiating between the forbidden and the permitted. All the minutest details in the teachings of the Torah and the sages will then be recognized

as an independent way of life, without which it is impossible to maintain a thriving national existence.

4. The moral defects that originate in a deviation from the natural moral sense complete their effect in a deviation from the divine moral norm by a defection from religion. The repudiation of and rebellion against the divine law is a frightful moral regression, to which a person succumbs only through an absorption in the vulgarity of materialistic existence. For a time, a generation, or some part of it, in some countries or provinces, may remain entangled in this moral blindness, to a point of not sensing the moral decline involved in abandoning the laws of God. But the moral sense does not lose its value because of this. Penitence is bound to come and to be made manifest. The sickness of forgetting the divine order cannot gain a firm foothold in human nature. Like a muddy spring, it returns to its purity.

5. The nature of existence, man's choice of action and his disposition constitute one chain of being that can never be detached one from another. What man desires is tied up with what he has done. The deeds of the past, too, are not eliminated from the thrust of life and its basic disposition. Since nothing is totally eradicated the will can impose a special configuration on past actions. This is the secret of penitence, which God established before He created the world. I mean to say that He expanded the potency of the spiritual life with reference to actions and to existence so that it also embraces the past. The evil deed continues to be reenacted, it causes ugliness and evil, deterioration and destruction, as long as the will did not put a new complexion on it. Once the will has put on it a configuration of the good, it itself becomes a stimulant for good and delight, the joy in God and His light.

6. Actions speak within the soul. Every noble action is generated by a chain of many causes in the realm of the good, the holy. There is no limit to chains of circumstances that were activated in the mysterious realm of the inner life until

this noble action became manifest. And just as every noble action originates in the realm of holiness, so, once it has been effectuated, does it release a light back to its source. It sends waves reverberating backward and enlarges the activities of the zone of the holy, and enhances it through the influence of the lower on the higher. The same process is at work in the opposite direction, with reference to every activity corrupt at its source; just as the impure source generates every corrupt activity, so does the corrupt activity manifest its sickness in the inwardness of the spirit that fashioned it. This will go on until the person who is master of his action and his will, will uproot it from its source through the power of penitence. Then, once it has been integrated within the pattern of love, it will transfer its abode to the depths of the good, and it will send up waves from below to above, just as the good actions, generating the good.

7. At the inception of creation it was intended that the tree have the same taste as the fruit (Genesis Rabbah 5:9). All the supportive actions that sustain any general worthwhile spiritual goal should by right be experienced in the soul with the same feeling of elation and delight as the goal itself is experienced when we envision it. But earthly existence, the instability of life, the weariness of the spirit when confined in a corporate frame, brought it about that only the fruition of the final step, which embodies the primary ideal, is experienced in its pleasure and splendor. The trees that bear the fruit, with all their necessity for the growth of the fruit have, however, become coarse matter and have lost their taste. This is the failing of the "earth," because of which it was cursed when Adam was also cursed for his sin. But every defect is destined to be mended. Thus we are assured that the day will come when creation will return to its original state, when the taste of the tree will be the same as the taste of the fruit. The earth will "repent" of its "sin" and the way of the practical life will no longer obstruct the delight of the ideal, which is sus-

tained by appropriate intermediate steps on its way toward realization, and will stimulate its emergence from potentiality to actuality.

Penitence itself, which activates the inner spirit that had been sunk in the depths of the chaotic and the antithetical to the ideal goal, will enable the aspiration for the ideal to penetrate all the conditioning influences, and in all of them will be tasted the splendor of the ideal goal. It will do this by enlarging the scope of action for the ideal of justice. Man will then no longer suffer the disgrace of indolence on the way of true life.[3]

Chapter Seven

The Value of Thoughts about Penitence, its Vision and Conception

1. It is in the nature of penitence to endow a person with peace and with solemnity at the same time. Even the mere thought of penitence is a comfort to him. In one tiny glimmer of its great light there is already to be found the noble happiness of a whole world, but together with this it confronts his spirit constantly with the obligation of completing it. This saves him from pride and invests him with a sweet light, which endows his life with great and abiding value.

The vision of penitence transforms all sins and their resultant confusion, their spiritual anguish and ugliness, to concepts of delight and satisfaction, for it is through them that a person is illuminated with the profound sense of hatred for evil; and the love for the good is strengthened in him with a mighty force. Beyond all calculation and knowledge, he finds delight in the joy of remorse wherein he feels that divine

---

3. This passage is based on the Midrashic homily that attempts to account for the inclusion of the earth in the curse that was pronounced on Adam after his sin in the Garden of Eden (Genesis Rabbah 5:9).

satisfaction uniquely experienced by penitents. This feeling comes appropriately together with the sense of refinement released by the heartbreak and the troubled spirit that are linked with the deep faith in liberation and continued assistance.

2. Every thought of penitence joins all the past to the future, and the future is uplifted through the ennoblement of the will inspired by penitence out of love.

3. Through the thoughts of penitence a person hears God's voice calling him, from the Torah and from the feelings of the heart, from the world and its fullness, and all that is contained therein. The desire for the good is strengthened within him. The flesh itself, which engenders the sin, becomes increasingly more refined to a point where the thought of penitence penetrates it.

4. The thoughts of penitence disclose the profound potency of the will. The heroism of the soul is made manifest thereby in all its splendor. The degree of penitence is also the degree of the soul's freedom.

5. I see how the sins serve as an obstruction against the bright divine light, which shines so brightly on every soul, and they darken the soul. Penitence, even if it is only entertained in thought, effects a great redress. But the soul can reach full liberation only when the potential of penitence is translated into action. However, since the thought is tied up with holiness and with the desire for penitence, there is no need to be concerned. God, may He be praised, will surely make available all the circumstances for the attainment of full penitence, which illumines all the dark places in its light. The degree of the penitence achieved is also the measure by which the person's study of Torah is blessed and made clearer. The study becomes clear and lucid. "A broken and contrite heart God will not spurn" (Ps. 51:19).

6. It is necessary to be so profoundly committed to the faith that even by entertaining the thought of penitence one mends a great deal in oneself and in the world. It is inevitable

that after every consideration of penitence a man should be happier and more at peace with himself than he was before. This is certainly the case if he has a firm decision to repent, and has become attached to the pursuit of Torah and wisdom and the fear of God, and especially if the disposition of divine love has begun to vibrate in him. He is then to comfort himself and console his weary spirit and strengthen it with every kind of encouragement, for we have the assurance of God's word: "As a person is comforted by his mother so will I comfort you" (Isa.66:13). If he should recall offenses he has committed against another person and he is too weak to redress them, he must not despair of the great efficacy of penitence. The offenses committed against God of which he has repented have already been forgiven. It is legitimate to assume, therefore, that the residual offenses are outweighed by the greater number that have been forgiven through penitence. However, he must not cease in his vigilance not to stumble over any offense against another person, and to rectify whatever he can of the past through wisdom and great resoluteness. "Save yourself as a deer from the hand of the hunter and as a bird from the hand of the fowler" (Prov. 6:5). But let him not become depressed because of the portion of offenses he has not yet managed to rectify. Instead let him hold firm to the pursuit of the Torah and the service of God with a full heart in joy, in reverence and in love.

Chapter Eight

The Pangs of Sin, the Suffering of Penitence
and the Healing of its Affliction

1. The pain felt in the initial inspiration to penitence is due to the severance of the evil layers of the self, which cannot be mended as long as they are attached to and remain part of

the person, and cause deterioration of the whole spirit. Through penitence they are severed from the basic essence of the self. Every severance causes pain, like the pain felt at the amputation of deteriorated organs for medical reasons. This is the most inward kind of pain, through which a person is liberated from the dark servitude to his sins and his lowly inclincations and their bitter aftereffects. "We learn this from the law that liberates a slave if he lost a tooth or an eye on being struck by his master." "Happy is the person whom You instruct, O Lord, and You *teach him out of Your law*"; the latter phrase may be read as meaning "this matter You have taught us from Your Law" (Berakhot 5a).

2. The great pains that overcome the soul as a result of the thought of penitence sometimes appear as a consequence of the fear of retribution. But in their inner essence they are intrinsic sufferings felt by the soul because it is afflicted by sin, which is contrary to all the condition of its being. However, these sufferings themselves cleanse it. The person who recognizes the goodly treasure imbedded in these sufferings accepts them with unreserved love and he is at peace. Thus he rises in many good qualities. His knowledge remains with him, his inner character is improved and the imprint his sins deposited on him is erased. His sins are transformed into reminders of the good, from which a spiritual beauty is revealed.

3. Every sin oppresses the heart because it disrupts the unity between the individual person and all existence. It can be healed through penitence, which is radiant with the light [of the higher influence] of the ideal embodied in universal existence. Thereby it becomes possible for the harmony with all existence to become once again manifest in him; when he repents he finds healing. However, the basis of the anguish experienced is not merely the result of sin itself. It is rather due to the basic nature of sin and the nature of the life process that has become disoriented from the order of existence,

which is resplendent with divine light radiant in all being in unity and high purpose. It is for this reason that those whose lives are basically evil and whose sins are rooted in their thoughts and aspirations and in the dispositions of their hearts become pessimists and see the whole world in such unduly dark colors. They are the ones who complain against the world and against life. They are the masters of the "melancholy spleen" (Zohar II 227b), whose mockery of existence is the laughter of a fool who does not realize that the Lord is good to all (Ps. 145:9).

4. What is the reason for the rage evinced by evil doers? What is the meaning of their anger with the whole world, what is the basis for the bitter melancholy that consumes spirit and flesh, that poisons life, that is found among them? Whence comes this degenerate source? With clear inner certainty we reply to this: All this stems from the source of evil, "from the wicked emanates wickedness" (I Sam. 24:13). The will is free, life dawned that a person might be heroic and truly free. When the will refuses to leave evil reposing in the depths of the soul, it unbalances life, it disturbs the equitable relationship of the soul with all existence, its overall character and its constituent particularities. The disruption of harmony brings about many pains. When it penetrates to the spirit there is an aggravation of suffering that manifests itself in fright, anger, impudence, dishonor and despair. The righteous, the people of goodness and of kindness, the men who know the happiness of life, therefore, call out to the miserable wrongdoers: Come and live, come back, come back from your evil way—why should you die? (Ezek. 33:11). Find delight in the goodness of the Lord and enjoy a life of pleasure and light, of peace and of quiet, of faith and honor, "as dew from the Lord, as showers on the grass" (Mic. 5:6).

5. Every righteous person experiences great anguish because he does not feel sufficiently close to God, and his great thirst remains unquenched. Because of this anguish all his

organs are tense with endless longing, and he finds no peace in all the delights and pleasures of the world. This is in essence the anguish of the *shekinah*, the anguish of the divine Presence, for all life in all the worlds is astir with longing that the supreme perfection of godliness be made manifest in them. This manifestation, in all its expanse and its delights, is contingent on the perfection of the free will in people, with all the talents and the good works that hinge on it. It is for this reason that the righteous always long for the penitence of the general public, and in the inwardness of their hearts they seek to see offenders in a light of innocence, as one seeks life itself, for in truth this is our very life and the life of all worlds.

6. When the righteous perform acts of penance, they reveal the holy light that they find in the dark and broken-down alleys in their own lives. The strategies they devise for themselves to rise out of depression and despair into the bright light of holiness and a nobler level of equity become in themselves great lights to illumine the world. Every person who feels within himself the depth of penitential remorse and the anxiety to mend his flaws—both those whose redress is within his reach and those he hopes to redress in time by the mercy of God—should include himself in the category of the righteous. Through their thoughts of penitence the whole world is renewed in a new light.

7. The whole world is pervaded by harmony. The unifying congruence penetrates all branches of existence. The inner moral sense and its mighty claims represent an echo of the unitary voice of all parts of existence, all of which interpenetrate, and the self is permeated with them and united with all. Every moral severance in thought or deed, in character or disposition, creates many wounds that inflict many inner pains in all aspects of the soul. The basis of these spiritual pains is the disturbing force of withdrawing the light of life emanating from the general order of existence from the life channels of the sinning soul. The purer a soul is the more it will

experience the disturbance of its pains, until it will still the pain in the life-stream of penitence, which flows from the divine source, which mends all the torn parts, and sends forth a life-restoring dew flowing directly from all realms of existence. There will be a reunion, the life-restoring flow will reach the soul that has been restored to its higher life in great mercy and abiding joy.

8. When the anguish, which is the pain of penitence brought about by the person's own spiritual state and that of the whole world, becomes very great, to a point of blocking the creative sources of thought, speech, prayer, outcries, feeling and song, then one must rise in a leap to seek life-giving lights in the source of silence. "The parched land will become a pool, and the thirsty ground springs of water" (Isa. 35:7).

9. When the thinking person withdraws into solitude and his inner spiritual strength is activated, he then feels all the flaws that have damaged his soul because his actions and dispositions are not what they should be. He then suffers a deep sense of anguish and he probes within himself how to mend his flaws. When the inner anguish becomes outwardly manifest with full gravity or when his outer condition deteriorates, as in times of disaster and trouble, then the inner feeling will not be firm. But even then it may lead to its climactic end, for penitence, even when induced by suffering, is still penitence.

10. The inner anguish that is a concomitant of penitence is excellent raw subject matter for poets of melancholy to express through their music and for artists of tragedy to show through their talent.

11. Sins are the essence of melancholy. When the soul undergoes cleansing, it experiences the very essence of its sins, and then does the melancholy of penitence assert itself; a fire of anguish, remorse, shame and a terrifying fear burns inside it. But in this very process it is purified. After some time, when the agitation subsides, it will return to its state of

health, to function again with self-control and self-respect.

12. One must be very cautious not to fall into depression to the extent that it will inhibit the light of penitence from penetrating to the depths of the soul. Otherwise the feeling of depression might spread as a malignant disease throughout the body and spirit; for sin grieves the heart and causes feelings of depression to settle over the festering bitterness of the agitation for penitence. The latter has melancholy aspects but they are like cleansing fire that purges the soul and sustains it on a basis of constant natural joy appropriate to its state.

13. Every sin produces a special anxiety of the spirit, which does not recede except through penitence. Depending on the level of penitence, this anxiety itself is transformed into a feeling of security and firmness of heart. One can recognize the anxiety that comes through in marks on the face, in gestures, in the voice, in behavior, in the handwriting, in the manner of communication, in speech, and especially in the style of writing, in the way one develops thoughts and arranges them. Whenever sin has obstructed the light, there is the defect noticeable. And according to the gravity of the sin, and its relevance for the viewer, will its imprint be discernible to those who look with clear eyes.

14. One cannot overestimate the distress caused by a lack of will for goodness and holiness. Wisdom is of no efficacy except to the extent that it is pervaded by the blessing of the will for the good. Sin inhibits the will from rising to a higher state. One must, therefore, repent in order to purify the will, that wisdom might appropriately assert itself. Especially is it important to repent of offenses against another person, above all, of robbery, which obstructs the ascent of the will. One must vigorously attend to this and trust in God's help to reach a state of perfection that will inhibit one's hands from touching anything tainted with oppression.

15. The despair that registers in the heart is itself an

indication of a refined inner revolt, which stems from a higher recognition of morality and holiness. It is, therefore, fitting that the despair itself shall strengthen a person's heart to be unafraid and to repent of every sin, which will bring him peace and firmness of spirit.

16. When a person entertains the thought of penitence and of mending his actions and feelings, even if it is only in thought, he must not be disturbed because he feels agitated over his many sins, of which he has now become more conscious. This is the nature of this phenomenon. As long as a person is being driven by the coarser aspects of nature and by bad habits surrounding him, he is not so sensitive to his sins. Sometimes he feels nothing, and he sees himself as a righteous person. But once his moral sense is awakened, the light of the soul becomes at once manifest, and by that light his whole self becomes subjected to probing and he sees its defects. Then he becomes agitated with a deep sense of anxiety because of his low state of perfection and his grave deterioration. It is, however, precisely then for him to consider that this awareness and this anxiety that comes with it are the best signs pointing to full deliverance through the perfection of the self, and he should strengthen himself thereby in the Lord his God.

Chapter Nine

The Significance of the Will that is Manifest in Penitence

1. The steady concentration of one's thought on penitence forms a person's character on a spiritual foundation. He continually draws into himself a refined spirit, which places him on a spiritual plane of life.

When the concern with penitence is always active in the heart, it confirms to a person the great value of the spiritual life. The important principle that the goodness of the will is basic, and all the inclinations in the world are only its implementation, becomes a fixed conviction within himself through the light of penitence that is constantly active in him. Automatically there settles upon him the great influx of the holy spirit as a permanent attribute. A quality of will ennobled by holiness, higher than what is customary among ordinary people, asserts itself increasingly within him. He then comes to recognize the true value of genuine success that depends on the person himself and is independent of external conditions—and this is a will for the good.

This success yields greater happiness than do all treasures and possessions. Only this brings happiness to the whole world and to all existence. For a good will that always abides in the soul transforms all life and all existence toward the good. By looking at the basic nature of existence with an eye for the good, one exerts an influence on existence and on the complicated processes of life so that they emerge from their deficiencies. All things then bloom and live in a happy state, as a result of the spiritual riches and the abundance that is contained in the good will.

This concept, that these fundamental issues hinge only on a good will, is disseminated in the world through "the masters of penitence," for whom penitence is indeed a constant preoccupation. Thus the will is increasingly refined and made better and the world moves toward greater perfection.

The nature of the will that is forged by penitence is an expression of the will immanent in the depth of life, not the shallow will that embraces only the superficial and external aspects of life. The will we speak of represents the most basic essence directing the life process, and this is the authentic nature of the soul. As the will is conditioned to the quest for the good through the profound commitment to penitence, the good becomes a fixed attribute of the soul, and all the resultant effects, all the benefits seeded in the world by the true penitent, derive from the realm of good. These are the people with enlightened souls in whom is embodied the ideal light of the higher holiness.

2. One's perspective is enlarged through penitence. The basic ideal of the good grows in its embrace to include the beginning of the world to the end, to the last generations. In the sweep of this view, because of its length and width, height and depth, there stands revealed the divine good and mercy in its authenticity, and personal as well as collective existence take on more nobility by being rooted in full equity. The defects that are manifest in the order of life come to be recognized as distortions that are smoothed out in the grandeur of the life of goodwill that flows like a mighty river over generations and epochs. Only fractional aspects of existence are disclosed in each particular generation, but the complete view becomes revealed in the course of the generations when the sweep of the will inspired by penitence endows them all with life and peace abounding with delight. When this becomes revealed it becomes clear that the happiness and the righteous joy have their fixed place from the very inception of things. All that seemed deficient, all that seemed ugly in the past, turns out to be full of majesty and grandeur as a phase of the greatness achieved through the progress of penitence.

3. The essence of penitence brings healing veritably to the entire world. The thrust of the will completes its work with force precisely after it emerges from confinement. Penitents carry on with special vigor the life-force emanating from the good. All actions and all creatures are included within the scope of the will that crystallizes in the person, in all its beauty. The basic essences, the forces and their resultant effects, are thrust in all directions—who has invested them with the light of life, system and order to stimulate the good to avoid evil traps? It is the exalted will, the moral force that is illuminated with divine light. Through the projection of the sensibilities of a holy people do all actions merge into an

integrated whole to carry out the will of the holy King who is exalted in justice and is sanctified in mercy.

4. A weakening of the will through the constant immersion in penitence represents an enfeeblement of body and spirit, which needs therapy. Nevertheless, it also partakes of the refinement and spirituality that purify the spirit, and love covers up every transgression.

5. When one is concerned with penitence it is necessary to differentiate carefully between what is good and what is evil, so that the feeling of remorse and the agitation of spirit oscillating between affirmation and negation focus only on the evil and not the good. Moreover, it is necessary to identify the good that is embodied in the depth of evil and to strengthen it—with the very force wherewith one recoils from evil. Thus will penitence serve as a force for good that literally transforms all the wrongdoings into virtues.

6. Sin blackens the illumination of the higher wisdom that is manifest when the soul is in edifying harmony with all existence and its divine source. This relationship is discernible in such souls in which enlightenment and will function as a unitary entity. Every sinful act disrupts this ideal unity and places the orbit of life outside it. The illumination that flows like a clear spring will not resume its influence on the will that has been profaned unless the person will turn back and be remorseful. Then will the light of penitence, to the degree of its clarity in perception and depth of acceptance, restore the original harmony. "Restore to me the joy of Your deliverance, and let Your generous spirit uphold me" (Ps. 51:14).

7. There is a defect in the lower level of penitence, in that it weakens a person's will and thereby damages his personality. This defect is rectified when the thought of penitence rises to maturity. Then it becomes part of the higher penitence whose aim is not to weaken the will or break the personal character of the individual but to strengthen his will and to heighten his self-esteem. Thereby the willful sins are trans-

formed into a positive force. "When the wicked turns from his wickedness and does that which is lawful and right—he shall live thereby" (Ezk. 33:19).

8. Penitence removes the thrust of the will, which has already been materialized in action and which has reached such a level of potency that it was able to satisfy the mighty claims of morality and religion. But since the divine light has been activated intensely and the will has been disoriented from its original focus, it does not become inert. Instead it acts with its potency on the basic core of the world, to plant in all existence a firm will for light and for good. Thus the previous acts of wrongdoing are transformed into real virtues.

9. Every sin stems from a defect in a person's capacity. The self has become weakened and it cannot resist the inclination to evil. This lack of capacity, when translated to action, weakens the will for the good, and this begets a weakness in perception, and the recognition of the good becomes confused. Penitence sets in after discernment, when one is more keenly sensitive in recognizing the good, which develops fully with the sensitivity to recognize what is evil. Evil authenticates the good. When the basic evil is readily recognized as evil, then does the basic good shine more brightly in its goodness. The more clearly we know the nature of the good and the obscuring effect of sin is lifted through the restoration of the will for the good and the inclination to pursue it, the more is there stirred in the person the resolution to fortify the will for the good in itself and to save it from the defect of sin. The self that has been weakened is compensated by rising from its lowly state and improving its capacity, so that it may function with full vitality in its commitment to the good. Thereby is the capacity to choose truly free, and the good is evaluated without impediment. Automatically the attraction of the spiritual, which is present in every person to draw him to the good, will be activated to strengthen the preference for the good, and to establish the structure of life in the individual

and in society on the basis of the absolute good, whose final word is—the light of God.

10. Penitence, with all its derivative applications in action, together with the underlying spirit that pervades it especially during the days dedicated to penitence, bestows a great benefit in purifying souls, in refining the spirit and purging behavior from its ugliness. But together with this it necessarily bears within itself a certain weakness that even the most heroic spirits cannot escape.

When one shrinks the will, when one restrains the life-force through inner withdrawal and the inclination to avoid any kind of sin, there is also a shrinking of the will for the good. The vitality of the virtuous life is also weakened. It turns out that the person suffers from the cleansing of his moral state the kind of weakness experienced by the patient who was cured from his illness through a strong current of electric shock. It may have eliminated the virus of his illness but it also weakened his healthy vitality. The penitential season is therefore followed by days of holy joy and gladness for the self[4] to restore the will for the good and the innocent vitality of life. Then will penitence be complete.

Chapter Ten

The Interdependence of Penitence and the Torah in their General Nature and in their Highest Significance

1. Truly full penitence presupposes high vistas of contemplation, an ascent to the rarefied world that abounds in truth and holiness. One can achieve this only through the pursuit of the deeper levels of Torah and divine wisdom concerning the mysical dimension of the world. This calls for

---

4. The festival of Sukkot and Simhat Torah.

physical purity and moral purity as aids, so that the clouds of lust shall not obscure the clarity of the mind. But prior to all these must come the study of the Torah, specifically the higher Torah for only this can break all the iron barriers that separate the individual and the community from their heavenly Father.

Penitence comes about as a result of a clear assessment of the world, and it in itself, by virtue of its own potency, serves to clarify and elucidate the world.

2. A good indication of valid penitence is a state of inner satisfaction and an illumination of the intelligence in higher perspectives, clarity in the formation of concepts, and holy vigor and purity of the imaginative faculty to concretize the higher perception that embraces all the diverse manifestations of the world.

3. Every sin impedes the calmness needed for the illumination of the mystical dimension of the world. Penitence opens vistas of understanding, even as it in itself is a byproduct of understanding.

4. Penitence is a necessity if one is to gain enlightenment concerning matters divine. The strength of will and its enlightenment and intellectual vigor are interdependent. Activities shed light on the higher sources that generate them, and the sensibilities rooted in the realm of the holy, by the very fact of their existence, reveal this source. Therefore whoever is ready for constant cleaving to God cannot be content with any state below this, and there are already present within him conditioning factors, physical and spiritual, that prod him to return to the full cleaving to God. But one cannot reach this except through a profound sense of humility, experienced when the spirit expands with great joy in the light of God. This is engendered in the heart when the perception has registered that cleaving to God, in all its manifestations, is the greatest happiness in life, and that the more impressively this perception is entertained and the more it is adorned by under-

standing, by a lofty spirit, by action, by an established life-
style, by public enlightenment and by greatness and nobility
of soul—the more the happiness of life will increase. As a
result of all this the joy of the soul will become more pervasive
and the state of cleaving to God will rise to its highest climax,
to a point where the grandeur of God will become manifest in
the soul. There is no limit to the depth of humility that will be
stimulated by this, for how can any person bear himself with
pride when he stands before the source of all perfection, the
infinite light of the supernal realm that transcends all blessing
and praises?

5. How wrongdoing dulls the intelligence, both the intelligence of the individual and the intelligence of society, of a
generation and of an epoch! The divine word reaches a person
from all its sources, from the Torah, from religious faith,
from ancestral customs, from social mores, from his inner
sense of equity—all these are channeled from the core reality
in the spiritual order and its fullness, in the laws of heaven
and earth, and their most basic essence. When degeneration
leads him to embrace an outlook on life that negates his higher
vision, then he becomes prey to the dark side within him, to
his weaker self. The result is that he cannot muster the
strength to hold on to the orderly structure of life as it makes
its claims on him, whereby he is held back from sin and
steered in the way of integrity as God fashioned him. Then it
is not merely one aspect of his being that has declined and
fallen, it is not merely his fluctuating will that has been
weakened, while his spirit in its essential nature, his intellect,
and the whole direction of his life have remained in their
previous state. It is not so; all things have changed. The
operative light of the mind, which is united in the depth of the
spiritual essence with all the life forces, which is woven together in one pattern with the moral order embodied in all
that surrounds it, below and above—this light is darkened.
And this light is the secret of life itself, the vitality in which

the soul finds its sustenance. It is only in purification, in penitence, that the light and life will again become manifest. Thus penitence is the basis of that human culture which is so much sought after.

6. Transgressions and unrefined morals dull the heart, and as long as one's spirit is darkened by them, it is impossible for any objective self-assessment to be cultivated on a broad basis. The seeker who seeks to elevate himself to higher enlightenment will feel this himself, and he will experience a compulsion to reach out for full penitence, so that his higher enlightenment shall not be defective. However, while in the case of all offenses between man and God spiritual penitence restores at once the joy of deliverance, in the case of offenses between man and man there cannot be any restoration until they have been redressed in action. At times there may be impediments that cannot be overcome, and as long as these wrongs have not been redressed they inhibit the light of knowledge, and they automatically impede the full recognition of the general sense of justice and the longing for its expression in life. Nevertheless, through a firm resolution to beware at least for the future of wrongdoing against other persons and to endeavor to mend the past—in the measure that he will fulfill these commitments to penitence, will the spiritual light shine on his soul. And the resourcefulness of the spirit itself will then find him ways to complete his penitence in action, so that the spiritual light, in all its fullness and beneficence, may alight on the soul that is so thirsty for it.

7. When a person raises himself to a higher perception, his sins will act at once to obstruct the supernal light, and the great thoughts decline as a result of the chilling effect of the sins, which are registered inside the heart. Let him then at once repent with a clear penitence, which will restore to him the more happy life as in the twinkling of an eye. To the extent that penitence will be authenticated in action, in his pattern of life, will the fruits of his thought be enhanced and the flow of his perception blessed.

8. This is certain, that one cannot succeed in the study of the mystical dimension of the Torah without penitence. In the study of those lofty subjects the will is joined with the understanding in one entity. When one comprehends the core of those subjects in congruence with the firmness of the will for the good, then one is spurred by a longing for it, and one projects many general and particular strategies as to how to reach it. But when sins form an obstruction, the will is damaged. Since the person cannot rise to the highest level of the will, and, being sunk in the filth of sin he cannot appreciate the importance of the will for the general and the particular good, knowledge cannot grow in him, and the channels for comprehending the secret teachings of the Torah are blocked. It is, therefore, important to strengthen oneself to do penance and to purify the will in order to attain a lucid understanding in the supernal subjects.

9. One cannot enter the spiritual world of mystical knowledge and gaze at the supernal light except through a preceding act of full penitence. When a person confronts the supernal illumination, there is at once revealed to him the splendor of absolute justice and beauty in the supernal holiness, and a fierce pressure is generated in him that he too shall be embraced by that splendor and beauty and that his life shall be rooted in them in all their manifestations. At once he assesses his actions and his morals and sees their defects. Then he experiences remorse and he repents out of genuine love. To the extent that he resolves to walk in the good path, in congruence with the light of the logic of equity—which becomes more ascendent with the illumination in the Torah, in which alone a Jew can find the deepest level of his responsibility—will he become rooted in the supernal world. Without any inner contradiction will his thoughts then become radiant, and the spiritual visions of the higher enlightenment that focuses on the mysteries of the world will rise before his eyes in their full radiance, in accordance with his previous state and preparedness, and in accordance with

his true spiritual vitality and freedom.

10. When one pursues the study of divine subjects by the method of pure contemplation, one experiences within oneself an obstructing veil that screens him from clear perceptions. The soul itself recognizes that this veil consists of the actions and morals that are not good. At once there is astir within the heart the longing for full penitence, for the highest kind of penitence. At times this will not be realized fully until it will be accompanied by sincere prayer. Then will the mighty fountain send forth its flow upon the soul.

11. Prayer and outcries to God and penitence from the depths of the heart expressed in a mending of behavior must precede every grasp of a higher perception. It is impossible for a truly important literature radiant with life-giving illumination to appear without the energizing presence of penitence, which renews the character of the whole world. However, the radiance of the literature of the future appears in sparks of understanding that precede penitence and pervade the spirit in full freedom that stimulates full penitence. This brings with it liberation, preceded by inner and outer forgiveness. This will at once be followed by healing and sustenance and the restoration of the exiles, and a renewal of the authority of judges and counselors who are the pillars of this literature and its founders; evil will then be subdued; justice will ascend; the heart of the people will begin to beat mightily toward Jerusalem; a crown of a fully sovereign nation will appear and all the heart's desires will be fulfilled, in accordance with the prayer of the upright,[5] which abounds with the love of Him who sustains the universe, who promised and brought it into being.

---

5. The blessings here anticipated are included in the weekday Amidah prayer.

Chapter Eleven

The Sources of Penitence in the Universal Realms of Being and the Highest Dimension of the Spiritual

1. Penitence comes as an aspect of discernment, and in its highest expression it transforms willful wrongs into merits, and they thus become a force for life. However, penitence, in all its forms, suffers initially from a weakening of the will related to the remorse felt for past misdeeds. It is only subsequently that it changes to joy and a relaxation of the mind due to the higher perception, to the transformation of willful wrongs into merits. More than this is the perspective of wisdom,[6] which was never involved in the weakening pain of remorse. It sees the merits [of the recycled wrongs] shining as the noon day and it brings with it the joy of God in full splendor without any blunting of shame or sadness, for everything has been converted to virtue, *from the very beginning*, through the manifestation of discernment in the soul. Higher than this is the manifestation of the light of the "universal crown,"[7] Here is the mysterious vision of the all, that begets all delight, all holiness and good, that includes everything in its holy treasure. This light does not operate by releasing the remorse felt when the divine emanation of discernment is stirred to action. By its light it is revealed that there is no deficiency or darkness at all. There is only the holy light and supernal beauty, the blossoming of life and uplifting illumination. It is beyond the action of discernment that voids [the wrongs, through penitence]. "For the Lord of hosts ordained

---

6. In the Cabbalah the *sefira* or divine emanation of wisdom, which sees reality in an unfragmented comprehensiveness, is higher than the *sefira* of discernment, which analyzes reality into components.

7. The highest of the ten *sefirot* or divine emanations, in which the divine light or life-force is in its purity without any reduction by the descent toward a material world and hence untainted by sin.

it, and who shall void it?" (Isa. 14:27). It is beyond the action of the *sefira* of wisdom that releases. From here flows only all good, without impediment; evil and ugliness never had any place here, for in truth it was not, it is not, and it will not be. There is only the light of God and His goodness.

2. The holy spirit in its general manifestation embraces in one whole the juncture of all its constituent expressions, those of the will, of the intellect, of beauty, of strength and of morality. It is this, when it acts in its fullness and on its highest level, that gives speech to the prophets, moving them to speak with varying particularization and with thundering power, "like the sound of many mighty waters, a tumultuous sound like that of an army, like the voice of the Almighty" (Ezek. 1:24). This is the spirit that embraces within itself the five expressions of the holy spirit mentioned elsewhere. This spirit also sends forth sparks of penitential light, it manifests itself in the spirit of penitence that is always present in every heart that desires to rise from the pit of sin and its failure—to the holy heights, to visit in the Temple of the Lord.

3. The more deeply rooted penitence is, the more there recedes the fear of death until it stops altogether. It is replaced by the condition commended in the woman of valor: "She laughs at the last day" (Prov. 31:25).[8] The spiritual reality of the person's true self, like the spiritual reality of the whole world, assumes its projected character, its authentic self becomes explicitly revealed, and death loses its name, and with it the fear and the terror it inspires. The individual identity continues to expand, it becomes part of the general being of the people in a very real fusion, and from there it is absorbed in the general existence of the whole world. As part of universal existence it finds its happiness in the divine splendor, in its great strength, its light and its delight, a richness of life that sends forth the flow of eternal being.

---

8. In accordance with the literal meaning of the text.

4. The life process is built on the basis of penitence. Particular existences become manifest in progressive descent from the divine to the worldly. This is a kind of deterioration and frightful death, to which the usual declines in the world from level to level, from more to less talent and mastery, cannot be compared. The descent is governed by divine providence, according to an assessment of justice that determines the fate of existences before any creature is created. Included in the supernal mercy alluded to in the verse "the world is built on mercy" (Ps. 89:3) is something of sternness and rigorous law as alluded to in the statement that the spirit of God "hovers over the face of the waters" (Gen. 1:2).[9] But this descent bears hidden within itself the basis of subsequent ascent, and even before the ordered structure of time emerged, the ascent was contained in it, and "the great depth of justice and the great heights of mercy" (Ps. 36:7) have kissed. Thus the nature of existence continues to clarify itself, it achieves greater authenticity in the spirit of man. For penitence is his portion and inheritance, and it serves as a symbol for all existence in the greatest heights and the lowest depths. "Lord, You have been our dwelling place from generation to generation, before the mountains were brought forth and You fashioned the earth and the world, from everlasting to everlasting, You are God. You humble man saying, Return to Me, you children of men" (Ps. 90:2-3). When we realize to what extent the smallest particularities of existence, the spiritual and the material, in miniature, all embody the general principles, and the smallest fragment has elements of greatness in the depths of its being, we shall no longer be surprised at the mystery of penitence that penetrates so deeply the spirit of man, that pervades him from the inception of his thought and world outlook to the minutest details of his acts and the ex-

---

9. The term for God here used in *elohim*, which describes God in His more austere manifestation, as Judge.

pressions of his character. This process is reenacted in the historical processes of humanity. When we shall understand better the qualitative value of man and his spirit, and the character he gives to existence through his influence, we shall at once discern clearly the luminous relationship between the great, cosmic form of penitence, in its broadest, deepest and highest aspects, and the penitence of the person, the individual and the collective, on whose orbit revolve all the strategies of the practical and the spiritual life. "Out of the depths I have called to the Lord" (Ps. 130:1).

5. The phenomenon of penitence indicates that the basis of every action is the spiritual imprint it leaves on the essence of the self. Since the content of every action is only the concept it symbolizes, which is woven into the basic structure of reality, we must necessarily say that the real world, as it is, is indeed a divided world. Its elements harmonize with each other, but the core of its being is its ideational element, which embraces it but is higher than it and transcends it. Penitence elevates the person and his world to that level, where all existence stands in the clarity of its spiritual content. That world, in the firmness of its spiritual state, is sovereign over our limited world of action. The order of our world of action then follows the imprint deposited in us in the phenomenon of penitence through the process of thought.

6. On the basis of the mystery by which life is governed, every good deed of an evil person takes its place in the realm of evil and impurity, even though, despite this, God does not deny his reward and compensates him in this world for even the slightest virtuous act. This is the way of evil. Certainly every act of wrongdoing and sin of a righteous person, though "he suffers retribution on earth" (Prov. 11:31) and "all about He has set raging storms" [of retribution] (Ps. 50:3), everything follows the rule that the measure of the good bestowed exceeds the measure of retribution exacted, thus enhancing the light of the holy and the good. From this we may infer a

general principle governing the status of nations, that any good action of a wicked nation strengthens the domain of the world's evil and that "acts of kindness of [evil] nations is a sin" (Prov. 14:34). The people of Israel, "a righteous nation committed to faithfulness" (Isa. 26:2), is subject to the rule that those close to Him are held accountable by the Holy One, praised be He, for even the slightest infraction, and are governed by the principle: "You only have I known of all the families of the earth, therefore will I visit on you all your iniquities" (Amos 3:2). All sins that are engendered from such a source that is for the most part good, that indicates that in its inner essence it is all good, must truly contain in the core of their being, in its hidden inwardness, a great light and much good. Thus we note that the transgression of the tribes[10] became the means of feeding the whole world.[11] In this spirit did the sages ordain the prayer: "Even when they transgress may their needs be before You" (Ber. 28b, 29b). However, this is the rule: The good and the constructive force that emanates from sin needs considerable refining before it can be transformed for the strengthening of all creation, and this refining takes place in the crucible of suffering that purges away pain, that is, it refines the sin that derives from a source that is good. It purges it from its outer ugliness, and establishes it on the basis of its inner essence in which abides the life of truth and holiness. And because nothing of the actions of a righteous person is lost as is alluded to in the verse "His leaf will not wither and in whatever he does, he shall prosper" (Ps. 1:3), every sin of his, even the most minor, must go through refinement. Thus it will be reconditioned to serve the general higher and beneficent purpose for which every gesture of a holy soul has been destined. This is suggested in the verse "For the Lord knows the way of the righteous" (Ps. 1:6)—the

---

10. The ten brothers who sold Joseph into slavery.

11. When Eygpt's food supply, under Joseph's management, fed the world during the time of famine, Gen. 41: 54-57.

Lord knows a realm where the thoughts of no creature can reach. Every form of penitence inspired by love reaches to that inner source, whence all that occurs is good and serves retroactively as an edifice of perfection and equity. The willful transgressions that are transformed into virtues do not need to become new creations, but only their basic source needs to be disclosed. Even the new heaven and the new earth that the Holy One, praised be He, is destined to fashion in the days of the Messiah do not involved a new creation. They are already in existence, as it is written: "As the new heaven and the new earth which I shall make stand before Me"[12]—the text does not say "shall stand" but "stand."

Chapter Twelve

The Influence of Penitence on the Ways of the Spirit, on Life and on Behavior Generally

1. Penitence raises a person above all the meanness to be found in the world, but it does not alienate him from the world. On the contrary, he thereby raises the world and life itself with him. Those impulses that engendered sin are refined in him. The mighty will that breaks all bounds, that influenced him to sin, becomes a living force that engenders great and lofty things for good and for blessing. The grandeur of life inspired by the highest domain of the holy hovers always on penitence and on those who are its champions, for they are the choicest representatives of life, who advocate its perfection, who call for the removal of stumbling blocks and for the return to the authentic good and true happiness, toward the lofty height of true liberty, which becomes a man who ascends toward the higher realm in accordance with his

---

12. The literal meaning, the usual translation is "shall stand," Isa. 66:22.

spiritual origin and his creation in God's image.

2. The more a person contemplates the nature of penitence, the more he will find in it the source of heroism and the most basic content for a life of practicality and idealism.

3. How we need penitence, how vital it is to illumine the horizon of all life! The spiritual channels are closed because of man's sin. The thirst for God and all its expressions, which embrace the radiance of the moral disposition, its practical aspect and its inner stirring in the soul, are in convulsion. It begins to jerk and stir with a movement of life, but falls again, because the burden of the filth of the transgressions weighs it down. Not only personal sin weighs it down, but even more so, the sin of society. The few noble spirits who seek the light of God suffer because of the sins of society as a whole. Their love for people is boundless. The core of the good in their souls is drawn especially toward the good of society and society is prone to contaminate them with the sins in which it is enmeshed. However, the truly righteous suffer willingly all the obstructions, all the physical and spiritual suffering, their only concern being to serve their goal, to enlighten, to improve, to enhance the good and the light of holiness, to hew a path toward the light of God and His delight, that it might enter every heart and spirit so that all may enjoy the goodness of the Lord, that God might rejoice in his works.

4. Every sin, even the slightest, plants in a person hostility toward some creature and through penitence love is again radiant.

5. When a person sins he has entered the world of fragmentation, and then every particular being stands by itself, and evil is evil in and of itself, and it is evil and destructive. When he repents out of love there at once shines on him the light from the world of unity, where everything is integrated into one whole, and in the context of the whole there is no evil at all. The evil is joined with the good to invest it with more attractiveness, and to enhance its significance. Thus the

willful wrongs become transformed into real virtues.

6. It is impossible to assess the importance of practical penitence, the mending of one's behavior according to the Torah and absolute equity, to make possible all the benefits of the spiritual ascent of the community and the individual. Each practical step in this process holds within its smallest gesture endless thrusts of idealism and breadth of perception that condition it to play its role in the world and in life. But when this step becomes defective, then is voided the strength of all the ideals released into the world. These ideals are analogous to the enormous potential energy imprisoned in one nucleus of an atom to give it its substantive force.

7. Penitence came before the world. The moral law encompasses everything. The claim of the supernal goal becomes particularized into many components. Any action that deviates from the norm, that is not oriented toward its source, is reoriented to its source when the will is mended.

8. The higher form of penitence is inspired by an inner force that derives from an external force emanating from the divine realm. The whole world, the physical and the spiritual, is embraced in a unitary whole. Morality, the impulse for equity and good, represents the central direction of the will of existence. This center, in the particularization of life, must conform to all the surrounding reality, to all existence, in its inner essence as well as its outer expression. Through the inner perception deep within the heart of what is equitable and good one recognizes the action of the moral law that pervades all existence, in the form of a vital, vibrant idealism. In the Torah this moral conformity in all its manifestations is represented in the light of holiness, adapted to each community according to its stature, and to the Jewish people in its most authentic form. The personality that finds in its way of life and its spiritual disposition defects and disharmony in relation to the absolute all, the inner and the manifest, will suffer endless pain and will seek to return to the source of life

and being. It will experience remorse over its straying, and it will return with an anxious heart and with the joy of deliverance. "I have strayed as a lost sheep, seek Your servant, for I have not forgotten Your commandments" (Ps. 119:176).

9. Penitence is, in essence, an effort to return to one's original status, to the source of life and higher being in their fullness, without limitation and diminution, in their highest spiritual character, as illumined by the simple, radiant divine light. The life process lowers us to proliferating fragmentation, which tends to solidify our limited existence, the more it reaches out and becomes involved in action, in undertakings and accomplishments. This creates the impression that our lives are firm and stable. It is for this reason that we feel weak and failing as the will prods us to return to the primary source that transcends all its proliferating particularities. As a result of this weakening of the will, even our spiritual aspiration is weakened. As we ascend on the ladder of penitence we must also hold on to the practical particularizatons, with their stirrings, the thoughts and strivings they conjure up, and raise them as well together with the ascent of our inner being toward the divine, to be reunited with our original source. However life breaks down into particularization, it continues to draw light from the original divine light, and it needs to return to the higher realm, together with the essence of our souls. Then we shall not ascend devoid of riches and we shall not fail because of feebleness, for we shall not return naked to the higher realm. We shall have with us our multicolored robes we acquired as a result of the proliferation of all life. We ascend and move on in time, with all the fruits of activity and life that go with it.

10. The moral impulse, with its divine call, enters the soul from the life thrusts of all the worlds. Existence, in its overall character, is sinless. Sin appears only in the goals of particular beings. In the perspective of the whole everything is related in eternal harmony. The actions that manifest the

eternal harmony are pure, devoid of any sin, error or transgression. This kind of life, which inspires such actions, is what the soul seeks. It finds it in the light of the source of all life, the light that is radiant with the light of the En Sof,[13] to which it is so ardently drawn, to which it is bound and for which it yearns with endless longing. It reaches for it with the higher penitence, the highest freedom, the excited joy of liberation and the awe of the holy of holies, abounding in the wisdom of all realms of being.

11. Penitence is the renewal of life. It is impossible for penitence not to change the quality of life while life continues, and it automatically changes its quality for good even if it takes place on the last day. "Remember your Creator in the days of your youth, before the evil days come and the years be reached when you will say, I have no pleasure in them, before the sun and the light and the moon and the stars grow dark" (Kohelet 12:1-2). Other consolations for wrongdoing are meant only to serve as embellishments to strengthen the will to penitence and to clarify its significance. However, when a person remains fixed in such consolations to a point of neglecting to embrace the values of a life of holiness, remaining sunk in the deep mire of sin, and saying, I am saved—this is the way of death of the idolatry of compromise that summoned the people to worship at the idolatrous shrines of Beth-el and Gilgal, calling: "Bring your sacrifices in the morning, pay your tithes every three days and offer a sacrifice of thanksgiving from leavened bread" (Amos 4:4). The behavior that abandons truth and justice and follows the temptations of the heart is heresy that drags along with it every kind of violence and lewdness, while exhibiting its outer facade and saying: See, I am clean. It abounds in empty consolations that cannot stand up in a world of falsehood that is devoid of stability. "The lips of a strange woman drop honey, her mouth is

---

13. The Infinite, a synonym for God.

smoother than oil, but her end is bitter as wormwood, sharp as a two-edged sword" (Prov. 5:3-4).

The fruits of beliefs and morals of those raised on the idolatrous culture reflect on its inner character. Its only vitality derives from the holy sparks it appropriated from the living treasure of Israel's faith, which it rejects little by little, until it will make itself bare altogether. "He swallowed up riches and he threw it up, God ejected it from his inside" (Job 20:15). But then will the holy spark that has been absorbed by the nations as something unwanted stir the hearts of many nations, to "turn them to a pure language, to invoke the name of the Lord" (Zeph. 3:9), the God of Israel, "in the spirit of the Lord, the spirit of counsel and might, the spirit of the knowledge and the fear of the Lord" (Isa. 11:2). This is not an alien spirit, a spirit of folly and weakness, a spirit of ignorance and moral callousness, that bases its false premises on compromise that is a disgrace to every leader and righteous judge. Only such "virtue" of nations is the source of every cruelty and meanness. "Our God will come and not be silent, a fire devours before Him, and storms rage all about Him. He will call the heavens above and the earth to judge His people. Let His faithful gather, those pledged to Him by a covenant at a sacrifice offering" (Ps. 50: 3-5). "The Lord is a God of justice, happy are those who trust in Him" (Isa. 30:18). "I will make an everlasting covenant with you, fulfilling the mercies promised to David, I have made him a witness to the nations, a prince and commander to the peoples. You will call a nation you know not, and a people that does not know you will run to you, for the sake of the Lord your God and the Holy One of Israel who has glorified you" (Isa. 55: 3-5).

12. It is necessary to summon people to penitence also for the sake of the survival of our people. In what sense is this to be understood? We must be united in our togetherness for the oncoming generations. But our spiritual unity needs to be nourished, and its nourishment consists of a way of life, and

an ideology. When our people are faithful to their pattern of life and thought, then the link of unity remains firm, and it endows additional strength to the ethnic and other forms of unity, though these in themselves are of a passing and changing nature. But when the spiritual phase of our life is weakened, then the spiritual dissension becomes stronger, and the basic unity of race and other external factors will be powerless to hold together the many fragments into which life in its objective and subjective conditioning fragmentizes them.

13. At times an idea descends from its grandeur and from its original purity, because after its realization in practical life unworthy people became involved in it and they darkened its lustre. This descent is not permanent, for it cannot be that the idea embodying the spiritual good shall be transformed into evil. The descent is only temporary and it is also a stepping stone to a new ascent. The people of lowly quality are numerous, and though this attribute [of popularity] is as nothing in comparison with quality, when it is added to quality it becomes its adornment; "when there is a multitude of people the King is glorified" (Prov. 14:25). It is not only preponderant in number but also in physical prowess, the energy and the desire to pursue and to achieve, to establish one's objective through practical steps and a display of strength—all these are more common among people of physical strength who are lacking in spiritual sensibility, which generally tends to blunt physical strength. When an idea needs to acquire a physical base, it tends to descend from its height. In such an instance it is thrust toward the earthly, and brazen ones come and desecrate its holiness. Together with this, however, its followers increase, and the physical vitality becomes increasingly more visible. This continues until the time comes when sensitive spirits girded with the might of divine righteousness are aroused. They rise to the peak of the idea in its original purity, they enter into its inner depth and bring to it the

purity of their own souls, their noble intentions and their innocent thoughts. As a result of this, the general idea, which has been weary and enfeebled, in the numbness of death, because of the spiritual pains inflicted on it by the stabs of the surrounding thorns, so that it is almost devoid of life, becomes aroused and begins to release on all who approach it the dew of life with majestic prowess out of its inner being. Then all who cling to it ascend with its ascent. Even those who embraced it at the time of its decadence, who willfully deviated from the straight road toward the goal embodied in the idea, also ascend with it. As a result of its influence, they turn toward a pure and higher penitence, with wondrous ease, which has no parallel in the manifestations of penitence through the stirring of the good in some individual soul. This process here envisioned will come and will not be delayed. The light of God, which is obscured by dark clouds, which is hidden in the core of the vision of Zion, will appear. It will raise from the lower depths the kingly city, the shrine of God with all its tributaries. With it will ascend all who cling to it, those near and far, for a true renaissance and for permanent liberation.

Chapter Thirteen

The Ways of Spiritual and Practical Penitence

1. One cannot be attached to the core of Israel's nationhood unless one's soul has been cleansed by penitence of its vulgar human traits and low moral attributes or unless one's soul is from the very beginning a pure soul. For the basic disposition of the Israelite nation is the aspiration that the highest measure of justice, the justice of God, shall prevail in the world. Whoever has been stained by any kind of sin, then to the extent of his stain, the desire for justice and for good

will not be operative within him properly. Therefore, he will not be truly linked with the national character of the Jewish people until the stain has been cleansed.

2. In order to remove every barrier between the general divine good and the individual person who thirsts for it, it is necessary to shed every moral defect, in the broadest connotation of the term. This embraces the cleansing of his character traits and the purification of his intellectual presuppositions that condition action. For these register the impact of the divine light on all humanity and all existences in its application to the realm of morals. Similarly, in order to remove the impediments to the perfection of the character of the Jew who robes the abstract essence of the divine good in his own distinctive expression, it is necessary to purge every practical obstruction that acts on the Jewish soul. This goal necessitates full penitence for all the detailed acts of wrongdoing and transgression, on the basis of the written and oral Torah, all of which express the divine soul embodied in the Jew.

3. It is necessary for a person to be united with the divine good in the soul of the community of Israel as a whole, and thereby he will be aided toward penitence. At all times he will be confronted by his shortcomings and sins, which stem from his alienation from the people of God that gave him being and is the source of all the good in him. Let him not hesitate to link himself with the soul of the people as a whole, despite the fact that among some of its constituent individuals there are also wicked and coarse people. This does not diminish in any way the divine light of the good in the people as a whole, and a spark of the divine soul is radiant even in the most fallen individuals. And because the community of Israel holds within itself the divine good, not for itself alone, but for the whole world, for all existence, by cleaving firmly to the soul of the people he will come to cleave to the living God, in harmony with the divine blessing that abounds in all things. The divine presence will them embrace him in all its majesty and might.

4. It is impossible for a person to feel afflicted with the afflictions of the community unless he hallows his ways and perfects his character and undergoes full penitence. The identification with the afflictions of the community with fullness of heart is itself the reward for obedience to divine precepts experienced by those pure of soul, who walk in innocence, who follow the teaching of the Lord.

5. The most original and the best approach to penitence, which is inspired by the light of the Torah in the world, consists in the study of civil law and all those precepts that govern man's relation to his fellowman, as set forth in the legal code, the "Hoshen Mishpat." This is to be studied with the clearest stress on becoming conversant with the contents of the text and with the most profound kind of thematic analysis possible. This will mend all the lapses to which the heart may have drawn one in life, it will establish the principles of divine justice on a firm foundation and it will liberate the soul from the trap of doubt and confusion. It will do this by illuminating the practical life with its clear light. However, one must always sensitize the heart and the mind through the other branches of the Torah, especially so through exposure to the moral influence, on a contemplative level, that is firm and broad, in the life-giving light of meditation on the concepts of God, on the spiritual life, so that the soul may be conditioned for attachment to the divine justice immanent in the legal branch of the Torah, which shows us the way of life. Then will this pursuit serve like a balm to raise the soul and to strengthen it.

6. When the desire for absolute justice, as envisioned theoretically in its spiritual form, grows stronger in the human soul because one has been ennobled by good character and good deeds, and by full penitence inspired by love, then this desire will break out from the ethereal realm and thrust itself to the ground below, and proclaim with force its mission to establish justice on earth. This engenders a special love for the study of those laws that define man's obligations to his

neighbor, and the largest section of the Torah, the laws dealing with money matters, expands further and becomes more
clarified, together with all branches of the law that governs
the practical life. And since the spiritual dimension of divine
justice becomes incorporated in the practical life it becomes
stronger, the soul becomes more firm, and its spiritual influence rises to a higher level of clarity.

7. If a person should expect that all his inner impulses
and all his faculties rise to holiness all at once in accordance
with the spiritual ascent he has attained and, similarly, that all
his defects of behavior be mended all at once and be transformed to absolute perfection, he will be unable to maintain
his stability and he will not be able to maintain his desire to
pursue the way that leads to true perfection. The basis of
everything is the ascent of perception, the intensification of
the light of the Torah, and penitence in action is to follow
closely, at first with reference to future behavior, then with
reference to matters of the past that lend themselves to easy
mending. Then this will reach out as well to matters difficult
to mend, and thus he will continue until he will mend everything. But he must not neglect anything in his spiritual progress as the inner claim of his soul demands of him.

8. The basic difficulty in comprehending the higher life
derives from the weakening of the will for goodness and perfection, a result of defects of character and sinful acts. It
might indeed be prudent to fast in order to break the potentiality for evil inherent in the realm of the material that impedes the ascent of the will toward higher qualities. But one
must consider whether one's spiritual and bodily stamina
would be supportive of this. In any case, one must not despair
of the will's openness to improvement. Even if many flaws
should remain in one's disposition and action, he should anticipate the help of God for a higher deliverance, since God is
good and upright, and He shows sinners the way to go.

9. The inner moral sense calls out to man: Son of man,

turn back from your sins! Sometimes the call is so loud that it disturbs all the harmonious balance of life. A person must then rise to a higher spiritual standard in order to stabilize his inner world, but here he will need the help of courage. A person's inner courage must come to his aid when he goes through the most serious spiritual crisis. As a result of the force with which the moral sense exerts its claim on him, a person is sometimes confused and he cannot liberate himself from his imprisonment; his evil traits, his evil deeds, which stray from the way of the Torah and morality, oppress him. He sees his path hedged in with thorns. He sees no way of mending. He feels himself in the grip of outside forces and he cannot withstand them. But out of all these the light of a sun radiating mercy will shine.

10. A person should not be disturbed by impediments in meeting the claims of penitence. Even if his difficulties stem from offenses against other persons, and he knows he has not redressed the wrongs and he finds himself too weak to mend his relations with his fellowman, let him not entertain in his heart any discouraging thoughts that disparage the value of penitence. Undoubtedly, once he redresses wrongs where no impediments interfere, God will also help him to redress satisfactorily those wrongs where he confronts great impediments that he cannot presently overcome.

11. The focus of penitence must always be directed toward improving the future. One should not begin by making the mending of the past an indispensable prerequisite. If he should immediately begin by mending the past he will encounter many obstacles, and the ways of penitence and the nearness of God will seem too hard for him. But if he concentrates truly on improving his future behavior, it is certain that divine help will also be granted him to mend the past.

12. There is a type of person in whose soul the moral claim shines with unusual clarity. After every lofty moral vision that he conjures up, he feels at once the demand to

conform his life to it. Since the flow of images moves with greater speed than the natural process of planning and acting, this person is always grieved and embittered at himself because he cannot meet his obligations and bring to full realization what has been revealed to him by the precious light of morality. At times out of this very holy sensibility comes a fear of the creative process; the person will be unwilling to confront the lofty images where the moral, the scientific and the most spiritual concepts in the realm of the holy all merge—lest he suffer undue anguish. In such a state it is necessary to invoke one's inner strength and to resort to the perception that the core of penitence is in the will, a perception that guides all who follow the path of a higher life, and a higher sensitivity, to enhance the riches of holiness, to strengthen the Torah and magnify it. Let him not shrink because of the moral claims that overwhelm him, but let him confront them with the confidence that the influence, generated by the light of the Torah, will always turn him in the direction of the good, in its highest form, and let him add to his intellectual and imaginative wealth in the free action of the soul that is most relevant for his individuality; and let him not be afraid. "Let the righteous smite me in kindness and correct me, precious oil my head will not refuse" (Ps. 141:5).

13. Great and majestic is the happiness of penitence. The consuming fire of the pain engendered by sin itself purges the will, cleanses the character of the person so that the great wealth in the treasure of the life of penitence grows for him. The person continues to ascend through penitence, through its bitterness and its sweetness, through its grief and its joy. Nothing purges and cleanses a person, raises him to the full stature of a human being, like the profound experience of penitence. "In the place where the penitents stand, even the fully righteous are unworthy to stand" (Ber. 34b).

14. The flame of remorse, which is engendered in a gentle person, through the inspiration of the light of penitence, is a holy fire, a fire that is full of light and warmth, full of life.

When it arises in a pure spirit, in a soul alive and illumined with the light of grace and good sense, endowed with the knowledge of people who have risen to holiness, then it is changed into a mighty, vibrant force, an active force that refines and cleanses, that engenders strength, that removes obstruction and begets a new spirit into all living things. It brings with it a new awakening and a bestirring full of a mysterious vitality. The person becomes a new being, refined and purged; his gaze is toward the heights, toward the higher vistas of knowledge and understanding, which is the generating impetus for penitence. From the light of the vision of the Messiah, from the entire Torah and all the commandments, from all the good deeds and good character traits, will come to him rays of light to illumine his dark paths and his barren ways. Together with his own edifice he will build an edifice for the world and many will walk by his light, which at first he had kindled for himself alone. It was at first a light for one and it became a light for a great multitude of people, and "you will be called a repairer of the breach, a restorer of paths to dwell in" (Isa. 58:12).

Chapter Fourteen

The Ways of Individual Penitence

1. Just as one must raise evil dispositions and thoughts to their original source in order to mend them and to moderate them, so is it necessary to raise low-level dispositions and thoughts to their original source and to illumine them with the light of greatness. Although the latter are good, they are not on a high enough level of goodness, and they do not offer enough illumination. And just as one serves the world by raising the degraded dispositions and thoughts, even more so does one serve and improve the condition of the world by raising the low-level dispositions and thoughts to a higher

level. This quality of raising what is lowly in life toward greatness never ceases at any time, at any hour. This is the meaning of full penitence, which qualifies the truly righteous to attain the virtues of penitents.

2. When one engages in spiritual contemplation one recognizes that his faculties for spiritual perception are dulled because of the defects in the soul caused by sin. The anguish caused by the paucity of light leads to remorse over one's sins generally, and over one's particular sins. Then one will desire with a full heart to cleanse one's actions and dispositions so that the obstruction does not continue to impede the flow of the divine light into the inwardness of the reflective soul. This is the way to the higher level of penitence, the penitence that is worthy of atoning for any misdeeds.

3. At times as a result of the endeavor to cling to a higher level of spirituality all the channels of the spiritual life will focus on the world of higher thoughts, and the body will be disoriented from the soul, with the result that it [the body] will come under sway of evil influences. Subsequently, when the contemplation of the higher spiritual realm has been completed and the life process resumes its normal functioning, the soul will find the body broken, through an impairment of its normal attributes. Then will commence a great and perilous inner conflict. For this reason, penitence, with its focus on mending one's style of life, should precede the ascent in contemplation. Then will one assure some contact between body and soul even during the period of the higher ascent.

4. When one wishes to embark on penitence one must realize that there is nothing to thwart this objective, not even the twenty-four offenses cited as difficult to redress through penitence (Maimonides, Mishne Torah, Teshuvah 4:1-6)[14]. One must not ignore any inclination to penitence, not even the

---

14. These cease to be impediments when one has begun to repent for them.

most trivial, saying that the thought that suggested itself is too insignificant for a person of his stature. Nor is he to ignore the call to the highest, saying that it is beyond his reach. Everything merges into one edifice, one world of penitence, which is more precious, greater and more ancient than all worlds.

5. The fact that the would-be penitent is at times confronted by great difficulties, whether in the duties between man and God or in the duties between man and man, should not impede the spiritual essence of penitence. Once there is a reaching for penitence, there is the reality of penitence, and the person involved becomes a new being. As to the misdeeds that require great vigilance to redress them, let him always anticipate that he will redress them; and let him cultivate a special humility as long as there is something he must redress that he has not yet done so; and let him look forward to the time when he will redress everything. Automatically it will turn out that God will help him mend everything, but even before he has had the opportunity to do this, whether because of objective or subjective obstacles, whether his will is not yet resolute enough or he has not yet reached a full determination as to the practical steps to be taken, let him nevertheless hold on firmly to the spiritual phase of penitence. Let him maintain firmly his conviction that in any case he has embraced penitence, which is more precious than anything else in the world, and let him increase his study of Torah, his good deeds, his pursuit of wisdom and his upright behavior to whatever extent he can. And let him offer prayer to his Maker that he be enabled to realize in action those aspects of penitence that still remain unfulfilled, for his own sake, for the sake of all Israel and the whole world, and for the sake of the *shekinah*, that the light of God shine in the world in all its fullness; and let him look forward to the time when all souls will be mended and enjoy the radiance of the divine presence, and all will be sated with goodness and with abounding life.

6. When one performs any action with a mundane motivation, for bodily or animalistic reasons, provided the act itself is permitted, if he has been aroused to repent for this, there is an immediate transformation of all impulses toward the spiritual and the holy. If one has violated a positive commandment and has repented, he is forgiven before he has had a chance to move from the spot (Yoma 86a). When one has performed a legitimate act,[15] immediately after the thought occurred to him to repent, he has risen toward holiness and the act and its generating energy rise with him. The melancholy that follows upon mundane pleasures is immediately turned into the joy associated with the performance of a divine precept. "For the upright of heart there is joy" (Ps. 97:11).

7. When one raises the question: What is the cause for melancholy? it is necessary to reply: The influence of evil acts, character traits and opinions on the soul. The soul, with its penetrating instinct, senses their bitterness and recoils, is frightened and saddened. When the light of penitence appears and the desire for good, in its original authenticity, asserts itself, there is opened a channel for delight and joy, and the soul imbibes from the river of delight. When the disposition to act absorbs the substance of these pleasurable feelings, there emerges the pure, higher moral sense that invests life with its splendor.

8. All melancholy stems from sin, and penitence illumines the soul and changes the melancholy to joy. The general melancholy prevalent in the world stems from the general foulness found in the universe as a result of the collective sin of humanity and the sin of individuals, and from the sins hidden in the earth that come to expression through the sin of man. The righteous who are the foundations of the world and especially the Messiah perform penance for this type of sin and transform it to joy.

---

15. But for improper motives.

9. If a person should eat with an improper or low-level motivation and repent immediately after eating, raising his thoughts and his faculties in penitence inspired by love, then he has mended the past. It is as though his initial eating was with a pure motive. The time when the food is digested, when it is appropriate to recite grace after the meal, is more appropriate for this act of elevation, which renders such eating worthy of the priests of God, who eat the bread offered to the Lord: "The priests eat and those who brought the offering are forgiven" (Pes. 59b).

10. Overindulgence in eating, even if it is necessitated by illness, has an element of impropriety, but it would seem that it can readily be elevated toward holiness. However, penitence must certainly be part of this mending and elevation. The increased vigor, when it is directed toward holy purposes, invests with its character the initial event that produced it, even if it was initially the act of overeating, since the latter was forced on the person due to illness or weakness, or the like. This is unlike eating forbidden food where the elevation is very difficult.

11. After the event, when a person has eaten with improper motives, or has stumbled on overindulging in food for which one is called an offender, if he should plan to repent with full penitence after the meal and elevate the holy sparks contained in that meal, there is hope that this would be efficacious. The sincere person should never tire of mending all he can after every meal with penitence out of love, in joy and gladness of heart, without sadness, with contentment in God, with remorse and contrition, pervaded by the grandeur and the strength of holiness. Then he will effect benefits for himself and for the world. Even if it should happen that in the course of the meal he be guilty of some low moments, let him repent and elevate himself and he will yet be worthy of eating "holy bread" in higher holiness, and the offense will be transformed to an influence for good, blessing, mercy and favor.

"He that is of a virtuous heart enjoys a constant feast" (Prov. 15:15).

12. At times it is well to avoid thoughts of holiness and penitence when they come in a spirit of melancholy. The joy that flows from the depth of holiness is greater than other expressions of holiness and penitence. When thoughts of fear and penitence occur to a person in a spirit of melancholy, let him distract his mind from them until his mind becomes more settled. Then he will take on himself all the claims of holiness and the fear of God in a spirit of joy appropriate for those sincere of heart who serve God in truth.

13. There is an inner sadness that stems from an afflicted soul. Especially when the pattern of action is deficient and the responsibility for action is not well defined, does the life force [nefesh] feel its lack, since the faculty for action is close to its sphere. It is otherwise with people who are close to the realm of the practical, whose deficiencies are more diffused in the distant realms of the spiritual. They cannot feel their lack to a point of sadness, and they can be more cheerful by nature. A person who is disturbed by his behavioral deficiency, who is profoundly spiritual in his aspirations, should try to enhance his spiritual sensibilities and harness them to serve the practical world, so that they will illumine the vistas of the practical. Through the resources of the practical Torah they will develop and become a beacon light of the higher penitence that will mend everything, the practical and the theoretical life as well.

14. It is necessary to repent even for deficiencies that stem from bodily weaknesses, for them and for their resultant consequences. However, one must strengthen oneself not to be overly fearful, especially of such deficiencies that were caused by the weakness of the body. We already have the great assurance of divine mercy that God does not regard as a sin anything to which a person was drawn against his will, whether in a positive act, or by a failure to act. And as it is

good for a person to be disturbed by a guilty conscience, so is it necessary for him to be firm of heart, to be ready for God's service in the study of Torah and sincere worship, with a clear mind, to whatever extent possible.

15. Even with reference to offenses that cannot be mended in thought alone, but must be expressed in action, as in the area of human relations, every thought of penitence is of inestimable value, even if it should be inspired by simple fear, the fear of sin. Even the slightest gesture of penitence stirs in the soul—and in the world—great and holy sensibilities. A holy light emanating from the divine realm illumines every inclination toward the good with the splendor of love and the delight of God. Even if there be imbedded in it much dross, its inner grace, its basic holiness—this is worth all the wealth, and all precious things cannot be compared to it.

16. Though sadness and fear are induced by the neglect of Torah and by all the wrongdoing, once we contemplate penitence everything is turned to good, and a person must strengthen himself to trust the mercies of God, praised be He, and to launch on the study of Torah and on acts of divine service, each one according to his level. If it should at times seem to him that the form of penitence suggested by reading books of morals does not correspond to his status, let him probe his status, and let him concentrate especially in doing what does correspond to his status. But let him not neglect altogether what is suggested in the books, and though he can embrace only a very small measure of the prescriptions that are not relevant to him, all levels of the good and the holy must be linked to each other. Together they fuse to form one whole, to be illumined by the light of God and His higher Torah, with the delight of God and His goodness.

17. At times when a person reads books on levels of holiness, he may feel an inner anguish. He must analyze his anguish into its components, and he will discover that occa-

sionally he is troubled because a particular good quality is remote from him, due to his sins. He should then strengthen himself in penitence in order to attain that quality. But he may also find that the quality alluded to in his reading has elements below his level, and he may be grieved over his inclination to content himself within the circumscribed zone of that quality. The person must then clarify to himself how fortunate he will be if he will strive to embrace what this quality has to offer him and to what extent his good fortune also depends on not remaining static at that level, but on going beyond it. "One must always ascend in the realm of the holy" (Ber. 28a).

18. There are two types of excellence in one's spiritual status. One is the effect of good deeds and study, the other is a disposition with which one is endowed at birth. One who attained his status through study and works, if he should suffer decline and need to raise himself again, it will be necessary for him to do so by slow steps and return by degrees. But one whose high stature is primarily due to the disposition with which he has been endowed at birth, through a greatness of soul, even if he fall from high station through inner or outer impediments, it will be necessary for him to return with a major thrust, speedily, with a leap as on the wings of eagles, without considering stages. However, there is also added to the latter type of return the penitence in little things, with attention to particular details relevant to them, except that those are not the primary labor of penitence for one whose core of being is of a higher order. They are only derivative additions, like embellishments that sweeten and aid the main goal—the great and exalted form of penitence.

19. In every stage, in every conception of life, there is a treasure of holiness. When a person leaps toward high visions, beyond his own level, he becomes deprived of the dimension of holiness in the lower levels, which are closer to his own, while he cannot achieve a permanent attachment to the higher

visions since they are too spiritual for him. He must, there-fore, return in penitence to the levels he has left behind, with regret and with joy. Nevertheless, let him not forget the im-pression made on him by the higher levels. Since he ascended let him not go down altogether. Then everything will be turned to the good.

20. A person may note that the more resolute he becomes in pursuing the upright way and the more committed he be-comes to the service of God, the stronger the evil impulse becomes in him, to bring him down toward lusts and lowly behavior. Nevertheless let him not regret his efforts, but let him continue with greater resoluteness. As to the obstructions that appeared on his way upward, it is for him to repent, and let him remember the principle that one who erred in the course of performing a divine commandment does not have to bring a sin offering (Shabbat 137a). And let him not be afraid of anything, but let him draw holy fear and penitence from all that happens.

21. The loss of vitality in the will, with its many negative results, is due in great measure to a lack of physical vigor. Though the latter itself is conditioned by many moral factors, in seeking redress through penitence one must analyze the various causes that have weakened the will. He should then attempt overall mending, both in the moral and purely spiri-tual realm, and in the area affecting the body and the strengthening of its faculties, so that the vitality of his will shall rest on a more perfect foundation.

22. When great visions occur to us, which seem beyond our reach, it is important to know that the remoteness is only physical, and is not due to a spiritual deficiency. Therefore, it is necessary to embark on penitence, so that we might come close to the light of the ideal that has flashed in our thought. But we must avoid depression or self-depreciation that blunts life's vitality. It is to be rather a gentle inner self-criticism, which reduces our unbecoming side and raises our good and

gentle essence. "The right hand of the Lord is exalted, the right hand of the Lord acts heroically" (Ps. 118:16).

23. When a person has little faith in the efficacy of his prayer, not because, God forbid, he lacks faith in divine providence, but because he feels depressed over his many sins and the anguish that accompanies his penitence, this will in the end be changed to a great and mighty faith in the power of God's mercy, which will work wonders for him, by the help of God, may He be praised, "who leads the humble in justice and shows the humble His way" (Ps. 25:9).

24. If a person is so low in his self-esteem that, embittered over his moral decline, with his many sins, he cannot find the poise to pursue the study of Torah and the performance of the commandments, to do his worldly work and to socialize with people in peace and with a healthy cheerfulness, then he must realize that with such dispirited condition over his sins, he is certainly a full penitent. This being the case, his status has risen, and he can now calm himself and renew his cheerfulness of spirit to perform all good deeds with a tranquil and glad heart, for God is good and upright.

25. The embarrassment experienced in the heart because of sin, although this is a natural reaction, brings with it, nevertheless, some atonement. If by reflection one deepens the embarrassment, one also extends the zone of forgiveness for all sins. They are all interconnected on the basis of the principle that one transgression stimulates another, and one who is embarrassed over one sin is embarrassed over all. The penitence that takes the form of the fear of God, which is in essence the feeling of shame, embraces a person's entire being and he is forgiven even for such sins as call for a high level of penitence sufficient to atone for all misdeeds.

26. Sometimes bad traits are themselves the retributory consequences of previous sins, and it is not enough for a person to try to cleanse himself of those traits. He will not return to his state of purity until he has taken stock of himself,

and will repent for the sins that caused, as a retributory consequence, the depreciation of his character traits.

27. Insufficient pleasure in the study of Torah results from a deficiency in the soul of a Jew, which needs to be mended through penitence directed to overcome this deficiency. Once one puts his mind to mend this deficiency, the higher light inherent in the nature of the soul begins at once to shine again, and the sweetness of the Torah becomes once again manifest.

28. The brighter the light of penitence shines before study, the clearer will be one's understanding of his study. The potency of the intellect rises as the potency of the will rises, and it attains clarity in proportion to the clarity of the will.

29. The higher penitence that is inspired by a great love and a clear understanding raises the content of study to a level of fruitfulness and creativity that has no parallel in any kind of study pursued independently.

30. Everything helps to elevate the spirit, to achieve a higher level of penitence: all one's knowledge of Torah, all one's general culture, all one's energies, everything one knows about the world and about life, every contact with people, every disposition to equity and justice. When a person feels inwardly ashamed, an unworthiness of body and spirit, he must probe with all his strength all aspects of his deficiency and mend them. He must not attend to this in a superficial way, because this will only lead bim to further decline. He must do this with penetrating concentration, and with pure vigor of spirit.

31. It is precisely after a truly pure kind of penitence that one must reimmerse oneself in the world and in life. Through this one restores holiness to its proper sphere and enthrones the *shekinah*, the divine presence, in the world.

32. Whoever neglects the study of Torah lacks the strength to hold his own in a time of trouble. This includes

the neglect of even a single commandment. The Holy One, praised be He, in His great kindness, stirs one to recall in time of trouble all the elements of good and the inspiration to holiness that derive from the teachings of the Torah and the commandments. As a result of the trouble one becomes conscious of every detail in the Torah and the commandments that have been neglected, and one returns in penitence. God accepts this penitence, and out of trouble He brings forth deliverance and relief.

33. One must hasten to repent for every sin, even if it be the most trivial. The delay in penitence is like the delay in removing an impurity in the Temple, or wool and linen in the same garment,[16] or leavened bread on Passover—every moment of delay is a sin by itself; and the accumulation of slight sins becomes a formidable force for evil. Similarly, one who is on a level of high spiritual attainment must repent for every needless word uttered, or even for every necessary and holy word uttered if without inner holiness, good sense or feeling appropriate for his state.

34. On the eve of the Sabbath one must do penance for all that transpired in the course of the week, in order to welcome the Sabbath without any impediment of sin or wrongdoing. At the end of the holy Sabbath, one must do penance for what was covered up by the illumination of the Sabbath, that it may be pure without admixtures, that troublesome matters that are rendered impotent by the holiness of the Sabbath shall not disturb the proprieties of the weekdays, when such defense is not available. This is the reason that the High Priest washed his hands and feet after removing the holy robes on the Day of Atonement. Elements of impurity invade the sanctuary, and because of the magnitude of the light of holiness, seek to attach themselves to him. While the holy service itself dominates the scene they are ineffective, but afterward it is

---

16. Forbidden in Deut. 22:11.

necessary to guard against them through a great penitence, in which there is much joy, strength and humility.

35. The fear of God must never be separated from wisdom, but must always be associated with it and draw on it, and automatically exert an influence on it. This applies to the general illumination that inspires the soul with the fear of God and with wisdom as well as to their derivative particulars. The light of wisdom must shine on every detailed element in the fear of God. From every element of wisdom must the fear of God, with all its values—the practical, the moral, the emotional and the imaginative—draw its nourishment. The soul will be illumined through the proper blending of these two great lights, and penitence, delight and joy and life will come to the world.

36. The clear intellectual aspirations raise man above the limited realm of the practical. When they are properly based they encourage him to mend his behavior in the future and they straighten out for him the way of life. But they also remove the obstacles from his doing penance for the past, for his misdeeds do not block his way, since he recognizes clearly to what extent the light of knowledge that prepares for and serves as the basis of penitence uproots all evil from its source, and turns them toward good, and willful sins are transmuted into virtues.

37. If a person should desire nothing less than to be wholly righteous, it will be difficult for him to be a penitent. It is therefore appropriate for a person always to concentrate on the aspiration to be a penitent, to be immersed in thoughts about penitence and in the endeavor to effectuate it in action. Then will his penitence be able to raise him toward the heights, to the level of the truly righteous, and even beyond it.

38. A penitent must walk in higher paths, in the ways of saintliness and holy thoughts. However, there are people born with a nature that enables them to be righteous from the

very inception of their being. If it happened that these people sinned and repented, they can, after their penitence, resume their former life-style, to walk in the way of the righteous, as before, without any noticeable intensification of the constant quest for holiness. But those who by nature have souls that are constantly in need of penitence, they are the ones summoned to be saintly[17] and people of holiness.

39. It sometimes happens that the spirit falls into depression, and the person cannot find any contentment, because he feels the paucity of his good deeds, because of an awareness of his misdeeds and his little diligence in the study of Torah. Such a person should concentrate on the secret potency of thought, realizing that "one who can infer one thing from another—his thought is more highly esteemed by the Holy One, praised be He, than all the sacrifices and burnt offerings." Holy thoughts and higher conceptual images therefore have all the efficacy of sacrifices, with all the rites pertaining to them. They also have the efficacy of the practical aspects of the Torah involving speech [study and prayer], those elements of the Torah that correspond to the cult of sacrifices and derive from them. A man should encourage himself with the realization that at times the paucity of good deeds and study may have occurred because of his great inclination to pursue the secret realms of thought, and it may be that his low feeling is inspired to a great extent by the fact that he did not esteem sufficiently the significance of his thought. Therefore let him concentrate on the perception that the mending of the entire world and the healing of all souls depend on the basics of thought, and let him raise his thoughts to higher realms, to whatever extent he can, and he will reach a level of penitence out of love. "Happy is the people that knows the sound of the shofar[18] O Lord, they will walk in the light of Your presence" (Ps 89:16).

---

17. Hasidim.
18. The summons to penitence.

40. There are righteous people of such stature that if they should miss for one moment the full measure of cleaving to God, according to their standard, they will feel themselves in the depths of sin, and they meet their crisis through a high level of penitence, through a complete, mighty and august kind of penitence. Even if their cleaving should be complete in only one aspect, in the element of fear alone or love alone, they will already feel a great lapse, and a disruption of the unity of the divine order in the world; and their soul will yearn for the higher penance to redress the wrong.

The upper strata of the righteous who are full of mercy and divine compassion for all creatures, for all the worlds and all who inhabit them, from beginning to end, who are guided with heroism and adorned with the beauty, the beauty of truth—they feel the imbalance in the level of their cleaving to God. If the fusion of fear and love of God should not be fully in proper balance, or one element should outweigh the other, they will return in penitence and raise themselves to the highest realm, whence flow the treasures of holy influences, and they will restore the holy balance to its position. They will mend the defect symbolized by Jacob's limping because of his thigh (Gen. 32:32),[19] and will walk straight. "My foot stands in an upright place, in the assembled multitude will I praise the Lord" (Ps. 26:12). These are the people of integrity to whom God's secret teaching will be revealed always; "with the upright is His secret" (Prov. 3:32). From the radiance of its striving for spiritual excellence, every seeking soul is filled with splendor and life, "and their search for glory releases glory" (Prov. 25:27).[20]

---

19. So interpreted in many mystical texts.

20. The usual interpretation interprets the opposite way, as disdain for those who seek glory, but Rabbi Kook detaches this part of the sentence from the rest to give a homiletical interpretation.

Chapter Fifteen

The Basis of Penitence for the Individual and the Community

1. The perception of truth is the basis of penitence. The recognition that the world in all its manifestations is only an emanation from the lowest point of the light of absolute truth in God implants in the heart a clear love for truth, and every expression that negates the essence of truth, whether in speech, in gesture or in action has no basis in the world, it has passed out of existence, and is read out of life. Self-criticism, when it probes deeply into the inner recesses of the soul and assesses properly all that has been done and thought, deepens the feelings of regret for every absence of truth in the phenomena of a person's life. It makes him feel his baseness, his ugliness, his nothingness. Then the person turns back in penitence out of love for the light of truth. A sage in the knowledge of Torah must also recite a verse invoking God's mercy when he retires for the night, to entrust his spirit to God who is the source of truth, to renew him in strength to the service of truth in the Torah, which invokes the attributes of truth, as is suggested in the verse "Into Your hands I entrust my spirit, You have redeemed me, O God of truth" (Ps. 31:6).

2. By right, every endeavor of knowledge should be directed toward the basic ideal of shaping the human will in its noblest form possible, to refine the will, to strengthen it, hallow it, cleanse it, to condition it through various educational disciplines that it shall always aspire to what is noble and exalted. Let the different branches of knowledge concern themselves with finding a way of translating into action all the particulars toward which the fund of goodwill prevalent in the world aspires, and which make up the necessities of the good life, both the material and the spiritual. The peak of their objective, however, must be the refinement of the will itself, its rational clarity and its ideal essence. But woe unto human-

ity when it digresses from the right course, and instead of making the center of all efforts the elevation of the will, leaves the will in its coarseness, without refinement and elevation, and directs all its efforts to satisfy the will's lusts, which flow on like a stream of brimstone, and which bring with them every manner of hell. Then humanity as a whole falls into the frightful and vulgar trap of idolatry, which will be paid for in blood, and out of its depths it will cry out to the God of truth, to return to the holy objective of making the basis of its general endeavor the elevation of the will. Then "you will call and the Lord will answer, you will cry out, and He will say, Here I am" (Isa. 58:2), for "the Lord is near to all who call on Him, to all who call on Him in truth" (Ps. 145:18). This is the entire basis of penitence: the elevation of the will, and changing it to good, to go out of darkness to light, from the valley of despair to the door of hope. "My people are in suspense about returning to Me" (Hos. 11:7); "return, backsliding Israel" (Jer. 3:12); "return, Israel, to the Lord Your God" (Hos. 14:2).

3. The natural remorse that burns in the heart as an expression of penitence derives from the anguish felt by the soul because it has remained static, instead of meeting its need always to ascend toward higher levels and surely so if it feels within itself that it has suffered decline. If it has altogether fallen from its status, then it has also lost the sensitivity to feel spiritual pain; at the very least it has damaged it and thereby its poignant bitterness will diminish. But the anguish caused by remaining static pierces to the depths of the soul and the pain is very great. The spiritual sensitivity of a soul undamaged by decline is alive and active, and the pain of remaining in a static state, which is against its nature and the antithesis of its reason for being, burns within it like a fire. This can be transmuted into the flame of a great love abounding in a spiritual delight, when the soul will gather strength to return to its objective of ascending, and maintaining firmly at all times this objective to ascend toward greater spiritual heights. "My soul will sing to You and not be silent, Lord my God, I shall

always praise You" (Ps. 30:13).

4. At times the heart suffers inner distress without reason or cause. This emanates from the source of penitence. The supernal light of God's presence reveals itself in the depths of the soul in a highly circumscribed form. This seed needs considerable watering from the fountain of higher knowledge and then it will emerge into the world with many great and celebrated lights, illuminating the whole mystery of life. The tree of life, with its precious fruit, will then manifest itself to the soul, and the person will be elevated and hallowed, and his mourning will be turned to joy, and he will be consoled and gladdened out of his sorrow. "Out of gloom and darkness, the eyes of the blind shall see" (Isa. 29:18).

5. It should not trouble a person's mind that he is highly esteemed in the eyes of people for his sanctity when he has claims against himself. This is the basis of penitence, what inspires all spiritual progress, which brings deliverance to the individual and the entire world. The high esteem accorded him should stimulate within him humility in full measure. By delving deeply into its essence he gains the crown of wisdom. To be vigilant in preserving humility, to infuse it into all the hidden recesses of the soul, one needs the quality of heroism. The outer honors accorded by society strengthen the basis of heroism, which can show itself in full splendor after it has been purged of the abomination of pride.

6. The higher level of penitence whose essence is a holy enlightenment and a firm perception of the delight in God is the basis of the lower level of penitence, which consists of mending behavior, raising the refinement of one's temperament; the basis of the higher penitence is also the basis of the Torah in all its ramifications of roots and branches. If a person should judge that he cannot temporarily fulfill the claims of the lower level of penitence to completion, let him hasten to attend to the higher penitence. In the end he will attain his goal since inwardly he desires to complete both levels of penitence. In due time, the higher penitence will also lead him to

the lower penitence, which consists in hallowing the particularities of behavior and one's bodily characteristics, the cleansing of one's temperament and elevating one's natural disposition. Then his heart and his flesh will sing to the living God.

7. To the extent that a person is aware of his sins, the light of penitence shines with clarity on his soul. Though at the time he had not yet reached a firm resolve to repent in his heart and his will, the light hovers over him and acts to create in him a new being. Even the impediments to penitence diminish in potency and their damage is lessened to the extent that the person knows of them and does not ignore them. As a result of this, the light of penitence begins to shine on him, and the holiness of the higher joy robes itself in his soul's being. Gates hitherto shut begin to open for him, and in the end he will attain that high station in which all the steep places will be made straight. "Every valley will be raised and every mountain and hill will be lowered, and the rugged place will be leveled and the rough places will be turned into a plain" (Isa. 40:4).

8. A person who embarks on penitence may encounter in himself wrongs that impede his penitential efforts, because he feels that he cannot overcome them. But if he does not desist, and holds on to his penitential goal, he will finally succeed in renouncing those wrongs which impede his penitence. Then will the light of retroactive penitence be most potent in him. By its liberation from confinement, from the obstruction of the grave impediments, it will act with a mighty force, and it will become one of the most precious forms of penitence. It is such penitence that effects a breakthrough to render acceptable penitents deemed unworthy of acceptance, like Manasseh and his comrades.[21] As the fully righteous is deemed unworthy of standing where a penitent

---

21. The reference is to King Manasseh of Judah who was notorious for his wrongdoings, for his idolatrous practices and his persecutions of the worshippers of God (cf. II Kings, 21: 1-18).

stands, so are ordinary penitents unworthy of standing where penitents who had to overcome impediments stand. Penitents who had to overcome impediments to penitence are to ordinary penitents like the fully righteous is to ordinary penitents.

The principle that is at work in the phenomenon of penitence also applies to prayer. There are conditions that impede prayer. But the person who sees himself confronted by those conditions but who nevertheless holds on firmly to the principle of prayer and calls to God at all times, will, in the end, find all those impediments receding. The illumination that emerges from the obstructions then moves forward with a mighty force, with a higher resolution, and hews a path for many "straying" prayers, his own and those of the world. It is precisely in such a person that the verse in Psalms (118:5) will find its fulfillment: "Out of my distress I called on the Lord, He answered me and set me free. The Lord is with me, I will not fear. What can men do unto me? The Lord has come to my help, and I shall see the fall of my enemies."

9. The desire for penitence, which always abides with a person, is the source of all his virtuous attributes. The depressing thought that is released from the deep domain of penitence is the source of joy. The basic disposition to penitence is inspired by the sense of the awesome perfection of the divine, and it is this that causes sin to be glaringly conspicuous. "You have placed our iniquities before You, our secret sins in the light of Your presence" (Ps. 90:8). The very realization that the feeling of being in a state of sin comes, in every case, as a result of a divine illumination acting on the soul—this very thought engenders endless joy and exaltation. The spiritual delight grows together with the depressed feeling in the heart of the one who is involved in the process of penitence. Penitence, according to this, effects liberation for the particular individual. As the divine illumination grows in him, he is liberated from every servitude to the alien forces that have come to dominate him. The whole community, too,

when it is ready to experience the desire for penitence, is at once liberated, through the divine illumination that exerts its influence upon it as a concomitant of the desire for penitence.

10. When one forgets the essence of one's own soul, when one distracts his mind from attending to the substantive content of his own inner life, everything becomes confused and uncertain. The primary role of penitence, which at once sheds light on the darkened zone, is for the person to return to himself, to the root of his soul. Then he will at once return to God, to the Soul of all souls. Then he will progress continually, higher and higher, in holiness and in purity. This is true whether we consider the individual, a whole people, or the whole of humanity, or whether we consider the mending of all existence, which always becomes damaged when it forgets itself. If one should envision that they sought to return to God, without setting themselves in order, this would be a deceptive penitence, through which God's name will be taken in vain. It is only through the great truth of returning to oneself that the person and the people, the world and all the worlds, the whole of existence, will return to their Creator, to be illumined by the light of life. This is the mystical meaning of the light of the Messiah, the manifestation of the soul of the universe, by whose illumination the world will return to the source of its being, and the light of God will be manifest on it. From the source of this mighty level of penitnece will man draw the life of holiness embodied in penitence in its true authenticity.

11. Our people will be rebuilt and established, and be renewed in vitality in all aspects of its life through the expansion, vitalization, and perfection of its religious faith, its piety, that is, the divine dimension of its life. All the builders of the people will come to recognize this profound truth. Then they will call out with a mighty voice to themselves and to their people: "Let us go and return to the Lord." And this

return will be a true return. This return will be a base for heroic action. It will release strength and vitality to all the practical and spiritual concerns, to all the pursuits necessary for the rebuilding and perfection of our people, to reawaken it to life, and to make firm its position. Its eyes will open, its soul will be made pure, its light will shine, its horizon will be enlarged, and a born again people will arise, a great, mighty and numerous people will arise, bearing upon it the light of God, and the greatness of peoplehood. "It will arise like a lioness, and like a lion it will lift itself up" (Nu. 23:27).

12. The realization that a decline in the moral state impedes the flowering of literature is a feeling unique to the Jewish people. Only we realize in truth that in order to improve the quality of literature, there is a necessary prerequisite, that the writers first cleanse their souls. We feel in ourselves the great need for penitence so that we might rise to the sublime heights of the noble literature that is uniquely ours, that stems from the wisdom of Israel, whose source is holiness and purity, faith and spiritual heroism.

Chapter Sixteen

The Roots of Penitence and Its Inner Action

1. The basis of penitence is an assessment of the state of the world. The roots of this assessment are above any particular assessment, just as the theory of numbers is above the actual numbers and their detailed configurations. For this reason the essence of the higher penitence is above any detailed assessment of one's condition; such assessment is its derivative. Thus a special installation for accounts was established outside Jerusalem, because Jerusalem itself was "the joy of all the earth" (Ps. 48:3), the place where one experienced the joy

of the higher penitence.[22] Concerning this did Adam sing: "It is good to praise the Lord, to sing to Your name, O most High, for You have caused me to rejoice in Your work, I will exult in the work of Your hands" (Ps. 92: 1-2).[23] The latter sentence is to be read in conjunction with the following: "How great are Your works, O Lord, Your thoughts are very deep" (Ps. 92:5), beyond all assessment, for "His understanding is without limit" (Ps. 147:5). The above is higher than the category that declared: "How many are Your works, O Lord," a term subject to number that is relevant for earthly assessment, as stated: "The earth is full of Your possessions" (Ps. 104:24). But the basis of penitence at its source is described thus: "As heaven is above the earth is His mercy toward those who fear Him, as far as east is from west so far has He removed our sins from us" (Ps. 103:11-12). The inspiration to penitence always moves from above to below — from an ascent to a realm beyond assessment to a confrontation of assessment, and from below to above — from an involvement in assessment to the realm of "the lovely everlasting hills" (Gen. 49:26), which was "before the mountains were brought forth" (Ps. 90:2), when "He weighed the mountains in a balance, and the hills in scales" (Isa. 40:12), "for from everlasting to everlasting You are God, You bring man to contrition, saying, Return, you children of man" (Ps. 90:2-3).

2. One of the foundations of penitence, in human thought, is a person's recognition of responsibility for his actions, which derives from a belief in man's free will. This is also the substance of the confession that is part of the commandment of penitence, in which the person acknowledges that no other cause is to be blamed for his misdeed and its

---

22. Kook gives a new turn to the statement in Midrash Exodus Rabbah, end, that commercial accounts were kept outside Jerusalem because the disturbing uncertainties of the market place were not to mar the peace of Jerusalem.

23. Rabbi Kook alludes here to a Midrashic statement that this psalm was composed by Adam after he had experienced the grace of God's forgiveness.

consequences but he himself. Thus he clarifies to himself his free will and his competence to order his life and his behavior. Thereby he clears the way for returning to God, to renew his life in good order, recognizing that his success will hinge on his turning to the source of knowledge, which is part of the holiness of the light of the Torah, that restores the soul.

After we make it clear to ourselves that the problem of two seemingly contradictory concepts (involved in the issue of free will) pertains only to us, because of our finite minds, but does not pertain to the Creator of everything, the Lord of all laws, the cause of all causes, the source of all wisdom, the architect of all understanding, praised be He, we shall realize that there is room for the concept that man chooses and is free, and also for the one that asserts that he does not choose and is not free, and these matters are continuous with all the forces at work in existence. As long as man has not repented of his sin, has not yet arranged his order of penitence, he remains under the servitude of his own choice and his guilt for all his misdeeds, and all their evil consequences weigh on him. However, after the process of penitence has begun, all his life's deficiencies, all his misdeeds and their bitter results, are transferred into the divine domain and all are reassessed outside the factor of his own freedom and his choice; they are merged within the domain of the higher providence, the providence of God, who effectuated all our works.

All this applies to the evil side of one's behavior. The good side is totally related to man's freedom. As the penitential process is deepened, and the evil dimension of his behavior is severed from his zone of free choice and is surrendered to the higher domain where all is good, for "evil cannot abide with Him" (Ps. 5:5), the deeper becomes the attachment of his good side to his domain of free choice. Thus are the light and the spiritual riches of his life magnified now and for all time, and the person and to some extent all existence rises to greater heights. They are illumined with a higher perception of the highest good, that a disposition for the good is the universal foundation, the beginning and the end of all existence. "The Lord is good to all, and His mercies are over all His works" (Ps. 145:9).

3. In unenlightened quarters of existence there prevails a false fear that extends to the souls of individuals and groups living under oppressive conditions and laws that impinge on their freedom. The penitent is afraid that his sins have already destroyed him, and he is without hope, without realizing that in his very fear lie hidden all the lights of his rescue. The earth itself was afraid and did not grow the tree to its perfection, that its taste be like the taste of its fruit; the moon was afraid of the competition of two kings serving with the same crown.[24] Humanity is afraid of the clear and exalted values of freedom; this world is afraid of the emergence of the world to come, which is robed in holiness. But the treasure of faith yields tranquillity, and the basis of fear disappears. "The name of the Lord is a mighty fortress, the righteous run to it and feel secure" (Prov. 18:10). In the holiness of faith the defects of all worlds and all who inhabit them will be mended. "Trust in the Lord always for the Lord God is an everlasting stronghold" (Isa. 26:4).

4. The gentle pain caused by the spirit of holiness and purity embodied in penitence yields a happiness of inestimable magnitude. In this condition man is immersed in the exciting thought of full remorse for all his sins, all his misdeeds and transgressions; his soul yearns with love for everything holy and perfect, it longs for its beloved, its Creator, the Creator of all things, praised be He; with all his heart and soul he seeks ardently to walk with integrity, to be a righteous person who performs acts of righteousness, to be upright and deal justly. Although at the time he may be perplexed how to extricate

---

24. An allusion to a Midrashic homily that God created sun and moon to shine with the same intensity, but the moon complained, and God diminished it, in Hullin 60a.

himself from the mire of sin, although he may still be unsure how to mend all his past and his course is not yet clearly marked out to him, with many stumbling blocks yet facing him, the will to be good—this is a wind from the Garden of Eden blowing on the soul and filling it with contentment, to a point that even the hellish fires of remorse are turned into a source of delight.

5. Penitence goes together with personal strength. Commenting on the verse "Happy is the man who fears the Lord" (Ps. 112:1), the Rabbis state: "Happy is one who repents while a man" (Avodah Zarah 19a). The context suggests that this means: "Happy is one who is a man [in full strength] when he repents."

6. The pain experienced when one approaches some holy act derives from the fact that at such time the soul is in a state of greater illumination and is more keenly aware of what absolute perfection involves. As a result, it realizes its own limitations and nothingness, and becomes embittered at the circumstances responsible for its lack of strength and vision. But in truth this is the basis for penitence out of love, and every sensitive person should be able to accept this bitterness with a glad heart. The depth of pain will then be changed to the substance of a higher pleasure, in which is manifest an abundance of holy delight.

7. Penitence does not come to embitter life but to make it more pleasurable. The joy of life resulting from penitence emerges out of all those currents of bitterness in which the soul is entangled in its initial steps toward penitence. This is the creative higher prowess, to know that sweetness is drawn from all bitterness, life from all the pangs of death, abiding delights from every disease and pain. This abiding truth registers increasingly in our minds, our feelings, our physical and spiritual natures. The person becomes a new being, and he releases with a resolute spirit the vibrations of a new way of life on all about him. He brings to his generation and to future

generations the glad tidings of joy for the upright, the joy of song out of faith in redemption, with celebration and acclaim. "The humble will increase their joy in the Lord, and the needy ones will exult in the Holy One of Israel" (Isa. 29:19).

8. Full penitence registers two seemingly contradictory effects on the soul: on the one hand anxiety and grief over the sins and the evil in oneself, and on the other hand confidence and satisfaction over the good, since it is impossible for the person not to discover some element of good in himself. Even if at times his assessment is confused and he cannot find anything good in himself, the very realization that sin and evil have produced in him anxiety and distress is itself of great merit. He should be happy, confident and full of vitality because of this measure of good. Thus even while seriously troubled by the emotion of penitence, he should be full of vitality, girded with the zeal for achievement and the joy of life and the readiness to experience its blessing.

9. Penitence in thought precedes penitence in action and penitence in the hidden realm of the will precedes penitence in thought. Penitence in the hidden realm of the will is always penitence out of love, even in the case of those whose penitence in thought is inspired by fear.

10. The higher penitence, the intellectual and the emotional, embraces within itself all lower forms of penitence, with all the details of their arduous self-searching on a spiritual level, in a manner that is gentle and agreeable.

11. A master of the Torah can only repent according to the norm represented by the Torah, and a master of the spiritual life can only repent according to the norm represented by the spiritual life. If a master in Torah should say, I will fast and this will be my penance, his words are meaningless and a dog might as well eat his leftover meal. If a master of the spiritual life should say, I will repent by performing scrupulously some physical, outer act, this is for him no penitence. His penitence must be free, on a high spiritual, refined level,

abounding in the light of the holy of holies, adorned with the elements of the higher life. Then it will bring healing to him and to the world.

12. Penitence has two aspects that we embrace under the categories of higher and lower penitence. The higher penitence is intended for oneself, and the lower is for the world. The one that relates to the inner life of the person himself is always on a higher plane that the one that is directed outwardly. Many a person, when embarking on personal penitence, will require more reflection and to that extent he will diminish his study, he will have to increase his conceptual pursuit and as a result reduce his activities. His primary concern will be to refine his inner being so that he may be cleansed and truly free. All this applies to the higher penitence, the penitence directed to oneself. It is otherwise with the lower penitence, the penitence intended for the world. Here the opposite process prevails, and the necessity is to increase the involvement in study and action, though thereby reducing the attention to thought. At times the very act of reducing the brilliance of thought is a service to the world. The outer world does not grasp thought as it emanates from the divine realm and the logical process operating in full clarity. It is precisely by dulling thought that one can reach the world more readily. It is important to know, however, that we are summoned to embrace both levels of penitence together, and that the lower penitence is like the body or the vessel for the higher. It is necessary to arrange the two in such a way that every gesture of higher penitence will also stimulate the lower penitence to move in a higher direction, and every movement of lower penitence lend added strength to the higher penitence. In their outer forms these two seem to be contradictory, but in their inner essence they are as two lovers who are inseparable.

13. The righteous who have been graced with illumination, who see the whole world in the perspective of the good,

justify everything. In the purity of their illumination, and in their fervor for the good, they remove the defects of the world and every form of wickedness from the source. They see the folly and evil in the world as veils, which only facilitate the shining light, making it possible for the light to illumine our world, but they do not damage or destroy it. This is needed because of the nature of the light itself. A limited holy light would not require dimmers to make possible the enjoyment of its illumination. From its perspective, all coarseness, all materialistic inclinations, and certainly all wickedness and folly are real defects, perverse and sickening, and the soul is soiled by them; the self is filled with indignation and is enfeebled by this existence. It is otherwise with the truly righteous, the masters of pure, divine enlightenment, the men of pure will in whom abides the glow of a higher light. They recognize that the pure light is too potent for the world to bear, and yet it must shine in the world! It is therefore necessary, because of the nature of the world, that there be many veils to screen the light, and these veils are evil and its ramifications. It thus turns out that the latter are included in the providential order of the world. The pain induced by this condition is the pain suffered by the people of limited light who cannot see how all evil is only a veil to facilitate the shining of the light. It is for this reason that the Messiah will come to direct the righteous toward penitence. When these righteous will ascend to the higher penitence it will become clear to them that the great light is infinite and that it is manifest in the world as an expression of great mercy, and that, were it not for the many veils formed by all kinds of wickedness, physical and spiritual, the world would be blurred by excessive light. As a result everything turns out to be a necessary element in the perfection of the world; all the wicked will be reformed and turned toward the good, having become aware of their function. The primary reason for the punishment meted out to the wicked is that they caused pain to the righteous in the world of finitude. The righteous who stand in the broad realm of the divine come and liberate the wicked from the narrow pit, and all is turned to firmness and joy. "Passing through the valley of fears, they make it into a place of springs; the early rain clothes it with blessing. They go from strength to strength, every one of them comes before God in Zion" (Ps. 84: 7-8).

Chapter Seventeen

The Great Revelation of Penitence in the Life of the Jewish People and Its Revival in Our Lord

1. The revival of the nation is the foundation of the great penitence, the higher penitence of the Jewish people, and the penitence of the world that will follow it.
2. When one desires truly to repent, he may be held back by many impediments, such as mental confusion, or weakness, or the inability to mend some misdeed in the area of human relations. The hindrance may be very great, and he will necessarily suffer heartbreak because he knows the great obligation facing a person to mend his defects, in the best and most complete manner possible. However, since his desire to repent is firm, even if he cannot as yet overcome all the impediments, he must accept the reality of illumination of the will to penitence as the force that purifies and sanctifies, and not allow himself to be swayed by obstructions that have not allowed him to complete the process of penitence. He should reach out to every type of spiritual elevation appropriate for him, on the basis of the holiness of his soul and its holy desire. And as this is true in the case of the individual, it is also true in the case of the community as a whole. There is at work an illumination of penitence in the Jewish people. The renewal of the desire in the people as a whole to return to its land, to its essence, to its spirit and way of life—in truth, there is a

light of penitence in all this. Truly this comes to expression in the Torah: "And you shall return to the Lord your God" (Deut. 30:2); "When you return to the Lord your God" (Deut. 30:10).[25] The penitence spoken of is always an inner penitence, but it is covered over by many screens. No impediments or lack of completion can keep the higher light from reaching us.

3. Out of the worldly, too, will emerge the holy, and out of the brazen libertarianism will also emerge the beloved yoke. Golden chains will be woven and arise out of the poetry of free thinkers and a luminous penitence will also arise from the secular literature. This will be the great wonder of the vision of redemption. Let the bud come forth, let the flower bloom, let the fruit ripen, and the whole world will know that the holy spirit is speaking in the community of Israel, in all the manifestations of its spirit. All this will culminate in a penitence that will bring healing and redemption to the world.

4. There has been a rejection of the concept of nature as taught in Judaism and this is responsible for all our confusion in thinking. People try to be wise, and find in speculation and logic what one must find in the nature of being, in the nature of the physical and of the spiritual, in the collective life of the people, and of every individual Jew. This is a violation of the covenant, an abandonment of the Judaic nature in action, in imagination, in feeling and in thought, in will and in existence. There is no other therapy for those who violate the covenant than a return to the covenant, which is firmly linked with the people of Israel. "Return to Me and I will return to you" (Mal. 3:7).

5. The feelings of penitence in all their splendor with all their most profound disturbance of the spirit must come to expression in literature, so that the generation of the renais-

---

25. Interspersed between these verses are verses that speak of the restoration of the people to their land.

sance will understand in the depths of its being the significance of penitence as a living and vital force, and it will return and find healing. There will surely arise for us a poet of penitence, who will be a poet of life, a poet of rebirth, the poet of our national soul on the way toward redemption.

6. We are delayed on the path toward perfection and we neglect it, because we feel an excessive anxiety when the thought of penitence occurs to us. We feel anguished and feeble because of the disturbing impact of penitence, and for this very reason we push away from our minds this thought that is the source of every happiness, with the result that we remain straying in the wilderness of life. But this condition cannot last. We must gird ourselves with spiritual strength, with the might of the song of penitence. All its engendered distress must be turned to a vibrant song that revives, strengthens, comforts and heals. Then will we have penitence with all its associated reflections as one sweet, pleasant whole, in which we shall meditate always and according to which we shall order every step in life, for our individual and our collective good, in this world and in the next, for the redemption of the individual and of society as a whole, for the renewal of the people and its return from captivity, as in ancient days.

The Moral Principles

A Note On The Text

Rabbi Kook's writings include a volume, *Midot Harayah*, that offers a succinct formulation of the basic concepts of morality. It is published as part of a volume entitled *Musar Avikha* [The Admonitions of a Father], Mosad Harav Kook, Jerusalem, 1971.

Morality for Rabbi Kook is not an autonomous order of values, but is integrally related to the larger world of religion. While the roots of morality are to be found in human nature itself, its fullest unfolding is dependent on the influences of the teachings and disciplines of religion and on the refining service of reason. The moral life expresses the higherst response to God's existence. The call to link one's life with God is beyond human reach, but man can link his life with the divine attributes we encounter in all the life-enhancing forces active in the universe.

The specific moral principles mentioned in this collection are striking affirmations of Rabbi Kook's basic teachings: a universal love for all people regardless of religion, race or nationality; faith in man, and the attribution of his defects to changes wrought by circumstances; the caution that religion is often expressed in distorted forms and the need to raise it to higher levels before it can be a source of light to the world; and his vision of the Jewish people as committed to a vocation of world perfection.

The format in which these discussions are presented follows the style of a similar treatise on morals, the *Sefer ha-Midot*, by the Hasidic master Rabbi Nahman of Bratzlav. The treatise is divided into the various moral categories and arranged according to the order of the Hebrew alphabet. The conceptual development of each moral category is not presented through a systematic exposition but through separately numbered paragraphs or sections, each expounding some aspect of the general theme. These sections are often concluded with a Biblical or Talmudic quotation that tends to place the expressed thought in the context of classic authorities, but in many cases those texts are used in a nonconventional way, interpreting them in a manner different from the traditional.

The moral categories in this treatise are the familiar categories in all moralistic literature, but occasionally Rabbi Kook invokes concepts that are distinctive to his unique Jewish experience, especially his involvement in Jewish mysticism. One of his moral categories is "A Covenant," without specifying what type of covenant he means. The context suggests that it refers to a voluntary commitment that a group of pietists assumed to pursue with special zeal some phase of religion or morality. We have records of such covenants entered into by mystically inclined individuals who sought higher levels of holiness than that represented by the conventional pietistic discipline.

Another category is "Bringing up Holy Sparks." This is a concept derived from the Cabbalah and popular as well in Hasidic thought. It refers to the divine dimension that is present in all things but that often remains in a submerged state until man fulfills his vocation to liberate it and activate it as the dominant force in all life. Even in its lowest manifestation, even when under the sway of evil and negativism, life is also inhabited by these "holy sparks." It is for this reason that Rabbi Kook argued against rejecting any expression of the life-force. Instead of rejecting it, it is for us rather to raise it to a higher level, when the so-called evil component can be overcome or, better still, sublimated or transformed to serve a positive end.

The treatise is introduced by the following preface:

The refinement of morals by reason must precede their cultivation in feeling, for unless a person can distinguish between good and evil, how will his feelings help him to acquire the good as an attribute of his nature, and to purge his nature of evil after he has become accustomed to it?

"Every good attribute bears with it some accompanying defect and this is the full service of God: to express the good attributes cleansed from all the dross of their defects."

LOVE

1. The heart must be filled with love for all.

2. The love of all creation comes first, then comes the love for all mankind, and then follows the love for the Jewish people, in which all other loves are included, since it is the destiny of the Jews to serve toward the perfection of all things. All these loves are to be expressed in practical action, by pursuing the welfare of those we are bidden to love, and to seek their advancement. But the highest of all loves is the love of God, which is love in its fullest maturing. This love is not intended for any derivative ends; when it fills the human heart, this itself spells man's greatest happiness.

3. One cannot but love God, and this sweet and necessary love must engender as a practical consequence an active love for everything in which we perceive the light of God. One cannot but love the Torah and the commandments, which are so intimately linked to the goodness of God. One cannot but love equity and righteousness, the benign order that engenders good for all, which is firmly linked to the reality of existence, and in which the heart envisions excellence, that, because of its majesty and beauty, we designate as the will of God. The divine will is manifest in it, but it is greater than all this, and distinct from all this, and it nourishes the soul of every living being with delight beyond anything to which thought could reach. And it is impossible not to be filled with love for every creature, for the flow of the light of God shines in everything, and everything discloses the pleasantness of the Lord. "The mercy of the Lord fills the earth" (Ps. 33:5).

4. The flame of the holy fire of the love of God is always burning in the human heart. It is this that warms the human

spirit and illumines life; the delights it yields are endless, there is no measure by which to assess it. And how cruel is man toward himself, that he allows himself to be sunk in the dark abyss of life, troubles himself with petty considerations, while he erases from his mind this that spells true life, that is the basis for all that gives meaning to life. It is for this reason that he does not share in it, and walks this world bound by the heavy burden of his material existence, without light to illumine his way. But all this is contrary to the nature of life; indeed it is contrary to the nature of all existence. The grace of God's love, a boon from on high, is destined to break out from its confinements, and the holiness of life will hew a path toward this delight, so as to enable it to appear in its full splendor and might. "No eye has seen what God alone will do for those who wait for him" (Isa. 64:3).

5. The love for people must be alive in heart and soul, a love for all people and a love for all nations, expressing itself in a desire for their spiritual and material advancement; hatred may direct itself only toward the evil and the filth in the world. One cannot reach the exalted position of being able to recite the verse from the morning prayer (I Chron. 16:8), "Praise the Lord, invoke His name, declare His works among the nations," without experiencing the deep, inner love stirring one to a solicitousness for all nations, to improve their material state, to promote their happiness. This disposition qualifies the Jewish people to experience the spirit of the Messiah.

Whenever in our classic tradition we encounter allusions to hatred, clearly the reference is to the phenomenon of evil, which has disrupted by force the unity of many nations at the present time, and certainly in ancient times when the world was in a much lower moral state. But we must realize that the life process, its inherent light and holiness, never leaves the divine image, with which each person and each nation has been endowed, each according to its level of qualification, and this nucleus of holiness will uplift all. It is because of this perspective on life that we are concerned for the fullest progress to prevail in the world, for the ascent of justice, merged with beauty and vitality, for the perfection of all creation, commencing with man, in all the particular groupings through which he functions. This is the essence that lies at the heart of the Jewish outlook, that, by the grace of God, we are now reviving on a practical and spiritual plane.

6. The degree of love in the soul of the righteous embraces all creatures, it excludes nothing, and no people or tongue. Even the wicked Amalek's name is to be erased by Biblical injunction only "from under the heavens" (Exod. 17:14). But through "cleansing" he may be raised to the source of the good, which is above the heavens, and is then included in the higher love. But one needs great strength and a lofty state of purity for this exalted kind of unification.*

7. When love is challenged by impediments, whether emananting from nature or from the teachings of the Torah, it goes through a refining process until it ascends to the very essence of divine love, which created all beings and sustains them in life at all times.

8. Though our love for people must be all-inclusive, embracing the wicked as well, this in no way blunts our hatred for evil itself; on the contrary it strengthens it. For it is not because of the dimension of evil clinging to a person that we include him in our love, but because of the good in him, which our love tells us is to be found everywhere. And since we detach the dimension of the good to love him for it, our hatred for evil becomes unblunted and absolute.

9. It is proper to hate a corrupt person only for his defects, but insofar as he is endowed with a divine image, it is in order to love him. We must also realize that the precious

---

* Kook believed that an evil deed is an impulse that at its highest source of origin was good but became distorted and went astray. The righteous judge everything from the perspective of its highest motivation and therefore include everything in the good.

dimension of his worth is a more authentic expression of his nature than the lower characteristics that developed in him through circumstances. It is for this reason that the Talmud (Pes. 49b) limits the permission to attack an *am ha-aretz* [a coarse person] to his back [his past] but not to his "front" [the open aspect of his life that is illumined by the divine light].

10. Much effort is needed to broaden the love for people to the proper level, at which it must pervade life to its fullest depth. This must be done in opposition to the superficial view, which suggests itself initially on the basis of inadequate study of the Torah and of conventional morality, and where it would seem as though there is a contradiction to such love, or, at least, indifference to it. The highest level of love for people is the love due the individual person; it must embrace every single individual, regardless of differences in views on religion, or differences of race or climate. It is essential to understand the mentalities of different nations and groupings, to study their characteristics and life-styles in order to know how to base our human love on foundations that will readily translate themselves into action. It is only a person rich in love for people and a love for each individual person who can reach the love for his own nation in its noblest dimension, spiritually and practically. The narrow-mindedness that leads one to view whatever is outside a particular nation, even what is outside the Jewish people, as ugly and defiling is a phase of the frightful darkness that undermines altogether every effort to reach that state of spiritual development whose dawn is awaited by every sensitive spirit.

11. One must discipline himself to the love of people, especially the love of the noblest among them, the sages, the poets, the artists, the communal leaders. It is necessary to recognize the light of the good in the best of the people, for it is through them that the light of God is diffused in the world, whether they recognize the significance of this mission or whether they do not recognize it.

12. Who can restrain the light of the higher love of God that stirs in the hearts of the righteous remnant, the devotees of holiness, who are upright of heart? It beats like a gentle wind filled with delightful fragrance, at the same time roaring like the waves of the sea. The soul is agitated by the intensity of the higher delight, and the love of this supernal delight enhances all the spiritual and the moral dispositions of the self, and every soul is hallowed. Whoever has the most distant contact with the radiance of the holy souls of these heroes of God is elevated. The whole Torah, the moral teachings, the commandments, the good deeds and the studies have as their objective to remove the roadblocks, that this universal love should be able to spread, to extend to all realms of life. The fruits generated from the roots of this supremely holy love comprise the good and upright qualities, the particular and the general, the personal and the social, until we reach a state where the world is judged by "righteousness and nations by equity" (Ps. 98:9).

FAITH

1. Conventional education begins when the child attains some powers of comprehension, education as a conditioning to nature begins when the child is born, and education as a conditioning in faith begins from the moment of the child's conception. "And you shall sanctify yourselves and you will be holy" (Lev. 11:44).*

2. All clarity derives from faith, and faith is initially a composite of fear and love. The soul in its inner being senses that faith, fear and love, in their essence, are directed only toward the divine. To whatever extent these values are encountered toward other objects, it is all made possible through some illumination from a divine spark that reaches there.

Faith in God is the most exalted concept. Because of its profundity it is lowered to reach all levels, even the lowest. It is interpreted on each level according to its capacity of comprehension.

3. The sophisticates who claim to be of little religious faith raise themselves above the lower plane of existence. The portrayal of faith on the lower plane does not suit them, while faith in its higher dimension they are not inclined to accept. Thus they remain suspended between contradictory concepts, until their relief will come from the realm of the holy.

4. A person in whom faith appears in its purity will love all people, without any exception, and his conern will focus primarily on how to improve and perfect them and the ways in which he will seek to perfect them will abound in morality

* A call to parents for holy sensibilities during conjugal union.

and equity, in accordance with the depth of faith that pervades his heart.

5. Faith in God is the soil in which all values of life blossom. As the knowledge of cultivating the land brings riches to those who pursue it, while everyone once thought that the peasantry were on the lowest plane of the economy, so will the teachings associated with religious faith bring a great and enlightened happiness to the entire populace that is sincerely devoted to it, when they will be shown the riches stored in its treasure. What was once the possession of the spiritually affluent will be readied and made clear to everybody, after the passage of those epochs that, through their spiritual advances, have adapted the knowledge of religion that it might be manifested in all the splendor of its clarity.

6. In all cultures and in all religious philosophies we see only the expansion of the central point, the natural feeling of faith and of simple piety. In order to broaden its horizon, to develop the potency embodied in it, it is necessary to pursue all the peripheral studies, the practical and the speculative, the intellectual and the emotional. The success of those studies depends on the extent to which they are linked to this vital essence of the human soul, which radiates a mighty radiance of life, the Jewish soul especially. This is the holy element of faith in God, which is the basis of true piety, and which is inspired by an inner quest for life, pervaded by keen emotion, expressive of the most basic principles of life. The soul with all its impulses, with all its potencies, its lights and its inclinations, is rooted in it.

7. The faith that has its roots in nature, with the natural vitality and fruitfulness it embodies, must then be planted in the field blessed by the Lord, in the foundations of the Torah then it becomes a Torahitic faith. Then it is refined and rises to greater heights, with all its potency, and it will continue to progress in purity and in strength. These are always enhanced when the divine light, emanating from the Torah of the Lord

ABRAHAM ISAAC KOOK

that restores the soul, shines on the basics of religion in full freedom.

8. The inner essence of conventional piety includes the illumination that derives from naturally based faith, the divine light that shines in the soul with great force automatically, apart from the illumination deriving from the Torah, our ancestral inheritance and our tradition. Tradition accompanies the light of the higher faith, guards it against errors and straightens its path. "Your word is a lamp to my feet and a light to my path" (Ps. 119:105).

9. When a mature faith radiates its light on the soul, the whole world is illumined thereby. A great resourcefulness, a mighty force of great nobility arises in the soul of the one who is consecrated to God, who cleaves to God who is the life of the universe. As this resourcefulness and potency is envisioned at first in the holy imagination, so does it raise itself in reason and in action. "Whatever you will desire will be established" (Job 22:28).

10. The great faith in the divine inherent in the heart of the Jew is beyond assessment and beyond comparison. Even Jewish heresy is permeated with faith and with holiness, more so than all the religions of the nations. Though it expresses sentiments of levity and atheistic denials, in the inner realm of the soul there is present the divine light of yearning for the living God and for attachment to Him to a point of readiness for self-sacrifice. Thus the Talmud comments on the verse "'And he [Isaac] smelled the fragrance of his [Jacob's] garments [*begadav*] and he blessed him' (Gen. 27:27), do not read the word *begadav*, which means 'his garments,' read it as *bogadav*, which means 'his traitors'" (Sanhed. 37a), like Yakum of Zerorot and Yose of Shuta* who later showed the loyalty hidden in their hearts with a remarkable readiness for self-sacrifice (Genesis Rabbah 65). What was revealed in the

_____

* They originally betrayed their faith.

142

end was also present in the beginning, but it was covered over by outer filth, a result of the unclean influences of the nations "who do not know God, and do not invoke His name, who devoured Jacob and laid waste His dwelling place. Not like these is the portion of Jacob, for He is the Creator of all things, and Israel is the tribe of His inheritance, the Lord of Hosts is His name" (cf. Jer. 10:25, 10:16).

11. That world view, which will become apparent to all in the hereafter, when the world will be renewed and emerge from its cursed state, when illumination will flow freely, without any blemish, is in truth the Jewish world view even now. But the world is not accustomed to it because it is too advanced in time. It persists only through the mighty force of the authentic faith that becomes manifest in some exalted event, even if without clear understanding. The heart senses it with a sensibility that is very delicate and hidden from the naked eye. The great multitude, whose natural sense is independently strong, is attached to it with a firm faith and is nourished by it with a vigorous life. People of understanding go about it and taste at all times tidbits of the sweetness of that higher delight to be disseminated by the universal enlightenment of the future. This is the delight of the Lord that is sought in every quest for holiness, as formulated in the prayer of Moses when the tabernacle was completed: "May the pleasantness of the Lord be upon us, and may You establish the work of our hands; the work of our hands—may You establish it" (Ps. 9:15).

12. Faith in God is robed in crude metaphors because reality takes on the shape of materiality as it comes within our comprehensions. Equally so is it robed in such moral attributes that the free moral sense finds defective. But these very defects stimulate us to raise our thoughts beyond every limited moral norm, even as the metaphors of the materialized version of reality stimulate us to rise beyond all negativism and limitations in God.

13. Faith in the Lord, with all its corollaries, must free

itself of its "shells" and stand in the fullness of its light, which illumines the entire world in its splendor.

14. Many a time it is necessary to reject analogies in order to remain on a sound basis in religion. But at times one would not be able to hold on to the basis of religion without robing it in analogies. This determination is entrusted to the heart of a wise man who knows what is timely and judicious, when to embrace and when to reject.

15. Faith in its purity is established through the possibility of atheism.

16. Faith in its purity is established through a denial of every vanity and wickedness.

17. Faith itself is pervaded by defects that are purged through morality and knowledge, and then it will be revealed in its purity.

18. Faith is pure when it is pervaded by inner feeling, without self-deception and without ulterior motives. It does not matter if it is not broadened by enlightenment. However, one who has been graced with intelligence will not be able to content himself without rational thinking, and for him a genuine faith will not be authenticated unless it is illumined by reason. If such a person should spurn reason, his faith will be full of distortion and falsehood.

19. The outward aspect of religious faith is sometimes expressed in an absurd form, but the light of God nevertheless abides in it. There are seemingly absurd situations throughout nature and existence, but the absurdity derives only from the limited vision and the inadequate conception of the grandeur that inheres in everything small as well as great.

20. When an individual or a group thinks on the subject of religion, it will project the ways through which religious faith may be made comprehensible, according to its own capacities. If it is on a low cultural level, and its imagination is pervaded by deceptive concepts, its explanations will also be on the same level. The substantive content of faith may then be

refined, but the ways in which the believers portray it, for its explication, will be confused and full of the errors of a mistaken imagination. But the citation of the ways of explication will not damage the substantive content of faith itself. As the individual or the group becomes more advanced, the more refined level of knowledge will make its claim also to refine the methods by which faith is explicated. When the person is indeed ready to associate with his faith clarifying methods of refinement, abounding in light and truth, then all his improvisations in clarifying religion during the transition period will not hurt the essence of religion. On the contrary they will make it even stronger, and lend it greater depth. On the other hand, if he should still be unprepared to accept the higher and more enlightened methods of clarification, then he will find in the critique of those methods great distress, confusion and peril. Simple feeling will then create a state of mind that will make him happy by avoiding any probing of the ways by which faith may be clarified, and he will depend completely on ancestral tradition.

21. An unbeliever is a lost soul, his life is no life. Since no ideal basis exists at the heart of universal existence, according to his position, there is no longer any room for a spark of true idealism within himself, and a life without an ideal at the heart of it is worse than that of an animal. Therefore, one who reaches for inner purity, and seeks to order his life on an idealistic basis, worthy of a good person's commitment, will at once be drawn mightily toward religious faith. The higher delight of the divine light will lend him vitality, and he will automatically desire to stamp the character of his life, which comprises his outer actions and behavior, according to the pattern that harmonzies with his idealistic, inner commitment. He will resolve by himself to mark his life with the tokens of the divine spark. He will certainly rejoice in the general commitments that embrace the tradition of his ancestors in its popular quest for closeness to the Rock who

endowed them with strength and to God for whom they longed. The clarification of this lofty and pure concept will win the world with its radiance. All creatures will then pay homage to the name of God, and they will form one fellowship to do His will with a full heart. "For the kingdom is Yours and You will ever reign in glory, as it is written in Your Torah (Exod. 15:18) 'God will be King forever and ever' " (quoted from the liturgy).

22. All the commandments are portrayals of faith, they derive from a depth of faith, and from what faith in the divine in its highest reaches implies for human behavior. Every commandment and its derivative particulars, as they are performed, deposit impressions in the inner life and in the world in which is spelled out the profound truth of faith in God. Every transgression and neglect of a commandment deposits in the inner life and in the world impressions that are completely contrary to what faith in God, in its fullest truth, requires. Whether this chain of causation is known or not, the effect takes place, and the strength of the divine dimension is enhanced with the keeping of the Torah, which derives ultimately from faith, and it diminishes with the voiding of the divine service or its neglect. The culture based on the Jewish people's inner quest for holiness spreads the perception of this profound truth. The love for the Torah spreads in the world to the extent that the hidden meanings of the Torah are clarified in the world, and the holiness of a pure faith is strengthened. The holy logic that is above our worldly logic stirs the strings of the violin of the divine soul in man and in the world, and one's eyes can then see clearly the great truth of faith that spreads from the entire Torah, in its writings and its traditions, and even in Jewish customs that are also part of the Torah.

23. The highest of virtues, the intellectual, the emotional as well as the practical, need to be linked with the simple faith that makes its early appearance in the heart of a child, but

whose inner essence is more exalted than anything we shall learn and come upon through thought.

24. Without convictions of religious faith, we have no basis for the acquisition of human values, and the more we recognize the necessity of these values in the life process, the firmer becomes our religious faith.

25. Two principles need to be clarified in order to perceive the nature of religious faith, which sustains the beauty of life: the truth about God, and the great need the group and the individual have for this truth.

26. Even if the criticism in the matters of faith were justified, with reference to its outer expression, to the manner of its functioning and the acts by which it is expressed, the condemnation pronounced would still represent a perversion of judgment. It is precisely through the robes of tradition and of simple faith that its inner essence is revealed, which expresses the nature of the inner life. The righteous of great stature, who are the sages of the highest excellence, will comprehend the inner essence of faith, which is robed in definition and simple tradition, by deepening their knowledge through responding to the claims of the criticism. Then they will quicken the heart with the life-giving light of their wisdom and fill the whole world with truth and faith and divine mercy.

27. What one finds in the holy books and in conventional discourse about faith constitutes a pedagogy to introduce us to its inner essence, which transcends comprehension and verbalization. There are people who have no relation to the conventional version of faith but deep in their hearts they possess its inner essence, and despite the repudiation of their faith, they perform good deeds of great magnitude. These people are bad on the outside but good inwardly, corresponding to the generation preceding the coming of the Messiah which is desribed as bad outwardly but good inwardly (Tikkune Zohar 60). It is like the case of the ritually unclean animal, the ass, in which there yet abides a dimension of the holy so that the Bible

prescribes that its first born needs redemption (Ex.34:20), placing it above the category of ordinary clean animals.

28. The fact that we conceive of religious faith in a distorted form, petty and dark, is responsible for atheism's rise to influence. This is the reason that the providential pattern of building the world includes a place for atheism and its related notions. It is to stir to life the vitality of faith in every heart, so that religious faith might be brought to its highest level. By including the good that is embraced in the theoretical conceptions of atheism, religious faith reaches its fullest perfection. Then will all the damage atheism effects in the world be transmuted to good, and the domain damaged by atheism will become an area full of delight. "He shall make her wilderness like Eden and her desert like the garden of the Lord" (Isa. 51:3).

29. Religious faith, on its highest plane, raises man to a position of strength that he cannot reach otherwise. But on a lower plane it serves to intimidate the human heart, that one should not be too firm. Timidity in itself is one of the weaknesses from which humanity, in the course of its development, tries to free itself. But this quality that is so hated by all who look for courage is needed for the world's existence and perfection. When the effort to free the human heart from this weakness engendered by religion proceeds by the way of a higher vision, that is, by the effort to raise man to a higher level of religion, where there is strength and courage, then it will be successful. But if it proceeds only by the negative method, to turn away the heart from religion, even if it be in its weak aspect, then there will arise other evil causes, which have an even more intimidating effect. Humanity will suffer from them even more than what it suffers from low-level religion.

30. In the domain of religion, there is also value in low-level religion, but one is not permitted to be a guide to life except on the basis of high-level religion. When the official

religious leaders are rooted in a low-level faith, cultural forces will drive them away from the leadership of life. There is only one therapy for this—to turn to high-level faith. *Teshuvah*, penitence—this means to turn toward the heights.

31. It is necessary, if there is to be a return to a firm faith, which is to have a vital role in every human soul, that we pursue the most subtle paths of reason, whereby one rises beyond all delimitations, and the soul becomes pervaded by knowledge and resourcefulness. Through such probing in depth the world is filled with light and with the energy of renewal, the slumberers will be awakened and the dead come to life again.

32. The great spirits of the world raise religious faith, in its natural form, from the lowest depths, and purify it until it becomes like purified gold shining in its splendor, and sending sparks to every side, and the entire world is illumined by its glory. This is the vocation of the great *zaddikim*, the world's mighty men of righteousness—to raise religious faith from its lowly state, to purge it out of its dross, and to bring it to its authentic character. At all times they raise specific elements of the light of faith to their highest level, they redeem them from their captivity and liberate them from their exile. Thus they renew the epic of the exodus from Egypt, "to redeem a people and its God."*

33. The inner experience of religious faith is so much more potent than the act of reason that to one who is not a free spirit, at home in the life of reason, it will seem as the antithesis of reason.

34. The primary purpose of faith is to express in the inwardness of the soul the grandeur of the Infinite (the En Sof).

---

* A verbal allusion to II Samuel 7:23.

A COVENANT

1. The basis of entering a covenant as a commitment to a moral discipline is so that the obligation to the ideal that emanates from the highest level of morality shall become deeply fixed in the nature of heart and soul and there will be no need for admonitions and precautionary measures to assure one's conformity. It will become a fixed sensibility as is, for instance, the revulsion of murder and similar offenses in the heart of upright persons, which the general moral sense has succeeded well in absorbing. When a person reaches this state in all his values he rejoices in God and trusts always in His mercy. Any violation of the covenant weakens the natural vitality in the moral sense, and it is for this reason that it begets anxiety and weakness in the depths of the soul. This anxiety is engendered by the act of straying from the right course and we then have the necessity of exercising special vigilance in thought.

However, through a higher form of penitence inspired by love, even this damage can be turned into a source of good, for instead of doing many good deeds through natural pressure, which is not rooted in reason, a person will now do them through the power of reason. On accepting as a good and with joy the fact that he previously did not experience sufficiently the satisfaction yielded to him by the goodly path and the service of God generally, and the anxiety and bitterness involved in the struggle to go in the upright way, he will thereby acquire the inner disposition to do what is good because it is the true good, that is, the will of God. If the covenantal obligation had not been weakened he would have continued to do everything confidently and contentedly. It is especially appropriate at such times to contemplate pleasure in the performance of every commandment, in every form of divine service and in every good inclination, for feeling will not disclose to him their full splendor, to draw his soul to them.

It may be that he himself will not feel his moral ascent through this particular good deed, or act of study and the like, but in the aggregate, in the general character of the Jewish people, it is certainly true that every conditioning in spiritual sensibilities and every phase of drawing closer to God on the part of any individual weighs in the scales for good. Surely in the general balance of spirituality what this person represents was missing in the world because of the great mass who are sunk in materialism. In his private life, when he has turned sufficiently toward the spiritual and his materialistic inclination has been weakened, he may no longer feel the delight that is distilled by the pursuit of holiness. However, in adding his own dimension of spirituality to the general treasure, the place of barrenness will be fructified by the influence of the holy. Then will his life attain its true fruition, and this should be to him a source of true joy. "Of those who do good deeds out of love and rejoice in their suffering, the verse states, 'Those who love Him will shine as the sun in its rising'" (Judg. 5:31, Shabbat 88b).

2. Whoever is truthful to his covenantal commitment to moral values can reach out in his way of life to material pursuits without disturbing his mind. However, to the extent that he violates this covenant it will be difficult for him, even when he commences to do penance, to concern himself with material pursuits, even if it be for a good purpose, for even little digressions will disturb him. The true therapy for this condition is to involve oneself deeply in the pursuit of wisdom and knowledge of God, that is, to study *haggadah*,* which leads to a more intimate knowledge of the Creator. As a result

---

* The homiletical and moralistic study of the Torah.

of the abundant inflow of the divine knowledge, it will also be possible for him to divest himself of his contemplation to engage in practical subjects and his material needs, all depending on the extent of his penitential therapy.

3. The violations of the covenantal commitment in the realm of basic moral principles and the most exalted of thoughts, which are basic to the world's existence and to the emergent life of the future, creates in man an inner blurring so that he can so longer recognize in their authenticity the worth of precious goals and the relation of things to moral objectives, all of which constitute aspects of the basic moral system due to govern the great future of the world in time to come. Morality, as he envisions it, will therefore be weakened and greatly in need of strengthening, and every little problem will impede his progress toward perfection. But after deepening his penitential pursuit out of his love for God, together with the study of the *haggadah*, which leads a person to a more intimate knowledge of God, the potency of the basic good will settle on him more firmly. Then he will experience a retroactive spiritual ascent through the assertion of the essence of faith, even if he will not feel inwardly a clear conceptualization of it. Then the inner light will also be perfected in him, and his initial alienation will turn out to be a force for greater nearness. The fact that the light of the habituated righteousness did not function to vitalize his moral sensibilities will have led him to find within himself the strength and the eagerness to raise his concepts to a higher level, and his transgressions will have been transmuted to merits.

PRIDE

1. It is essential for a person who loves true perfection to purge from his heart every semblance of pride, which undermines all spiritual beauty. When pride is overcome, in the conviction that its sordidness makes it impossible to reach for true perfection, it will be cleared away altogether, and leave in its place a feeling of joy together with true humility.

2. Of all evil traits, none vulgarizes a person more than pride, so that he cannot rise toward the majesty of the spiritual. Whoever yearns for the light of God to illumine his soul must despise pride so that he will literally feel its defilement.

3. Whoever yearns to have his soul illumined by the divine light will despise pride as though it were something foul to his senses.

4. As long as the heart is pervaded by pride, one is inhibited from penance and cannot comprehend any concept of purity.

5. A person who cleanses himself of pride will be enabled to turn in full penance without any impediment even from those offenses that normally obstruct penitence.

6. When a person becomes aware that he is proud, this itself is therapeutic for overcoming pride.

7. Pride blemishes the will and when the will is blemished there is no possibility for any virtue to develop in a person.

8. Pride engenders laziness.

9. Pride is the grossest kind of folly.

10. Pride is in itself the fiercest kind of retribution.

11. When a person yearns to purge pride from his heart his enemies feel a love for him in their hearts.

12. Whoever bestirs himself to purge his heart of pride

will make himself worthy of loving Eretz Yisrael.

13. One who truly loves Eretz Yisrael will attain the virtue of hating pride.

14. A person who truly tries to hate pride will be worthy to attain the virtue of humility, though at first it may seem to him that he is remote from it.

15. All thoughts that arise in the heart of one who truly hates pride become words of Torah.

16. One who hates pride will attain lucidity in explaining *Halakhah* (religious law).

17. One who hates pride will be made worthy of enjoying the bliss of cleaving to God.

18. The atmosphere about one who hates pride becomes sanctified.

19. One who suffered much from pride will know how to hate it.

20. Even if a person should be humiliated a great deal he must still avoid pride.

21. A great person does not have to be exacting about petty things in order to avoid the lowly state of being proud.

22. There is no problem of pride in the experience of inner purity in the depth of one's thought or the expression of the soul.

23. It is foolish to avoid study or any other worthy action or doing something original or even writing some original comments on subjects of Torah out of fear lest there be in such act an admixture of pride. Each person must pursue everything worthwhile, and endeavor that all his thoughts rise to a higher level. As to pride, either it will be displaced or it will be hallowed and raised to its source in holiness or it will be voided through lower and higher forms of penitence.

24. A person can find in himself exalted, great and important qualities, as well as lowly and mean qualities. It is for him to see himself as lowly because of his negative qualities, and as of high worth because of his good qualities. But he

must not boast even of his good qualities. On the contrary, even his good qualities should fill him with endless humility, for it is they that challenge him to develop his other qualities that are in an undeveloped state.

25. Everyone who probes deeply his own nature must assess the feeling of pride, which dimension of it is unworthy and alienates him from himself and from God, and which is refined and broadens the horizons of his mind and reminds him of his spiritual self that abounds in majesty and beauty. Many a time the heart of a person is full of firmness, a quality that initially appears like pride, but after clarification it turns out that his strength derives from the divine light shining in his soul, and envisions the grandeur of God. If he should try to detach himself from this pride, not only will he fail to achieve any good for himself, but he will stifle his spiritual powers, and, angry and depressed, he will go about sad and, bowed down. It will appear to him that dejection is an expression of nearness to God, whereas it is, in truth, a form of alienation and turning away from Him.

26. When it is difficult to rise to a higher level in slow stages, it is necessary to raise oneself all at once, to invoke the attribute of pride in holiness, to view oneself very positively, and to see the good aspect in all one's faults. Once a person has resolved to seek the good, all his defects are at once turned toward the good, and he can then find in himself much good. Then he will rejoice in the dimensions of the good in him, and he will increase daily his good deeds with a pure heart abounding in the hope of consolation.

27. At times a righteous person takes pride in the grandeur of God that he feels in his heart. Then he is holy of holies, his words "hew out flames of fire" (Ps. 29:7), and he is indignant at every lowly feeling that stirs in him to engender the wrong kind of humility. This kind of pride abounds in humility, which is an admixture of strength and joy and an eternal love for all.

ABRAHAM ISAAC KOOK

LINKING LIFE WITH GOD

1. The divine philosophy [the Cabbalah] teaches us the attributes of God, the divine *sefirot*, that we may know it is for us to link our lives with the attributes of the Holy One, praised be He.

2. We must study God's names, His attributes, the *sefirot*, so that we know it is incumbent on us to cleave to the attributes of God, that we have the capacity to cleave to them, and that we cannot cleave to God in His awesome transcendence. If this is not clear to us then we have no understanding of the concept of the divine attributes, of the basic meaning of the *sefirot*, and of the fundamental significance of the mysteries of the "chariot."*

3. Our ideals will always be advanced and they will bring to light each day and each moment new wellsprings of light and of a life of purity if we are convinced that there can be no morals and divine ideals in the world and in life, in the soul and in the spirit, unless there is a God, unless all existence is rooted in a source that transcends all existence.

4. We must attach ourselves to the divine ideals and we must always strive to realize them in life, in thought, in action and in the imagination, in the life of the individual and of society, in our deepest and most zealous aspirations.

5. One cannot avoid some semblance of idolatry unless one masters the concept that the cleaving to God called for in the verse "And you who cleave to the Lord your God" (Deut. 4:4), refers to the attributes of the Holy One, praised be He.

---

* An allusion to Ezekiel's vision of the chariot, in chapter 1, in which Rabbi Kook sees exemplified one of his basic positions, that man can identify with the forces through which God acts, but not with God as He is in Himself.

156

One cannot cleave to the *shekinah*** itself. We can cleave to His ways. As He is merciful and gracious, you be merciful and gracious; as He bestows kindness, so you bestow kindness.

** The divine presence.

BRINGING UP HOLY SPARKS

1. As there are holy sparks* in the food we eat, so are they in all human activities, and similarly so in everything we hear and read. At times worldly pursuits from the most remote order of being become associated with the profound principles of the Torah; and everything serves a divine purpose, in the perspective of the holy.

2. One need not be unduly concerned in having eaten to excess. Retroactively all the holy sparks will be raised to great holiness. But initially, one must be very careful to be in the category of the righteous person who eats only to satisfy his hunger.

3. The holy sparks imbedded in the food we eat rise together with the holy sparks that ascend from all movements, all speech, all actions and acquisitions. To the extent that there is good and uprightness in all expressions of life is there an ascent of the holy sparks in food and drink and in all things that yield keenly felt pleasures. What is naturally experienced in the soul in its relationship with all existence becomes the basis for perceiving the most profound wisdom concerning the nature of things, and serves as a free-flowing fountain and as a river that never ends its movement.

4. Impressions registered from the outside are raised toward the heights during sleep, and this is their perfection. The spiritual elevation that takes place through a transfer from involvements with the pursuits of the outer senses and the limitations imposed by the environment is manifested on the whole world, with great mercy. Many moral attributes,

---

* Elements embodying the divine purpose.

opinions, actions and dispositions are ennobled; the chain of life is lengthened, and a dimension of kindness is extended in the world.

5. When the dislocations of travel effect a spiritual impoverishment, it is necessary to make redress with firmness and courage, and not with timidity and sadness. The impoverishment that results from various encounters stems not only from negative causes. It arises also because new impressions seek hurriedly to force their way into the soul, displacing the old impressions as a result of the narrow zones in which they find themselves. On restoring the old to their place one must be careful not to distort the character of the new impressions. This can be effected only through high-level penitence, free of all lowliness. Then everything is strengthened, the perceptive vessels are broadened and the new impressions are accommodated with the old.

6. Eating in proper measure and in a holy disposition sanctifies the person and the world, and lends joy to life. Sadness induces overeating, and the act of eating takes on heaviness, and it expresses anger and despair. The holy sparks fall to a depth more dark than where they were before, and the soul is aggrieved. But a person can in the end turn everything to joy, and through the noble thoughts in the inwardness of his heart all forces that have any bearing on his life are elevated, and there is an enhancement of light. However, it is necessary to add to the dimension of the holy in the future, to eat in order to satisfy his hunger, and with ordered joy, without any timidity or sadness, thus raising the holy sparks directly, rather than in a roundabout way.

7. Excessive eating and drinking certainly induces pride, and likewise so if these take place without any holy intention. The extent to which proper intention is needed depends on the level of the person involved. The holy sparks in food and drink, by their nature, seek to ascend. When one eats with the proper motivation one paves a way for them to ascend in

holiness. The evil admixture in them descends, while the good rises for enduring benefit and holy and noble delight. In the soul of the eater there is automatically stirred an elevation of the good and a lowering of the evil. In the absence of proper motivation, there is no prepared path for the holy sparks and they reach to ascend without ordered selection. They take evil along with them in their ascent, thereby also stirring in the person who has eaten an elevation of evil attributes, which is the basis of all pride.

In the light of this, eating before prayer is very difficult, for it is difficult to gain the spiritual disposition needed to differentiate and select the good before enhancing one's spiritual state to evaluate life through prayer. Therefore all eating and drinking before prayer is in the category of pride. Concerning such a person does the verse say, "You have turned your back on Me" (I Kings 14:9). After he ate and drank and became proud, he took on himself the discipline of the kingdom of God! Only when this is done for medicinal reason is the concern about pride inapplicable, for the commandment to heal is associated with holiness. The Holy One, praised be He, sustains the sick person, and the divine presence is with him. The basis of holiness is humility, the sick person is needy and depressed because of his illness and his eyes are turned in prayer toward the mercies of God. The beneficial aspect of the holy sparks of the medicine always ascends on the path of holiness. It rises ever upward on a straight and readied path.

FREEDOM

The aspiration after freedom of thought has a good as well as a bad aspect, a dimension of the holy and a dimension of the profane. The good aspect is manifested when it is directed beyond the zone of the imagination and physical lusts. Then will thought proceed on its free course and bring happiness to the individual and to society. The bad aspect is manifested when the concept of free thought proceeds according to our natural impulses, in which temperament and imagination, lustful tendencies and all lower elements of our animal-like self are represented. Then free thought leads mankind to a frightful vulgarization, which is destructive of life's richness. It uproots the elements of beauty and eternity from the human soul in its individual as well as its social expression. "He who pleases God shall escape from it" (Eccles. 7:27).*

---

* The original speaks of a woman's temptations.

FEAR OF GOD

1. The fear of God is the profoundest kind of wisdom. It is built on a world outlook that more than any other focuses on life in its most inward aspect. It offers the in-depth foundation for every branch of science and of Torah, whether in the realm of the sacred or the secular. Even the secular, when it seeks profundity in its basic position, must reach this conclusion, that without the fear of God science must necessarily hover over the external layer of concepts. In truth these do not consitute wisdom. The fear of God alone is wisdom.

2. The fear of God, as envisioned in the soul, reflects a remarkable synthesis of two opposites in the conception of God: the absence of absolute knowledge concerning the essence of God, and the certainty of knowledge concerning His absolute existence. The wondrous synthesis of these two basic antitheses is most overwhelming. The sages saw an allusion to this in the faith of the patriarch Jacob. The reference to God in the Amidah as "awesome" was seen as the perception contributed by Jacob who had exclaimed after his vision of God following his dream of the heavenly ladder linking heaven and earth: "How awesome is this place" (Gen. 28:17). * He was called "a quiet man dwelling in *tents*" (Gen. 25:27). It was suggested that "tents" here alludes to the two conceptions of God, that of Abraham and that of Isaac, which Jacob synthesized (Zohar I 146a). "The peak of wisdom is the feeling of awe" (Derekh Eretz Zuta, chap. 5). The negation of knowledge**is a necessity. All knowledge blurs the object of knowl-

---

* The commentary of the Baal ha-Turim on Deut. 7:21.
** Of God's essence.

edge even as it clarifies it, because all human knowledge is blurred, as is the knowledge of every finite creature that began its existence in time. The essence of life is rooted in the relationship of God to existence, and this is part of the unknown, which can be discerned only by the most hidden love in the heart. It cannot be defined in precise terms, because it will become blurred through limitation, thus obscuring the continuity of existence. It is for this reason that no finite being can comprehend the divine being. This would contradict the divine existence. The ultimate goal of knowledge is to discern the continuity of life, that there be no veil separating it from the source of life and existence, and this can only be in the confession of our not knowing. In other words, it is not in the characterization of our lack of knowledge, but in the very negation of knowledge, in the higher darkness, that the essence of true knowledge is present, without any touch by a finite hand, which would diminish its stature. "Do I not fill heaven and earth? says the Lord" (Jer. 23:27).

3. The concept of the fear of God lends strength to the person who understands it in its purity. It endows life with interest and great aspirations, and with a high level of spirituality, which refine the potentialities of the soul with the light of holiness. But for fools it appears as a symbol of the confusion that engenders weakness and despair. This exerts a very bad influence, and when it spreads it inspires a rebellion against the general discipline of the divine kingship on the part of the young people who have tasted life in its vitality, who rightfully seek a life free of timidity and fear, but rather abounding in confidence and courage. But the conception that inspires any kind of fear also makes a contribution to the world in its moral development. It is in order to implant fear in those who stumble over moral principles since they will not halt at any transgression in order to satisfy their lust. In relation to such wicked people the fears envisioned under the category of the fear of God is a true vision, for truly the divine

order effects retribution from God's adversaries. There is an additional benefit in that fear weakens evil inclinations, and thereby returns wrongdoers to the right course. But those who come close to God through the study of Torah and the quest for moral virtues, who are obviously far removed from evil deeds, must understand the concept of the fear of God in terms that elevate and vitalize all the potentialities of the soul. They must define fear as awe, which bears with it love and inner delight. "Delight yourself in the Lord and He will grant the petitions of your heart" (Ps. 37:4).

4. When the fear of God first arises in a person, in the individual as in the group, it disorients him from reality. He suffers a loss of will and of independence. The fear of God has touched him only in its external aspects, and it has not changed for the better the crude and evil elements in his physical self and in the profane soul imbedded in the dross of human life. Instead, the divine sensibility, which is the antithesis of all evil and vulgarity, voids them* and the person thus becomes enfeebled in his life, and his social concerns are damaged. There is no vitality or continuity of will to perfect the life of society. But the spirit of a courageous person who recognizes in his inner being that this sensibility of the fear of God is everything, the essence of all life and all good, will not abandon his treasure, and no matter how he might suffer physically or spiritually, even if he should ostensibly be unable to meet the challenge of the freedom of modern life, of the great cultural aspirations of the times, the magic of beauty and the storm and stress of life, and at times even of the natural moral sense, to adapt them in every instance to the concept of the fear of God and its implications for life, according to his comprehension — all these will not be able to disrupt his life's conviction that only in the fear of God is there a firm shelter for man. He will refine it, purify it, raise it to the

---

* His lower concerns.

heights of authenticated knowledge, adorn it with illumination of a healthy moral dimension, beautify it with the splendor of modern life and its culture, and pervade it with the sweetness of love, of broadmindedness, and of the higher delights. Through it and for its sake he will revitalize the world and life in a new form full of majesty, of great beauty and courage. And "the stone the builders rejected will become the chief foundation stone" (Ps. 118:22).

5. The fear of God's punishment is to be differentiated from fear in the sense of awe before the grandeur of God and from the sensibility of love for Him, quantitatively as well as qualitatively. In the quantitative sense it is necessary to bring this concept to completion and to add the two missing elements [awe and love]. In the qualitative sense, however, it is necessary not only to bring it to completion but to enhance it and to perfect it and to develop new dimensions in the inner conception. The fear of God's punishment is like seeds planted in a garden, which are not eaten, but are planted in a small, narrow row where they will not reach their full fruition, but from where they will be plucked up and replanted in a large, spacious garden after they have grown to their first stage and are suitable to bear fruit. There they will reach their full fruition and become good food for people to enjoy.

6. In behavioral norms mandated by reason it is in order to invoke the fear of God's punishment only in relation to forms of illness afflicting the soul. In matters of general health there is no need to invoke the concept of the fear of punishment, and since this justification is not needed it is sometimes damaging to invoke it. However, as far as behavioral norms established by tradition, there is need to invoke this to some extent. But it is necessary to probe the rationale for the commandments, to expound it and to disseminate it, so that even the precepts that fall into the category of the traditional will also be seen as directed to some rational end, in their general scope as well as their detailed provision, like the rationally

based commandments. Then will the service of God reach out and proceed, in its embrace of all the Torahitic precepts, and there will not be any great need to invoke the fear of punishment, which is an external consideration, but we shall invoke the love of God and fear as awe before God's greatness.

7. We shall not uproot the crude basis of the fear of God's punishment from our thought, though it is only on the lowest level of the spiritual that it is needed and it is only there that it must be given scope. These sediments preserve the potency of the good wine, when they remain deposited on its bottom. Our life resembles the process by which the world came into being. The sufferings and afflictions of the world, the tribulations and humiliations, with all our struggles against them, with all the pain they cause us, they are all the salt that refines the world. These thoughts that are based on the fear of divine punishment, when they are properly defined and balanced, raise the spiritual dimension of the soul. They give stability to life and fill us with a seriousness of will fit to be a firm foundation for the building of the most happy kind of society. On this crude foundation are being built august edifices, noble thoughts and aspirations enchanting the eye with their beauty. An inner illumination, equivalent in nature to the fear of a mishap and the natural caution to which it leads—this is a basic concomitant of all life's strengths, and in the tiny and insignificant proportion in which it is experienced, it inspires a love for life and gives it a dimension of vitality and joyfulness. Whoever uproots this lower concept distorts life, and robs it of the capacity for development, and weakens the soul. The mark of this defect is bound to be discernible in every natural and intellectual endeavor. "The beginning of wisdom is the fear of the Lord" (Ps. 111:10); "The fear of the Lord is a fountain of life, to depart from the snares of death" (Prov. 14:27). "The path of life goes upward for the wise, that he may depart from *sheol* beneath"; "Pleasant words are as a honeycomb, sweet to the soul and healing to the bones" (Prov. 16:24).

8. In its initial appearance, the fear of God, by its nature, weakens man, but this weakness is the foundation for a higher courage to arise. The physical courage is weakened but it is replaced by a more ideal kind of courage, and it restores to man all he lost even on the physical level. The humility inspired by the fear of God engenders in man that august feeling which goes together with the exalted majesty of God. An insufficient sense of the fear of God, in its refined aspect, and every vestige of pride in its ugly state vulgarize the spirit by establishing a barrier between the person and the higher potency of the divine realm, and deny him the enhancement and vitalization of life through the majesty of God that crowns the righteous with a noble humility.

9. The lack of practicality that is sometimes a concomitant of the fear of God derives from insufficient clarity in distinguishing between good and evil as inner dispositions. The acceptance of the discipline of the divine kingship surely is intended to weaken the evil dimension in our nature, but in the absence of such clarity, it weakens one's faculties generally—the spiritual faculty, that is, the essence of thought—while its mission was to weaken the defective aspect of thought; and it weakens the physical faculty, that is, the vitality of life, the desire for work and the zeal for accomplishment. The proper perception must always restore to those who fear God this great loss, so that they know that the fear of God in its purity must add to our strength generally, and bring to realization all desirable potentialities hidden in our nature, to enhance our intellectual endeavors and our performance of good deeds, and that its inhibiting objective is directed only toward the evil dimension of our nature, the source of evil traits and defective actions. When life is purged of these, many good qualities develop, bringing with them great blessing.

10. The fear of God itself must submit to the discipline of the fear of God.

11. At times the imagined fear of God is more destructive

than all illusory notions in the world.

12. When spiritual decadence results in a decline of the fear of God in the world, and the decline reaches its lowest point, then everyone will realize how miserable he is, how devoid of significance, because of a lack of what constitutes the basic foundation of life, which is the fear of God. Then all will be drawn to cultivate the fear of God, with heart and soul, in a conception that is broad and free, which will be automatically linked with the most explicit acknowledgements of truth and the grace of the most refined feeling that adorns human life.

13. It is essential to understand the fear of God, in its simple meaning, and to conduct one's life on that basis, in self-determination. This will result in the opening of doors toward lofty concerns, with their respective values. The person will then realize that these are the entrance through which one reaches the realm of inwardness, and that they also settle a person's mind, enabling him to understand the affairs of the world, while contemplating lofty and spiritual subjects.

14. There is a customary exaggeration in relating the concept of the fear of God to inner weakness and excessive self-love to a point that it makes a person meticulous about everything; and it is further maintained that it is impossible for the authentic fear of God to be developed in a person until he frees himself from the weaker form of the fear of God. However, even the weaker form of that fear, when it is linked with the name of God, has within itself a semblance of the true fear, and one must not neglect it except to the extent that one has acquired the higher fear, which comes with inner courage and dignity. In truth this is the essence of awe at the glory and majesty of God, and the fear of sin is its automatic corollary.

15. Although the outer level of the fear of God [one motivated by the fear of retribution in this world or the hereafter] is not of much worth, the person who feels a great measure of the outer fear, even if it is only a great measure of

timidity, will possess many sparks of the inner fear, which he will be able to raise to a higher and more significant level when he repents out of love.

16. The fear of sin must focus on the person's own life; it is for him to be afraid lest he himself commit sin, whether a grave or a light one. Obviously this principle includes his responsibility for his circle to do what it can to ward off sin, for it is his circle. But as to sins committed in the world outside his circle, he must always remember that as God's praise rises from the righteous, so does it rise from the wicked and as it rises from paradise so does it rise from hell.*

17. When the fear of God is experienced in so profound a measure that it depresses one's inner disposition, and one experiences anxiety to a point of disturbing his equanimity, denying him the peace, even for spiritual pursuits, which are the basis of man's vocation, then it is necessary to conserve this great and holy force, to store it in the inner recesses of the soul in a manner that will be possible for it to be activated when necessary, in an appropriate measure. It is to be invoked at all times with a particular objective, while the reservoir of this potency of fear of God, which seeks to break out and disturb life and its manifestations, should be transformed into a spiritual and practical force through which to strengthen one's pursuit of Torah, wisdom and good deeds.

18. In seeking comprehension in divine matters, it is good to be imbued with the fear of God on the level of awe before the divine majesty, to be inhibited from breaking into the realm of the eternal mysteries, not to depend in these matters on one's own understanding. But how much darkness comes into the world, and how many unfortunate ones are lost to Judaism and are grazing in alien fields from which there is no return, when this trait is carried to an excessive self-depreciation to a point of avoiding altogether the probing

---

* An allusion to a text in Exodus Rabbah 7, where the wicked are described as eventually submitting to the retributive judgement that in effect bestows on them the graces of penitents.

of the hidden teachings of the Torah, of avoiding all investigations in the subjects of religious faith, and an exaggerated fear of all scientific research. The spirit becomes soft like wax and is devoid of strength to respond to challenge with knowledge and understanding, so that even those remote from our point of view might comprehend. All this was brought about by past abuses, and the present affliction has become necessary in order to mend them. In past generations there were times when we were alientated from God; "they denied the Lord, saying, 'Not He'" (Jer. 5:12). The corrective reaction to this in our culture in the course of many generations was a simple and excessive fear of God. But in the end this itself will stimulate the corrective therapy.

19. The august fear of God that fills the heart with great anxiety because of its many claims may at times disturb the joy of Torah study and of the divine service, and it is open to many abuses, which must be cleared away and against which one must beware. But since it stems from a pure heart that is anxious about the word of God, it will in the end elevate a person and robe him with confidence and strength, and all his profound anxieties will be turned to joy. "For this one will I have regard, for the one who is poor and of a contrite spirit who is anxious at My word" (Isa. 66:2); "You poured down a bounteous rain, O God, when the land of Your inheritance was weary, You strengthened it. Your flock settled there. In Your goodness You prepared it for the poor, O God. The Lord gave the word, those who announce good tidings are a great host. Kings of armies flee, flee, but she who stays at home divides the spoil" (Ps. 68:10-13); "I rejoice at Your word as one who finds great treasure" (Ps. 119:162); "Those who love Your teaching enjoy great peace, there is no stumbling for them" (Ps. 119:165); "God, the Lord, is my strength, He makes my feet like hinds' feet, He causes me to walk on my high places. For the leader, on my stringed instruments" (Habakkuk 3:19).

HONOR

1. When the duty to honor God is conceived of in an enlightened manner, it raises human worth and the worth of all creatures, filling them with largeness of spirit, combined with genuine humility. But a crude conception of God tends toward the idolatrous, and degrades the dignity of man and of other beings. It is for this reason the sages declared that the dignity of persons is so important that it supersedes a negative precept of the Torah (Ber. 19b). This illustrates that an enlightened conception of honoring God engenders as its beneficent by-product the principle of human dignity.

2. Much dross must be purged away from the concept of "honoring God" before it be comprehended in its authenticity, eliminating from it every defect and every false influence. A'l the world's suffering may be seen as a process of cleansing the concept of the honor of God from all its dross.

3. The concept of honoring God embraces courage and timidity. The disposition to honor God's name engenders human courage and the perception that the highest good is sovereign in the world. These become widespread as the more enlightened knowledge of God, which bears with it the noblest sensibilities of reverence, becomes dominant in the world. But timid and emotional people who, out of fear, are not reflective, and do not dare to probe the greatness of the divine conception and of what it means to honor Him, find in this conception itself a source of stumbling. The duty to honor God becomes for them a ruthless demand of a being eager for unlimited honors. It degrades their every refined and noble sensibility, and makes of them sad and cruel slaves who hate one another and who, in truth, hate God deep in their hearts,

though they always speak words of love and honor when they mention God's name. "With their mouth and their lips they honor Him, while their heart is remote from Him" (Isa. 29:13).

4. The more lacking one is in inner perfection, the more nature will seek to gain perfection on an outer level. It is only in a state of low-level spirituality that there will be aroused in a person a desire to glorify himself before others, both with the virtues he possesses and with others he does not possess. It is therefore important for a person to enhance his level of inner perfection, and his self-assessment in relation to others shall always be in the proper measure.

5. When a person is honored in the world, and he is concerned because the world erred in its esteem for him, let him put aside that concern and let him invoke it at such time when he should be visited by some insult. "Those who are insulted but do not respond with insult, who hear themselves maligned without replying, who do everything worthwhile out of love and rejoice in affliction—concerning them is it written, 'Those who love Him will be as the sun when it rises in its might' " (Shabbat 88b, Judg. 5:31).

6. At times it is in order to accept honor and to enjoy it, so as to strengthen one's spiritual energies for noble ac-complishments, even as one drinks wine to renew his vitality and to renew his joy of spirit. But one's eye must always exercise vigilance that the honor paid him is in recognition for true excellence in character. This distinguishes a person, and in his distinction he rightly invokes God's name.

7. When the shunning of honors expresses a profound inner sensibility, it engenders peace of mind and puts every-thing in an equitable perspective. It brings to fruition the best qualities that are dormant in the hidden levels of life. The spiritual powers blossom, they branch out and become in-tertwined, and send deep roots into the depths of life, and the person is elevated and becomes a blessing to himself and to

the world. Even the shunning of honor that comes under some necessity, though not so pure and idealistic, still bears on itself a holy light as though prompted by a generous impulse of the heart that is inspired by a clear perception in the person of his worth and of the holiness and nobility in genuine humility. It will strengthen a person who follows it. Necessity will be followed by freely willed decision. The spirit of genuine humility, the pride of all precious qualities, will pervade all tendencies of the person who assesses his path in a proper spirit and accepts joyfully all the ways that lead to the shunning of honor. Honor will pursue him in the inwardness of his being, it will elevate him, and it will guard the pure and holy dimension of the genuine humility developing in his spirit. "The reward of humility is the fear of the Lord" (Prov. 22:4).

8. It is essential to find the honorable aspect in every situation. Then will the light of the whole world, in its highest glory, become manifest, and begin to endure. "And the reproach of His people will be taken away from all the earth" (Isa. 25:8).

9. When the light of the Messiah shines in the heart, it conditions us to respect all people. "It shall come to pass on that day that all the nations will seek the scion of Jesse [the Messiah] who serves as an ensign of the people and his resting place shall [generate] respect" (Isa. 11:10).*

---

* The term for respect or honor, *kavod*, is generally translated here as glorious, but Rabbi Kook takes it to mean that the Messiah will inspire respect for all people.

ANGER

Anger for the sake of the Torah arises when the person of higher spiritual sensibility who soars in the realm of higher contemplation is forced to confront the narrow world of particularized teachings and precepts, which are imposed by necessity on the alluring heights of universality. And the higher soul is grieved, and thus is engendered irritation of spirit and anger for the sake of the Torah. At times this also develops because of a sudden confrontation with reality, which remains in its lowly state in the practical world, because life is on a low level of development. The soul that yearns for the delight of God and for the splendor of the divine light, in its great brightness, is grieved and is agitated, and there develops the semblance of a pent-up anger.

But a person of lofty spirit, with patience born of the breadth of enlightenment, rises above all this. The reflective person will understand how all the descents are in truth ascents, and that the particularizations and limitations bring into being a wide illumination of a higher divine light. Then will a divine inner peace once again pervade the soul and one will find rest and contentment; "the light of the righteous brings joy" (Prov. 13:9).

TOLERANCE

When tolerance in the realm of ideas is inspired by a heart that is pure and free of every kind of evil, it is not likely to dim the feelings of holy enthusiasm that are part of the contents of a simple religious faith, the source of the happiness of all life. On the contrary, it will broaden and enhance the basis of the enthusiasm dedicated to God. Tolerance is equipped with a profound faith, reaching a point of recognizing that it is impossible for any soul to become altogether devoid of holy illumination, for the life of the living God is present in all life. Even in areas where we encounter destructive actions, where ideas take the form of negation, there must, nevertheless, remain hidden in the heart and in the depths of the soul a vital light of holiness. It is manifest in the noble qualities we encounter in many of the characteristics even among our barren elements, those afflicted with heresy and consumed with doubts. Out of this great and holy perception and faith is engendered tolerance, to encircle all with the thread of compassion. "I will gather together all of you, O Jacob" (Mic. 2:12).

HUMILITY

1. "Here I am"* suggests humility and zeal.

2. Humility perfects the will, and it thus serves as the best vessel for the reception of every blessing.

3. Humility strengthens the memory.

4. Humility is associated with spiritual perfection. The more a person understands the world and life, their spiritual and material perfection, the many needs of humanity and of the individual person, the more he realizes his limitation of will to do good, and he becomes lowly in spirit, and is constantly elevated by his great desire to draw closer to the absolute good.

5. It is impossible to achieve any clear perception except through humility.

6. One cannot merit the achievement of humility except through cleaving to God. It is appropriate for one who is qualified for true cleaving to God to wear the *tephillin*** (Deut. 6:8, 11:18) often. Then he will truly be filled with humility.

7. When humility effects depression it is defective; when it is genuine it inspires joy, courage and inner dignity.

8. At times it is not necessary to be afraid of greatness, which inspires a person to do great things. All humility is based on such holy greatness.

9. From the time one begins to suffer with feelings of haughtiness, one gathers strength to overcome the evil traits

---

* The Hebrew *hineni*, spoken by Abraham when he was summoned to meet the test of the binding of Isaac, Gen 22:1.

** Phylacteries worn on arm and head during weekday morning prayer, in which are encased the passages calling us to love God.

rooted in feelings of self-depreciation, and to infuse a spark of life to the refined intelligence. One then combines the traits of humility and self-depreciation, and their good qualities, with the benefits extracted from the unclean trait of pride.

10. One is called on to invest much effort in clinging to humility. When a thought of pride or a feeling of self-exaltation arises in the person, it is for him to apply the good aspect of these sensibilities to reinforce the will to holiness, while the negative aspect let him discard with loathing. Then he will add to his feeling of humility, and he will always be in joy and in gladness of heart, in a continued feast. From everything he will receive the refined element, wrung from the depths where our moral dispositions are rooted, similar to the pressing of grapes so as to make the wine that rejoices the human heart.

11. Humility and true lowliness enhance one's health and strength, while the spurious forms of these virtues enfeeble and depress. A person must therefore choose for himself the qualities of humility and lowliness in their enlightened form that he may grow stronger and sturdier. "Those who trust in the Lord will renew their strength" (Isa. 40:31).

TIMIDITY

1. Timidity is an evil trait; it is the dross in the fear of God. Until timidity is purged from it, it [that fear of God] will not be crowned with love and joy.

2. Timidity is an evil ingredient of the fear of God, and its admixture effects the loss of the riches in the true fear of God. It is therefore necessary for a person to be trained in courage and firmness of heart, and then he will be fit to embrace a level of the fear of God that is itself the embodiment of courage.

3. The feebleness of timidity must be eliminated from the realm of the intellect, that the divine light be made manifest in its fullness, in all its freedom. This is the purpose of the aspiration for freedom of thought, whose dross is denial, the denial of everything holy and exalted, of everything beyond the customary and the crudest forms of reality. It parallels the dross of the fear of God that is based on the traditional faith deriving from the endearment of ancestors and solicitousness for their honor, the traditional faith when it is based *solely* on the endearment of ancestors and solicitousness for their honor. It is rooted in feeling more than in reason, in the prompting of the heart more than in the light of thought. The dross here referred to is the timidity and panic that release terror against the healthy act of reason and thought and are themselves the source of idolatry and the essence of its impurity. But the higher source of this quest for freedom of thought is the recognition of the authenticity of human nature. Just as science recognizes the authenticity of every general law, so it recognizes in every free expression, in every intuition, the eternal and precious truth that is at the heart of

religious faith, whose inner essence is so firmly based that all the dark forces seeking to distort it will succeed only in enhancing its light. The doubts that accumulate on the subject of religion through the generations, that are revived and gain popularity among the populace as fairy tales without substance as a result of [the antireligious] criticism, will only make clearer the profound enlightenment and the boundless heroism that are found in religion's basic essence. Religious faith is endowed with so much vitality, it embraces so much of being and general potency, that a tiny measure of it hidden in the waves of nihilism and destructiveness can give them life. This is the potency of God, which is manifest in all aspects of existence, in man's will and in the expressions of his intelligence, in all the domains of his imagination and his disciplines, the particular and the general, in all the changes of time and the seasons in their upward as well as their downward fluctuations.

4. Fear is complete foolishness. A person must not be afraid, he only needs to be careful. The more he is afraid, the more he falls, and when he is frightened, the fright itself produces the stumbling. It is therefore important for him to strengthen himself in the understanding that there is no reason for him to be afraid. All the frightening images are only the fragmented colors of a great vision that needs to be completed, and when it is completed they all merge to engender confidence and great strength that fill the soul with firmness and courage. All the evil fantasies and their terrifying ghosts are transformed into supportive forces, which gladden and satisfy the mind. The evil and damaging element they embody is altogether nullified, the life-giving energy they embody is turned into a force for holiness. "They shall attain gladness and joy" (Isa. 35:10); "The joy of the Lord is your strength" (Neh. 8:10).

MODESTY

The virtue of modesty effects many benefits in the world, and therefore is it deemed important enough to negate other virtues, desirable in themselves, but which, because of man's passions and weakness of character, might result in a breach of modesty on which the spiritual and material worlds depend. The virtues of love and friendship, in all their expressions, should have been the same for both sexes, but because of the high value of modesty is the virtue of good manners superseded so that the sages once advised a man not to extend a greeting to a married woman (Kiddushin 70b).

The modest person recognizes that it is not because of hostility to the feminine sex that he keeps his distance and establishes restraints, but because of a general rule that is sound.

We find a similar discipline in the realm of thought, in the proper aloofness from probing subjects that would turn us away from the moral order. At times it seems that we thereby reject freedom of thought, but whoever understands the objective will recognize the great value of the restraint, and will embrace it with love.

RIGHTEOUSNESS

The basic righteousness of the *zaddik** who "is rooted forever" (Prov. 10:25) is the constant feeling of a divine claim in his spirit to be linked with all his will, his mind, and his feeling to his Creator, to the Rock of all worlds, to the Source of all life and the Being from whom derive all beings. All the derivative concerns in action, in intellectual pursuits, in the study of Torah, are only branches through which is revealed at times the holy illumination of the higher righteousness. But its essence is the light permanently implanted in the soul, in the core of its being. It is manifested in the very center of the life-force, whose character is defined by the ever-stronger desire to be linked with the divine light.

---

* The righteous person.

THE WILL

1. It is necessary that the general will be developed to its full potency. Then it is to be conditioned toward holiness. The customary method of its training must be the same for old and young: the will must be enhanced, strengthened, purified and given a bent to idealism, all at the same time.

2. The Talmudic principle quoted in God's name, "I created the evil impulse, and I created the Torah as its therapy" (Kiddushin 30b) also means that the will cannot be perfected in its purity except through the influence of the Torah. If we encounter a God-fearing person who has not studied Torah, it is for us to realize that his will cannot be firm, and, for this reason, his perfections in life must be weak. The firmness of the will is enhanced to the extent that it is affected by the potency of the Torah, and together with this the will ascends toward holiness. This is the force prodding us toward the heights, which is active in the world.

3. Under all conditions it is important to find the element of good will in a person, and if its light be dim, it must be brightened through Torah and prayer.

4. How high man can rise! He can make his will an active and dominant force in the world, radiating blessing on anyone he chooses and influencing life according to his aspirations. "'And be a blessing' (Gen. 12:2)—you will be a channel of blessing" (Genesis Rabbah 39). One must note clearly this concept of the nature of man and the world, of man's controlling influence on existence. From this lofty height man descends into the practical world and exerts practical domination in external matters, to put nature under his sway. But this is only the outer robe of the inner control, of being a

blessing, of blessings being bestowed through him, according to his will and speech. "You shall decree, and it shall be established for you, a light will shine on you always" (Job 22:28).

REPROOF

It is well to reflect on how people generally reprove a person to make him change his way. It may well be that that particular way, though beset with defects, is good, in the light of his circumstances. These very defects may shield him against more grievous defects. May God lead us in the righteous path, for at times it is the evil impulse that leads us to concentrate on faultfinding with everybody. May He who is merciful toward the merciful forgive us.

IMPROVEMENT

1. Whoever imagines that he improves the world through his service, while being unaware of his own condition and of the nature of the spiritual life generally, must be full of delusions and deceptive fantasies. With every moral improvement, with every good attribute, every worthwhile subject of study, every good deed, even the smallest, even a goodly conversation, one raises his own spiritual state, and the spiritual dimension is the essence of its being. It thus turns out that by raising himself spiritually his whole being is raised to a higher status. Each particular individual is related with a firm bond to general existence, and automatically when one part of existence rises to a higher state, all existence is uplifted. Thus one truly improves endless worlds with every good action. When a person lives in the light of this conception, his mind is broadened and his thoughts move ever closer to the truth.

2. Whatever a person can correct it is well for him to concentrate on, and not neglect correcting it. But whatever he cannot correct, let him not continue to dwell on and let him apply the principles: "Worry in a person's heart —let him put it out of his mind" (Yoma 75a, an interpretation of Prov. 12:25).* Let him always concern himself with improving himself and with improving the world with the clear guidance of a higher intelligence, to the extent of his ability, and there will be exemplified in him the statement in the verse: "Commit your work to the Lord, and your thoughts will be established" (Prov. 16:3).

---

* The conventional interpretation is, "it will bow him down," but the Hebrew permits both interpretations.

Lights of Holiness

A Note on the Text

The three-volume work *Orot Hakodesh*, "The Lights of Holiness," is the most sophisticated of Rabbi Kook's writings. It is not an exposition of any one theme, and it is not structured in accordance with any conceptual development. It consists of a series of meditations on various aspects of a life of holiness, some no more that a few lines and the longest extending to several pages. The term *light* indicates a perception of the nature of these meditations. Rabbi Kook saw them as a series of illuminations that came to him from the mysterious realm of the divine. He wrote them as they came to him, in a kind of spiritual diary that filled eight volumes of manuscript. They were written over a period of fifteen years, from 1904, when he became rabbi in Jaffa, Palestine, to 1919, when he became the chief rabbi of Jerusalem after his return from internment first in St. Gallen, Switzerland, and then in London, England, during the First World War. The work of selecting and editing this material took twelve years. The titles of individual selections and the organization into sections and chapters was the work of the editors, principally that of Rabbi Kook's foremost disciple, David Ha-Kohen.

This work reveals Rabbi Kook as a mystic par excellence. The encounter with God is seen as an ongoing experience, and sensitive souls continue to be illumined by the divine light. The finitude of the human self blunts our capacity to receive the light, but man can continue to refine his receptive faculties and he will see more and understand more. We know, not though the process of dialectical analysis, but through inner vision that opens up to us the mystery of existence. However, Rabbi Kook prized highly the contribution reason can make in structuring the illumination, in refining it, and in guarding against distortions by the undisciplined imagination.

In empirical existence life is often fragmented and immersed in lowly pursuits. It often descends to the mire of evil. But the more we enlarge our perspective, the more evil recedes, and creation stands revealed in its true authenticity, which is all good. The evil encountered, moreover, is only an amalgam of the reality experienced, and it is possible to extract the good from the evil, and to embrace it for the enhancement of life's values. This is a task uniquely appropriate for the righteous. They enrich life's treasure of goodness and truth by releasing whatever goodness and truth they encounter beneath the facade of evil and falsehood.

The response of the soul to God is love, love for God and love for His creation, and inspired by this love one seeks to overcome fragmentation by linking all particulars into a comprehensive whole. The divine dimension in our natures is the most impressive aspect of our true essence, and it will continually assert itself, taking us to the heights toward which we are destined. This process moves to some extent by the momentum generated by the thrust of the life-force itself, but man can share in his own self-liberation. The Torah and the commandments aid us in this endeavor, but the disciplines of conventional piety alone cannot bring us to our highest goal. A more direct reach for the sources of illumination is needed, and here Rabbi Kook invoked the strategies common among mystics. He recommended greater attentiveness to one's inner sensibilities through meditation and withdrawal from worldly distractions, serious study of spiritual and moralistic writings and exposure to great spirits, the true *zaddikim* by whose light others can also see light.

But he often warned that man must not be an echo or an imitation of others. There is a distinctiveness in each soul that must be discovered and given free scope of expression. This process is universal and it touches all God's creatures. It acts across all boundaries of race, nationality and religion, but it is especially potent among the Jewish people, whose commitment to the oneness of God is also a commitment to the vision of universality in all its far-reaching implications. It is the vocation of the Jew to serve as a sensitizing agent to help make the whole world more receptive to the divine light.

Rabbi Kook's style in these pronouncements is poetic. In tone and content the meditations sometimes resemble prophetic utterances. He does not interrupt his thought with proof-texts but his exposition often draws on phrases and even whole sentences from Biblical, rabbinic and Cabbalistic sources, at times with slight variations, as the context requires. The first two volumes are accompanied by an index that lists the sources of these allusions, but the third volume has a more limited index, listing only the Biblical references. We have included here representative selections from each of these three volumes. They are meant to reflect the character of this work as a whole.

The Wisdom of the Holy as an Influence on Life

The wisdom of the holy ranks higher than all other aspects of wisdom in this respect, that it transforms the will and personal disposition of those who pursue it, drawing them toward those lofty heights on which its concern is focused. All branches of worldly wisdom, though they describe important and noble subjects, lack this impact, to draw the nature of the person who explores them to their own level of value. Indeed, they do not relate to the other aspects of the person's nature, only to his scientific dimension.

The reason for this is that all aspects of the holy emanate from the ultimate source of life, and the content of what is hallowed has the power to engender new being, "to stretch out the heavens and lay the foundations of the earth" (Isa. 51:16), and certainly to stamp a dramatic new image on the person probing it. The secular sciences lack this potency; they do not, in themselves, engender anything new. They only portray to the mind what is found in existence. Thus they cannot turn the one who studies them into a new being, to sever him from an evil inclination in his basic self and change him into a new type of person, pure and vibrant with the light of what is the true and abiding life.
Vol. I, p. 1.

The Summons to the Mystical

When an individual, and similarly a generation, has reached a state where its spiritual propensities are summoned to expression, then it will no longer satisfy its pressing thirst

192

with any fragmentary knowledge unless this very k owledge leads to a content that is broad and free, that will engender great ecstasy in the root disposition of the soul, deriving from the source of its being. Thus the mystical elements of the world, the hidden meanings of the Torah, the secret knowledge about God, are called forth from each generation.

The stubborness of seeking spiritual satisfaction in the outer aspect of things enfeebles one's powers, fragments the human spirit, and leads the stormy quest in a direction where it will find emptiness and disappointment. In disillusionment the quest will continue in another direction.

This is the mission of the strong, those for whom the light of God is the whole meaning of their lives. Even if they have been hurt by great disappointment, even if they have grown faint because of insufficient faith in themselves, even if they have become wearied by their battle against a great multitude that follows confidently its own opinion, let them not cease their beneficent labors, let them not allow their strength to give way. In their hands is the banner of the hidden meanings of the Torah, riches of knowledge, a comprehensible and inner-directed faith, abiding deliverance for the Jewish people and for man, for body and soul, for this world and for all worlds, for great and small, for old and young.

If we say something and turn speechless, if we commence an utterance and the concept is lost in silence, if we lack the strength to liberate the word, to find the expression, we will not, for this reason, become dismayed ane retreat from our fixed goal. The difficulty of speech will not serve as a restraint on the stream of the lofty desire in which the word of God is revealed, which bids us speak, to gird the stumbling with strength, to proclaim peace to the adversaries of the world. "I will cause a new utterance to be heard in the land: Peace, peace to the far and near, said the Lord; and I will heal him" (Isa. 57:19).

Vol. I, pp. 5-6.

The Mystical Dimension That Embraces Everything

Philosophy embraces only a given part of the spiritual world. By nature it is detached from whatever is outside its sphere. By this itself it is fragmented in its being. The grace of perceiving how all feelings and tendencies, from the small to the large, are interdependent, how they act on each other, how separate worlds are organically related—this it cannot portray. For this reason it must always remain an aristocratic discipline, set apart for special individuals.

Greater than this is the mystical quest, which by its nature penetrates to the depths of all thought, all feelings, all tendencies, all aspirations, and all worlds, from beginning to end. It recognizes the inner unity of all existence, the physical and the spiritual, the great and the small, and for this reason there is, from its perspective, no bigness or smallness. Everything is important, and everything is invested with marked value. There is no lost gesture, there is no vain imagining.

Corresponding to this there is no limit to the possibility of ascending toward the heights. There is no wisdom or perception concerning which one may say that it is enough, and that it cannot be linked to a higher illumination, in comparison with which it seems in a state of dimness. Even the supernal crown,[1] which is a dazzling light, a pure light, is darkness in comparison with the Cause of causes, before whom all lights are turned into darkness.

Because of this advantage, mystical vision, in being able to embrace within itself all thoughts and all sparks of the spiritual, is alone fit to chart for us the way to go.

Therefore, the mystical dimension is the soul of religion, the soul of the Torah. From its substance derives all that is revealed, all that is circumscribed, all that can be conceived by logic, and all that can be carried out in actions. The far-

---

1. The highest of the ten *sefirot* that emanate directly from God.

reaching unity of the mystical dimension embraces all creatures, all conditions of thought and feeling, all forms of poetry
and exposition, all expressions of life, all aspirations and
hopes, all objectives and ideals, from the lowest depths to the
loftiest heights. The source of life deriving from the highest
realm of the divine, which only the light of prophecy, the
clear illumination, the light seen by Adam,[2] the supernal
lights can disclose, streams into and passes through all stirrings of thought, all movements of the spirit.

Only the mysterious mind of the Supreme One fixes the
particular formations, what shall be regarded as first and what
as last, which phenomenon shall obscure the unity because of
its lowly state, and which is above it because of its greatness.
"And before the One what can you count?" (Sefer Yezirah,
ch. 1, Mishnah 7).
Vol. I, pp. 9-10.

The Spiritual Unification of the Future

One of the great afflictions of man's spiritual world is
that every discipline of knowledge, every feeling, impedes the
emergence of the other. The result is that most people remain
limited and one-sided, and their shortcomings are continually
on the increase.

The cloud that each discipline casts on the other also
leads the devotee of a particular discipline to feel a sharp
antagonism toward the discipline that is remote to him, whose
values are outside his concerns.

This defect cannot continue permanently. Man's nobler
future is destined to come, when he will develop to a sound
spiritual state so that instead of each discipline negating the

---

2. Prior to his fall.

other, all knowledge, all feeling will be envisioned from any branch of it.

This is precisely the true nature of reality. No spiritual phenomenon can stand independently. Each is interpenetrated by all. Only the limitations of our mental capacities impede us from glimpsing those aspects of the spiritual domain that are immanent in every part of it. When man rises in his spiritual development his eyes will open to see properly. "Then the blind will see and the deaf will hear, and the earth will be full of the knowledge of the Lord as the waters cover the sea" (Isa. 35:5, 11:9).

Vol. I, p. 22.

The Unification of *Halakha* and *Aggadah*

The *halakha*[3] and the *aggadah*[4] must be united. The necessity that moves us to concern ourselves with both must also lead to their spiritual unification. The fact that one who concerns himself with *halakha* feels he has entered a different world when he enters the realm of *aggadah* and vice versa destroys much of the spiritual stimulation that is inspired by the peace of mind that comes from inner unity.

We are summoned to chart paths in the methods of study through which the *halakha* and the *aggadah* will be merged in a substantive unity.

The concept of bringing together distant realms—this is the basis of building and perfecting the spiritual world. This is a basic tendency that runs like a distinctive thread through all manifestations of life, in all its dimensions, and it must emerge in ever broader form. After the analytical disposition has done its work of analysis in order to clarify each discipline

---

3. The legal side of the Talmud.

4. The nonlegal, principally the theological and the moral.

according to its category, it must make room for the synthesizing disposition to be activated in the soul, which has been illuminated by the concept of unification. Thereby will all knowledge, all the spiritual disciplines in their respective categories, be revealed as different organs in one enduring, multifaceted body that is illumined by one enduring, multifaceted living soul.

As we commence the process of unifying *halakha* and *aggadah*, many other unifications and harmonies will be stimulated in its wake. The heavenly and the earthy realms, our physical and intellectual selves, with all the hidden riches in each of them, will join to activate in each the process needed for its full growth and development.

This will release new light on the particular subject to which we have set our eyes and our hearts in our study of the Torah, the unification of *halakha* and *aggadah*.

This unification is only the disclosure of the unity that has always existed below the surface. Whoever has failed to taste the flavor of *halakha* has not tasted the flavor of the fear of sin. The pursuit of Torah and the fear of sin must always be blended. The labor of study must be seen as dedicated, in a systematic manner, to this principle of unification, whose consequences will be of immense importance.

In truth there is always a *halakhic* element in the *aggadah*, and similarly an inner *aggadic* content in the *halakha*. For the most part the *aggadic* content is present in the qualitative aspect of the *halakha*, and the *halakhic* content in the theory behind the quantitative proliferation of the *aggadah*. Without any searching or special sensitivity we are influenced, while studying *halakha*, by the *aggadic* dimension hidden therein; and while studying *aggadah*, by the particular *halakhic* formulations, which are merged in the *aggadic* content.

However, not everyone can see with a proper perspective these trends, each of which is at all times present in the domain of the other. The alienation from each other of these worlds that are so closely linked and substantively related has resulted in a sickly separation in the method of our study and its development, and confines in narrow circles both these domains, the *halakhic* domain as well as the *aggadic* domain.

We must stress the joining of these two forces in a proper form, so that each will give added strength to the content of the other, help clarify its particulars and shed more light on its general concepts, on the depth of its logic and its far-reaching significance. The *halakha* must be made more appealing through association with the *aggadah*, in an appropriate manner, and the *aggadah* likewise needs to be assessed in its relation to the clearly defined, fixed laws and the particularized delimiting logic represented in the established structure of the *halakha*. Thereby will the vitality and fruitfulness of both be doubled.

The necessity that moved the masters of Talmudic dialectics[5] in former generations to attempt at times to link the *aggadah* and the *halakha* derives in truth from this claim for unification of these two forces that act with such congruence.

We have already been called upon to bring together many talents and branches of knowledge for the clarification of our studies, of our whole way of life. The very nature of *halakhic* study demands that it include many approaches, the views of the early and later masters, who were so numerous in the course of the generations. Deep probing and wide horizons are especially a must for us. It is therefore necessary that we reach out as well with references to unifying the contents of the *halakha* and the *aggadah*, in which are included all the contributing factors of logic and history, morals and faith, sentiment and custom, and, above all, pure inspiration, which is pervaded with the dew of life embodied in the general light of the Torah. This should grace everyone pursuing the study of the Torah for its own sake, to give him special delight and

---

5. *Pilpul.*

blessing as he rejoices in the Torah, which strengthens the heart.

Vol. I, pp. 25-28.

The Masters of the Concealed and the Revealed

The arrangement that separates the revealed from the concealed, in the Torah and in all wisdom generally, has its basis in the different dispositions among the enlightened ones.

The person inclined to the revealed does not need any mystical vision for the perfection of his individuality. His inner refinement and his moral sense are satisfied through the assimilation of the spiritual elements immanent in every perception of the revealed. As far as the Jew, a disciple of the Torah, is concerned, his Jewish soul is well perfected with an inner dimension through the accumulation of perceptions that emerge within it, and he fashions out of them a rich spiritual content.

Fundamentally we are compelled to say that there is a certain richness of the mystical among the devotees of the revealed, which makes it unnecessary for them to labor over refined, spiritual subject matter. They already possess satisfactory substantive matter from the realm of the spiritual. This sufficiency leads them occasionally to feel impatient with all mystical concerns. On the contrary, they themselves feel a lack in the knowledge of particulars related to the practical, and their way of life is filled with impediments, to the degree that they lack such knowledge. It is this that prods them to profuse arguments and discussions related to action.

The devotees of the mystical are the very opposite. They find enough within themselves to satisfy them with reference to the outer level of existence. The practical way seems straight to them. They resolve doubts as they occur, without weariness. But the modest possession embodying the mystical spirit presents them with endless claims to complete it. They feel a kind of fierce hunger and mighty thirst for concepts relating to the hidden, the concealed. Questions about lofty matters, which touch on the highest mysteries, give them no peace. They press on them to continue the endeavor to find answers, at least for some of their details and the ways we may envision them.

It is rare to find a person who responds fully to the claims of the revealed and the concealed at the same time. There is always some opposition from one to the other. It is only when a person is sensitive to his surroundings and realizes the precious elements that each of the two sides have accumulated by their labors that he is seized as it were by a strong kind of the "envy among scholars" and he then seeks to nourish himself by both methods. For the most part he finds roadblocks on his way, but he tries to overcome them.

Such people are always oppressed by a heavy burden, by a troubled mind, but they bring much good to the world. It is they, after all, who by their spirit create a new world, in which the heavenly and the earthly embrace each other.

After they bring out this composite vision from potentiality to actuality, others can then come and accept what has been readied and there comes into being in the course of the centuries a regular spiritual disposition to embrace these separate and opposite disciplines together. Then there is indeed revealed a creative force of double potency. "Wisdom cries aloud in the street" (Prov. 1:20); "sound wisdom is double[6] for effecting deliverance" (adapted from Job 11:6); "write the vision clearly upon the tablets" (Hab. 2:2).
Vol. I, pp. 36-37.

---

6. Usually translated "manifold."

The Perception of Universality

It is the nature of a spiritual perception to embrace everything in togetherness. This is its distinctive characteristic, which differentiates it from an ordinary intellectual perception, which is always concerned with particulars, and which brings them together with difficulty into general categories.

Those souls that are especially drawn to see things in their inwardness are attached to universality with all their strength. They feel great pain when they are forced through their own habits or through the influence of their environment to particular concerns, whether spiritual or practical. But they take comfort in the realization that life imposes the necessity to concern oneself with all the conditioning factors through which ideals may be carried to realization. They are, however, moved by a great desire to reduce the conditioning factors, and, as soon as possible, to kindle the light of the ideal.

Vol. I, p. 41.

Those Destined for the Mystical

Whoever feels within himself, after many trials, that his inner being can find peace only in pursuing the secret teachings of the Torah must know with certainty that it is for this that he was created.

Let him not be troubled by any impediments in the world, whether physical or spiritual, from hastening after what is the essence of his life and his true perfection. He may assume that it is not only his own perfection and deliverance that hinges on the improvement of his character, but also the deliverance of the community and the perfection of the world.

Every soul that has reached fulfillment always perfects

the general character of the world. All life is blessed through the truly enlightened ones, when they press on resolutely on their course, without being restrained by life's obstacles. To the extent that the soul is enhanced inwardly by attaining its full character does it become the sustaining basis for many souls and an influence for life and multitudes of blessing are channeled through it. But everything is dependent on the degree of the person's humility.

And let him not be confused by the question that always confronts those inclined to the inner life, that if he should devote himself to the pursuit of his hallowed sensibilities, when will he attend to his own needs, to the affairs of the world, and to the other branches of the Torah necessary for action, the analytical study of the Talmud, the performance of deeds of kindness, and the cultivation of the active forms of piety. It is only as he remains attached to his fructifying roots, to that dimension of the Torah which is singularly relevant for his soul, as he remains immersed in cultivating his inner disposition and yearns continually to devote himself to its perfection, will doors open to him, for all aspects of his needs, whether in the pursuits of practical life, or of peripheral spiritual pursuits. It is precisely one who pursues the Torah *for its own sake* who merits many things.

But if he should detach himself from his source, and stray to draw his water from other wells not substantively appropriate for him, he will wander from sea to sea, from one river to another to the end of the earth, but he will find no rest. A person who wanders away from his place is like a bird that strays from its nest.

A person should, therefore, always take courage in the Lord and trust in the God of his life, who fashioned his soul within him, with a singular disposition and with an inclination to a unique kind of holiness, through which alone he can find what he seeks.

Out of the depth of inner peace he will discover that the times of straying, too, physically and spiritually, have been prepared from the beginning for his benefit and for his perfection. There are times when one gains his sustenance from distant places. But he must not be disdainful of trouble and exertion. Though for the most part those who seek God are sated with delight and inner peace, the righteous are content to suffer injury for the sake of the Holy One, praised be He. Vol. I, pp.88-89.

The Fear of Anthropomorphic Similes

It is foolishness, this fear of utilizing anthropomorphic similes in the study of the secret teachings of the Torah. Surely we know that these in no way damage the enlightened basis of the purity of faith in one God, praised be He. These only add to our clarity of understanding and condition us to a better adjustment to the divine illumination.

We have only to study, to adopt the physical and spiritual allusions in a manner appropriate for the regular expression of this divine light, which releases from its source at all times, every moment, fountains of pure illumination. In accordance with the magnitude of understanding and the depth of attachment to God does the full love for God flow from the hidden treasures of piety to renew the life of the spirit, turning it into a new being, each day continually.
Vol. I, p. 110.

The Value of Opposition

Ideologies tend to be in conflict. One group at times reacts to another with total negation. And this opposition becomes more pronounced the more important a place ideas have in the human spirit. To one who assesses all this opposition on the basis of its inner significance, it appears as illustrating the need for the spatial separation of plants, which serves as an aid to their growth, enabling them to suck up [from the earth] their needed sustenance. Thus will each one develop to its fullness, and the distinctive characteristics of each will be formed in all its particularities. Excessive closeness would have blurred and impaired them all. The proper unity results only from this separation. One begins by separation and concludes by unification. Vol. I, pp. 15.

The Confinement of the Specialties

In every branch of wisdom a person pursues he will find both frustration and delight. The delight will come through an expansion of his knowledge, through the spread of the spiritual life in his soul, while the frustration will result from confinement, because every branch of wisdom confines itself within its distinctive domain.

Especially a person of sensitive spirit, pervaded by a sense of the poetic and an appreciation for the beautiful, will suffer as a result of the confining nature of the different disciplines of study, which focus on objective and transient phenomena.

The pain will be particularly acute when the specialists who have not felt troubled by the need to expand knowledge, who are content with their portion and see themselves as great, as endowed with a high level of perfection, free of deficiency, pass to us dry grains of subject matter, like essays on history focusing on external events, which may abound in fruitful and far-visioned implications, but they sever their favorite material from the larger web of existence in all its majesty.

We must overcome our barrenness of spirit, and embrace what these seekers manage to discover, but thereafter we must revitalize this same subject matter by relating it to its vital, universal source.

Whether we seek the perfection of society, or of our own private selves, we shall finally be unable to bear with equanimity the impoverishment of knowledge, the diminution of life and the reduction of the majesty of the spiritual that the specialists bring to us with their great riches, with their vast information, which is ordered by a spirit that is confined in its specialization.
Vol. I, pp. 49-50.

From Particulars to Generalities

A person must first enrich himself with the acquisition of the particulars, so that his spirit may be liberated to contemplate general principles. This is the whole delight of the person who aspires to broaden the domain of a higher enlightenment.

After reaching a satisfactory level in the acquisition of particulars, the spirit then proceeds to formulate for itself general principles, which transcend all the particulars. When they are fully elaborated, then the principles embracing the higher enlightenment hover over the many particulars, as a dove hovers over its nest. They thereby evoke to full expression the vitality and the light hidden in each particular, through a penetrating perception that derives from the higher enlightenment, endowing richness to the many particulars in all their varied forms.

Then commences the time of man's greatness, which demands of him that his good deeds shall not be performed by rote, but that his every act, his every habit, his every service of God and his every performance of a commandment, his

every feeling and thought, his every study of Torah and his every prayer, shall be illumined by the hidden light, the universal light that is hidden in the higher soul, before their efficacy begins to be manifested in action.
Vol. I, pp. 53-54.

Enlightenment from Within and Without

The inner enlightenment that wells up forcefully within the person, and the enlightenment from without, the rational, that derives from the knowledge of the world and of reality, both contribute to building the human spirit. They perfect one's understanding and will, and they function jointly, even when a person is not conscious of it.

But the more the person puts his heart to contemplating the spiritual edifices that these two basic paths fashion within him, the more he perfects them, and he rises increasingly in a clear spiritual ascent. He is then filled with new strength and courage, which flow from the divine fountain of deliverance.
Vol. I, p. 58.

The Contribution of Natural Reason to Holiness

Natural reason cannot substitute for bodily strength. The person must endeavor to be full of life and bodily strength, so that reason can be operative in him with full potency in all its dimensions, in accordance with the principle of those knowledgeable in the ways of nature: a sound mind in a sound body. Similarly the intelligence that emanates from on high in the form of the revelation of the holy cannot substitute for natural reason, which is, in comparison with it, like the body in comparison with the soul.

At all times must a person cultivate the virtue of natural reason in all its aspects so that he might meet in his spiritual life as well the requisite of a sound mind in a sound body. By this I mean that the holy spirit be enlightened and developed in him, within the framework of reason, clear and lucid, enriched with all the perceptions that may come within the purview of man, in all the depth of their acuteness.

This is the way of the Holy One, that an empty vessel cannot be a receptacle of wisdom (Berahot 40a, 50a). Thus it is written, "He gives wisdom to the wise and knowledge to those who have understanding" (Dan. 2:21), and "To the heart of every wise man I have imparted wisdom" (Exod. 31:6).

Vol. I, pp. 66-67.

A Summons to Higher Contemplation

If you will it, man, observe the light of the divine presence that pervades all existence. Observe the harmony of the heavenly realm, how it pervades every aspect of life, the spiritual and the material, which are before your eyes of flesh and your eyes of the spirit.

Contemplate the wonders of creation, the divine dimension of their being, not as a dim configuration that is presented to you from the distance but as the reality in which you live.

Know yourself, and your world; know the meditations of your heart, and of every thinker; find the source of your own life, and of the life beyond you, around you, the glorious splendor of the life in which you have your being.

The love that is astir in you—raise it to its basic potency and its noblest beauty, extend it to all its dimensions, toward every manifestation of the soul that sustains the universe, whose splendor is dimmed only because of the deficiency of the person viewing it.

Look at the lights, in their inwardness. Let not the names, the words, the idiom and the letters confine your soul. They are under your control, you are not under theirs.

Ascend toward the heights, because you are of mighty prowess, you have wings to soar with, wings of mighty eagles. Do not fail them, lest they fail you; seek for them, and they will at once be ready for you.

The forms that robe reality are precious and holy to us, and especially to all who are limited in their spiritual perception. But always, when we approach a life of enlightenment, we must not swerve from the perspective that light flows from the incomprehensible to the comprehensible, by way of emanation, from the light of the En Sof.[7]

And we are summoned to share in the heavenly delight, in all the particularized perceptions, which are included in this universal whole, from which all the proliferations of life are engendered.
Vol. I, pp. 83-84.

The Enlightenment of Holy Men

The enlightenment of holy men is the basis for the spiritual illumination that arises in the world, in all human hearts.

The holy men, those of pure thought and contemplation, join themselves, in their inner sensibilities, with the spiritual that pervades all. Everything that is revealed to them is an emergence of light, a disclosure of the divine, which adds life and firmness, abiding life and spiritual firmness, which gives stability to the whole world with the diffusion of its beneficence.

---

7. The Infinite, a mystical term for God.

A life-giving illumination flows always from the source of the Torah, which brings to the world light from the highest realm of the divine. It embraces the values of the spiritual and the material, the temporal and the eternal, the moral and the practical, the individual and the social. These spell life to all who come in contact with them, and guard them in their purity.

Meditation on the inner life and moral conformity must always go together with those qualified for this. They absorb the light pervading the world, which abides in all souls, and they present it as one whole. Through the influences radiating from their life and their fellowship with others, through the impact of their will and the greatness of their spiritual being, through their humility and love for all creatures, they then disseminate the treasure of life and of good to all.

These men of upright heart are channels through which light and life reach to all creatures. They are vessels for radiating the light of eternal life. They are the servants of God, who heed His word, the messengers who do His will to revive those near death, to strengthen the weak, to awaken those who slumber.

And they cry out in the name of the Lord, the God of the universe, who tells every creature: Live and take delight in all that is good, ascend, rise higher and higher.

Vol. I, pp. 84-85.

The Impact of Mystical Knowledge

It is not the purpose of the highest level of mystical knowledge to be disseminated in the world in a quantitative manner, that many become knowledgeable of it. This is impossible. If the many become familiar with its outer expression, they will remain totally ignorant of its inner content, and this will prove more detrimental than beneficial. But this knowledge must reach those who possess the precious virtue of contemplating lofty subjects.

Those individuals, by their lofty state of spirituality, elevate the world from its lowliness by the mere fact of their existence, and not by any perceptible exertion. The secrets of the inner world they do not reveal, and they cannot reveal. But whatever the mighty illumination, with all its force, effects substantively through the diffusion of its sparks even on what is openly known, on the glance of every eye, on every utterance and gesture, on the nature of the will, on the thrust of life, exerts an impact and lends firmness, it strengthens and hallows everything.

The general goal of the influence exerted by the people of Israel in the world, too, is not a dissemination of concepts, in the manner of teaching, and the simple and open spread of influence. But when this people keeps faithfully within itself its unique attributes, this itself elevates mankind, because mankind possesses such inner predisposition in its treasure.

The efforts to give guidance envisioned by the prophets is of minimal significance in comparison with the higher efficacy of the impact exerted from within. The lower level of prophetic vision declares: "And many nations will go and say, Come, let us go up to the mountain of the Lord, to the house of the God of Jacob, and He will teach us of His ways, and we will walk in His path, for out of Zion shall go forth instruction, and the word of the Lord from Jerusalem" (Isa. 2:3). This is a proposal for the perceptible level of action, which is the second stage of prophecy. But the higher level of prophetic vision, which is the teaching of Moses, declares: "And now if you will indeed heed My voice and keep My covenant, then you shall be My treasured possession among all peoples; for all the earth is Mine, and you shall be to Me a kingdom of priests and a holy nation. These are the words that you shall speak to the children of Israel" (Exod. 19: 5-6).
Vol. I, pp. 86-87.

The Renaissance of Intention

Humanity must go through extensive development before it will recognize the great value of the *intention* and the *will*, of the hidden idealism in the depths of the soul, which continually adorns itself in an array of new colors that disclose some of its treasure and majestic greatness.

All the great moral deeds in the world among individuals and societies are only small expressions, tiny sparks of the great torch of intention when it has reached a state of perfection.

Intention is everything. The revival of intention is the revival of the world.

Prayer with intention, the affirmation of God's unity with intention, the commandment and the duty performed with intention, the direction and development of life with intention, and intention in itself, as a rational and moral concept—its beauty and majesty, its splendor and holiness, its endless unfolding, its divine aspects—and intention when it is expressed in letters, words, each letter and dot of which stands for vast oceans of life, will, aspiration, and enlightenment, of potency and courage, spirituality and nobility; and intention when incarnated in holy corporate beings, pure idealistic people, for whom equity and good, in practical affairs and in morals, is the whole joy of life; the living, creative intention—what a luminous phenomenon this is in the world.

And the divine mystery comes and links the soul stirred by intention with the sources of life's aspirations, with their ultimate roots, and the light of the En Sof, the light of the living God, continues to stream forth, reaching every thinker and man of action.

Intention is where action is conceived. And the higher intention, the intention that is permeated with the divine life, embraces every thought of peace, of the battle for righteousness and equity, every assertion of wisdom, of a good and

desirable order of things. Every act that perfects the world is embraced in it.
Vol. I, pp. 124-125.

The Phenomenon That is Like a Relic of Prophecy

Each time that the heart feels a truly spiritual stirring, each time that a new and noble thought is born, we are as though listening to the voice of an angel of God who is knocking, pressing on the doors of our soul, asking that we open our door to him that he might appear before us in his full majesty.

The more liberated a spirit with which we meet him, the purer the heart, the firmer and more resolute the feeling, the greater our inner love and desire for what is the most exalted, the most honorable, so will multitudes of noble souls appear to us, and with his light he will illumine our darkness.

Our encounter with the objective world of the spiritual will then grow in holiness, our relationships will be strengthened, habit will do its work to give us clarity and peace of mind, and the beneficence of the revelation, a relic of the grandeur of prophecy, will move us, bringing us healing in its wings.

We shall be protected against every kind of destructiveness, of evil and falsehood, with which the imagination might embarrass us if we hold on firmly to the tree of life that is ancestral tradition, with its noble standard of morality, with its laws affecting all aspects of life; to our faithful relationship toward man generally, toward the family and the nation; to all the claims of life.

But with all this we need not remain bound in the chains of convention, which choke the higher, free spirit, which desecrate the holy that emanates from a higher order, the world of freedom, where thought has been endowed with liberty, absolute freedom for aspiration, complete freedom for the inclination of the will, and for creation. And the greater the freedom, the greater will be the level of holiness. "I will rejoice in the Lord, I will exult in the God of my salvation" (Hab. 3:18).

Let everyone express in truth and in faithfulness whatever his soul reveals to him, let him bring forth his spiritual creativity from potentiality to actuality, without any deception. Out of such sparks torches of light will be assembled, and they will illumine the whole world out of their glory. Out of such fragments of inner truth will the great truth emerge.
Vol. I, pp. 167-168.

The Unfolding of Creation

Let our spirit fashion for us its creations. We recognize the angel, full of life, who attends to the act of birth, who brings into being his creations. He soars toward us from the great beyond, he draws close to us, he reveals himself in our souls. He has now come.

We shall welcome him with peace and with love. He is aware of our love in a more refined and pure, more vital and genuine form, than we who are confined in our physical frame can sense it.

Now our creation has come to a standstill, or it has been interrupted for us in the middle. "You but raise your eyes toward him and he is gone" (Prov. 23:5). The angel has flown away, he has ascended toward the heavens, and we are perplexed.

We concern ourselves with the pursuit of Torah and wisdom, with good deeds, with the cultivation of good character traits, to tie the holy angels to ourselves, to strengthen ourselves with the strength of the gracious God, who reveals Himself to us with His light and deliverance.

Our states change, courage and weakness encounter each

other, love is merged with anguish, confidence and panic are operative together, light and darkness in confusion. All this comes about because of our lack of refinement.

Let us raise ourselves higher. Penitence will arise with greater intensity, with greater potency, the will reaching toward a higher level of holiness. We raise ourselves above the flesh and its filth. We rise above the falsehood and hypocrisy of the environment. We cling in truth to truth, and the light grows stronger, and life ascends to a higher state.
Vol. I, p. 169.

The Soul's Illumination

As long as a person is constrained to wait for a time when the creative spirit will inspire him, and then he will create, meditate, sing—this is an indication that his soul has not yet been illuminated.

Surely the soul sings always. It is robed in might and joy, it is surrounded by a noble delight, and the person must raise himself to the height of confronting his soul, of recognizing its spiritual imprints, the rushing of its wings that abound in the majesty of the holy of holies, and he will always be ready to listen to the secret of its holy discourse. Then he will know that it is not at one time rather than another, on one occasion rather than another, that the soul engenders in us new thrusts of wisdom and thought, song and holy meditation. At all times, in every hour, it releases streams of its precious gifts. And the streams that flow from it are holy treasures, fountains of understanding, stored with good sense. God's compassions are new each morning, great is His faithfulness (Lam. 3:23).

On contemplating inwardly in the depths of the soul, one realizes that the activating thrust of the truly higher life does not cease even for a moment. It moves "forward and backward as the appearance of a flash of lightening" (Ezek. 1:14). Its work is that of the holy angels, it ever breaks out in song, joyously proclaiming God's glory.

When the person of a higher soul suffers a loss of faith in the power of his own identity, then he will walk about gloomy, he will be desolate, and the lustre of the whole world will be diminished for him.

But on turning back in a higher penitence, and regaining the glory of his faith in his higher powers, which stir in him always, his spirit will revive and be brightened, and all the worlds that reflect his disposition will be filled with splendor and light.

Vol. I, pp. 174-175.

The Inner Spark

The inner essence of the soul, which reflects, which lives the true spiritual life, must have absolute inner freedom. It experiences its freedom, which is life, through its originality in thought, which is its inner spark that can be fanned to a flame through study and concentration. But the inner spark is the basis of imagination and thought. If the autonomous spark should not be given scope to express itself, then whatever may be acquired from the outside will be of no avail.

This spark must be guarded in its purity, and the thought expressing the inner self, in its profound truth, its greatness and majesty, must be aroused. This holy spark must not be quenched through any study or probing.

The uniqueness of the inner soul, in its own authenticity—this is the highest expression of the seed of divine light, the light planted for the righteous, from which will bud and blossom the fruit of the tree of life.

Vol. I, p. 177.

Creation and Study

Whoever is endowed with the soul of a creator must create works of imagination and thought. He cannot confine himself in shallow studies alone. For the flame of the soul rises by itself and one cannot impede it on its course.

Scope for thought—this is the constant claim that a thinking person addresses to himself.

Superficial study sometimes narrows thought, it aborts it at birth. It is this that aggravates the sickness of narrowness of thought. With all one's strength one must liberate oneself from this, in order to free the soul from its narrow confines, to redeem it from its Egypt, from the house of bondage.
Vol. I, p. 179.

Originality and Acquired Knowledge

Understanding reached by one's own mind—this is the highest expression of spiritual progress. All that is learned by study is absorbed from the outside, and is of lesser significance as compared with what is thought through within the soul itself. All that is acquired by study is only a profound strategy as to how to draw on what is hidden in the heart, in the depths of the soul, one's inner understanding, from the knowledge within.

Knowledge in our inner being continues to stream forth. It creates, it acts.

The higher creative individual does not create. He only transfers. He brings vital, new light from the higher source whence originality emanates to the place where it has not previously been manifest, from the place that "no bird of prey knows, nor has the falcon's eye seen it" (Job 28:7), "that no man has passed, nor has any person inhabited it" (Jer. 2:6).

And with the emergence of such greatness of the self,

there is fashioned the faithful ear, the listening heart. Such a person will never utter a word he did not hear from his teacher. These are the prophets of truth and righteousness, to whom God has communicated the truth.
Vol. I, p. 180.

A Holiness That Destroys and a Holiness That Builds

There is a holiness that builds and there is a holiness that destroys. The benefits of the holiness that builds are visible, while the benefits of the one that destroys are hidden, because it destroys in order to build what is nobler than what has been built already.

One who understands the secret of the holiness that destroys can mend many souls, and his capacity for mending is in accordance with his understanding. From the holiness that destroys there emerge the great warriors who bring blessing to the world. They exemplify the virtue of Moses, the man of the mighty arm, who broke the tablets.

One whose spirit cannot reach out to the wide horizons, one who does not search for the truth with his whole heart, cannot tolerate spiritual destruction, but neither does he have any edifices he has built himself. He finds shelter in naturally formed structures, like rabbits who find shelter in the rocks. But man, one who has a human soul, his soul will be unable to rest except in edifices he constructs with his own spiritual toil, on which he works with increasing diligence.

At times the vision ascends toward the heights, enticing one with concerns of great universality and purity. Then the lower concerns, the narrower ones, which are sustained by the imagination, and the customary rules, together with such aspects of the good and the holy that were linked to them, totter, and the person is devastated. He remains so until a brighter light shines on him, to rebuild the ruins of his spiritual edifice into a more noble structure, and also to take with him the deeper elements of good and holiness that had been embodied in the lowly and shallow concerns. Out of these he will build a new world, a world pervaded by a great light. Vol. II, p. 224.

The Great Dreams

The great dreams are the foundation of the world. They are manifested on different levels. The prophets dream, as God is quoted in saying: "I speak with him [a prophet] in a dream" (Num. 12:8). The poets dream while awake, the mighty thinkers dream of perfecting the world. All of us dream of the time "when God will return the captivity of Zion" (Ps. 126:1).

The crudeness of conventional life, which is wholly immersed in its materialistic aspect, removes from the world the light of the dream, the splendor of its wide horizons, its ascent above ugly reality. Thus the world is in convulsion with pains engendered by the destructive toxins of reality, devoid of the brightness of the dream.

But these pains are the sufferings of love, they will purge the world, make it clear to it how grave is the error of those who boast of reality in its defective state, while only the uninhibited dream, which is in revolt against reality and its limitations, is truly the most substantive truth of existence.

Then the vision of the dream will return and it will become a clear revelation.[8] "I shall speak to him mouth to mouth, plainly and not in riddles, and he will behold the likeness of the Lord" (Num. 12:8).
Vol. I, p. 228.

---

8. As it was promised to Moses.

The Ascent of Everything toward the Holy

Differentiation is included in the scheme of creation. The difference between the holy and the ordinary is a fact. A blurring of their distinctiveness would be destructive. A concentration on understanding and experiencing this great fact of differentiation contributes to much fruitfulness of spirit. But after all this one comes to the clear perception that all these are passing phenomena, and that the exertion of everything toward holiness, toward brotherhood, toward equality and delight, is the eternal vision that animates every noble spirit. The perception of differences is a passing phenomenon, engendered by temporary circumstances.

The general conception of striving for equality, which is the basis of kindness and the pure love of people, is seen in the mystical interpretation as bringing up the sparks that are scattered among the husks of unrefined existence, and in the great vision of transforming everything to full and absolute holiness, in a gradual increasing of love, peace, justice, truth and compassion.

Vol. II, p. 322.

The Heroism of the Holy

The *zaddikim* and those pure of heart fail to appreciate sufficiently the function of the physical world, as a result of their spiritual ascent and the dissociation of their interest from the physical. This gives them in some respects a sense of spiritual exaltation, but for the world it results in decline, and this decline eventually penetrates from the world to these great people themselves. Even their detachment, their avoidance of familiarity with absolute evil and the filth of impurity, also effects a decline for the world, though they themselves escape the trap of the filth by turning their eyes away from it. In the end, however, the decline suffered by the world through the growth of the filth that might have been reduced by these pure of heart who know its nature and could have tried to break it comes back and afflicts them, and as a result they suffer general distress.

This condition remains only as long as those holy people of the world have not yet risen to the higher divine heroism, and a fear of familiarity with the physical and certainly of an encounter with evil is hidden in their hearts. They feel constrained to withdraw into holy retreats, allowing the filth of the world to spread, according to its crude nature.

But when they will reach the nobler epoch, and through the illumination of the light immanent in the Torah and the enlightenment of the holy reach the level of heroism adorned with holiness, then they will no longer be afraid of the knowledge of the physical and all its functions, or of an encounter with impurity and all its filth. They will be confident that wherever they will look with the eyes of the holy heroism, the physical will ascend and be ennobled by the holy, and the filth of impurity will come to an end, all bowing before the light of the holy. Then will be magnified and hallowed the name of the Lord, the God of truth, and " the eyes of the blind shall see out of obscurity and out of darkness" (Isa. 29:18), and the Lord will be king over all the earth, and "idolatry will altogether disappear" (Isa. 2:18).
Vol. II, p. 328.

The Doctrine of Evolution

The doctrine of evolution that is presently gaining acceptance in the world has a greater affinity with the secret teachings of the Cabbalah than all other philosophies.

Evolution, which proceeds on a course of improvement, offers us the basis of optimism in the world. How can we despair when we realize that everything evolves and improves? In probing the inner meaning of evolution toward an improved state, we find here an explanation of the divine concepts with absolute clarity. It is precisely the En Sof in action that manages to bring to realization the infinite potentiality.

Evolution sheds light on all the ways of God. All existence evolves and ascends, as this may be discerned in some of its parts. Its ascent is general as it is in particulars. It ascends toward the heights of the absolute good. Obviously the good and the comprehensive all go together. Existence is destined to reach a point when the whole will assimilate the good in all its constituted particulars. This is its general ascent: No particularity will remain outside, not a spark will be lost from the ensemble. All will share in the climactic culmination.

Toward this objective one needs to be sensitized spiritually to seek God on a higher plane. This is effected through a service of faith in God.
Vol. II, p. 555.

Conformity to the Light of the En Sof

The spiritual waves stirrring the individual and the world derive from the inner endeavor of all things to conform to the inflow of the light of the En Sof.

In one moment there is a flash of light, and life is enhanced as the will is filled with delight in the envisioned conformity to the absolute good in the light of the En Sof. A great satisfaction moves through all the avenues of life and of all existence.

Then there at once settles on us the realization how dark and deficient everything is in comparison with the En Sof, what endless abysses separate the Creator from the creature, and how impossible is this desire for conformity. And everything seems dry and empty.

But out of this very depression over the nothingness of

everything, and that the source of all is everything, and the mighty higher reality of the divine light, its affirmation and splendor, fills all the vital parts of body and soul. The pangs of insignificancy, of total annulment, brighten up existence, extend the boundary, and the possibility of conforming to the light of the En Sof becomes again promising to the spirit. Man then rises, his soul's confidence and the eternal significance of his life are again strengthened. He rises toward the heights until he feels crushed and desperate, but his spirit is at once renewed, and again becomes luminous. It "is a forward and backward movement, like the appearance of a flash of lightning" (Ezek. 1:14).

Vol. II, p. 345.

The Higher Attentiveness

Waves from the higher realm act on our souls ceaselessly. The stirrings of our inner spiritual sensibilities are the result of the sounds released by the violin of our souls, as it listens to the echo of the sound emanating from the divine realm.

Though we do not know how to delimit, and we cannot particularize, and certainly not sum up, or see an ordered content in the subjects with which the divine reverberation concerns itself, nevertheless, we listen with general attentiveness. We hear the sound of words.

Though we do not discern the configuration of letters and separate words, all our endeavor in Torahitic and scientific studies is only to clarify whatever comprehensible words it is possible to distill from this divine voice that always reverberates in our inner ear. We do this to be able to present them to ourselves and to others in a form that is conducive to action and to an ordered discipline of study.

Vol. II, p. 346.

The Glory of Life

The realm of mystery tells us, You live in a world full of light and life.

Know the great reality, the richness of existence that you always encounter. Contemplate its grandeur, its beauty, its precision and its harmony.

Be attached to the legions of living beings who are constantly bringing forth everything beautiful. In every corner where you turn, you are dealing with realities that have life; you always perform consequential acts, abounding with meaning and with the preciousness of vibrant life. In everything you do you encounter sparks full of life and light, aspiring to rise toward the heights. You help them and they help you.

The glorious wisdom that you comprehend is not a faint shadow of some spiritual mirage that is devoid of meaning, to be displaced by research and science. These phenomena are the children of a real world, introducing themselves to you, sending you good news from afar, news about their well-being and their state of health. Their well-being also contributes to your well-being.

When you ascend to greater heights you raise yourselves to a more noble fellowship, to surroundings of greater splendor.

And everything aspires, longs, yearns, according to a pattern that is adorned with holiness and girded with beauty. For this life of yours is not a meaningless phenomenon. The light of Your own presence, O Lord, our God, is imprinted on the law that governs life.

Vol. II, p. 355-356.

ABRAHAM ISAAC KOOK

The Spirit of the Masses and of the Elite

The intelligensia believes that it can separate itself from the masses, that then it will be healthier in spirit, more refined in its thinking. This is a basic error, an error that does not recognize the healthy side in natural perceptions, natural feelings, and in natural instincts, which have not been perfected but which also have not been damaged by any cultural influence.

The healthy sense of equity is much more common among ordinary people than it is among scholarly and intellectual moralists. The learned are more expert on particular aspects of morality, its rules and fine points, but the essence of its feeling is common among naturally healthy people, who make up the masses, the common people.

It is not only in the basic moral sensibility that the masses are above the elite. The religious sensibility, the feeling of the greatness of God, the sense of beauty, sensitivity— everything that pertains to a proper way of life, unfiltered in the murky vessels of knowledge and wisdom, is in a healthier and purer state among the masses.

But the masses by themselves will be unable to preserve themselves in the state of purity. They will be unable to integrate properly their concepts. They will also be unable to engage in battle when contradictory perceptions and feelings are in conflict inside themselves or in the outside world. For this they need the help of the great men of wisdom, to set straight for them the paths of their life.

But as the latter will extend to them counsel and wise guidance, so will they release on the latter an influence for a healthy life.

The partnership of the elitists with the masses is the force that keeps both sides on a sound basis, and guards them from moral and physical decadence.

Prophecy, which is channeled from the divine, has precisely this as its objective—to join the spirit of the masses

224

with the aristocratic spirit that is characteristic of the elitist few. The idiom of the common people is joined here with the sophisticated thought of the spiritually well endowed.
Vol. II, pp. 376-7.

The Revelation of Unity

The affirmation of the unity of God aspires to reveal the unity in the world, in man, among nations, and in the entire content of existence, without any dichotomy between action and theory, between reason and the imagination. Even the dichotomies experienced will be unified through a higher enlightenment, which recognizes their aspect of unity and compatibility. In the content of man's life this is the entire basis of holiness. In the life of the spirit it is the light of eternity, in which the temporal and the eternal merge in one whole.

This is the most august thought among the great thoughts that man's intellectual capacity can conceive. It is revealed to him through his receptivity to spiritual illumination. It may take him to the height of a revelation of the divine, by the way of reason, the knowledge called "face to face."
Vol. II, p. 425.

The Perfection of the Spiritual through the Material

When spiritual decline sets in because of a deterioration in one's bodily state, it is necessary to deal with it on the basis of its cause: to mend one's bodily state, according to a definite regimen and with firm understanding. Through the mending of the bodily condition the spiritual damage will be repaired.

In the course of life it often becomes apparent that spiritual deficiencies result from the breakdown in the proper order of the physical. The physical then asserts itself with full force, and it seems to many that it has risen as a destructive force against the spiritual order. In truth, however, it becomes clear in the light of developments that the thrust of the physical was directed to a general rehabilitation, which embraces all of the spiritual needs as well, in their purest form. Vol. II, p. 435.

A Love for the World

Great souls cannot dissociate themselves from the most universal concerns. All they desire and aspire for is the universal good, universal in its comprehensiveness, universal in its full width, height and depth. But the whole is constituted of numberless particulars, particular individuals and particular communities. The whole cannot achieve its highest fulfillment except through the perfection of its particular individuals, and the particular communities, whether small or large, of which it is constituted.

The higher unification, in which everything finds its completion, rests on the influence of the knowledge of God and the love of God, from which it necessarily derives, to the extent that one has embraced it. When the knowledge of God is suffused by a great love, when it is pervaded by its true illumination, according to the capacity of each soul to receive it, there radiates from its absolute light a love for the world, for all worlds, for all creatures, on all levels of their being. A love for all existence fills the hearts of the good and kindly ones among creatures, and among humans. They yearn for the happiness of all, they hope that all may know light and joy. They draw into themselves the love for all existence, differentiated into its many forms of being, from the higher love for God, from the love of absolute and total perfection in the Cause of all, who created and sustains everything.

When love descends from the spiritual realm to the created order, it descends by fragmentation into many particulars, to opposition and contradiction. It faces the necessity of confining the scope of the love bestowed to one individual for the sake of another, to many individuals for the sake of another group of many individuals, and to individuals in general for the sake of the all-embracing collective.

Love in its most luminous aspect has its being beyond the world, in the divine realm, where there are no contradictions, limits and opposition; only bliss and good, wide horizons without limit. When worldly love derives from it, it partakes of much in its nature. Even in its descent it does not become miserly or grudging. When it needs to confine itself, it confines love for the sake of love, it sets a boundary around the good for the sake of the good.

When these love-possessed people see the world, especially living creatures full of quarrels, hatred, persecutions and conflicts, they yearn with all their being to share in those aspirations that move life toward comprehensiveness and unity, peace and tranquillity. They feel and they know that the nearness of God, for which they yearn, can only lead them to joining themselves with *all* and for the sake of *all*. When they confront the human scene, and find divisions among nations, religions, parties, with goals in conflict, they endeavor with all their might to bring all together, to mend and to unite. With the healthy instinct of their noble souls, which soar with a divine thrust above all confinements, they feel that the individuals need to be enhanced, that the best of societies must rise to greater heights, and to enter with all the affluence of their individuals into the light of a universal life. They want that every particuar shall be preserved and developed, and that the collective whole shall be united and abounding in peace.

When they confront their own people, to whose happiness, continuity and perfection they feel committed in all the depths of their being, and find it splintered, broken into parties and parties, they cannot identify themselves with any particular party. They desire to unite themselves with the

227

whole people, only with the all-embracing whole, in all its fullness and good.
Vol. II, pp. 456-457.

A Fourfold Song

There is one who sings the song of his own life, and in himself he finds everything, his full spiritual satisfaction.

There is another who sings the song of his people. He leaves the circle of his own individual self, because he finds it without sufficient breadth, without an idealistic basis. He aspires toward the heights, and he attaches himself with a gentle love to the whole community of Israel. Together with her he sings her songs. He feels grieved in her afflictions and delights in her hopes. He contemplates noble and pure thoughts about her past and her future, and probes with love and wisdom her inner spiritual essence.

There is another who reaches toward more distant realms, and he goes beyond the boundary of Israel to sing the song of man. His spirit extends to the wider vistas of the majesty of man generally, and his noble essence. He aspires toward man's general goal and looks forward toward his higher perfection. From this source of life he draws the subjects of his meditation and study, his aspirations and his visions.

Then there is one who rises toward wider horizons, until he links himself with all existence, with all God's creatures, with all worlds, and he sings his song with all of them. It is of one such as this that tradition has said that whoever sings a portion of song each day is assured of having a share in the world to come.

And then there is one who rises with all these songs in one ensemble, and they all join their voices. Together they sing their songs with beauty, each one lends vitality and life to the other. They are sounds of joy and gladness, sounds of jubilation and celebration, sounds of ecstasy and holiness.

The song of the self, the song of the people, the song of man, the song of the world all merge in him at all times, in every hour.

And this full comprehensiveness rises to become the song of holiness, the song of God, the song of Israel, in its full strength and beauty, in its full authenticity and greatness. The name "Israel" stands for *shir el*,[9] the song of God. It is a simple song, a twofold song, a threefold song and a fourfold song. It is the Song of Songs of Solomon, *shlomo*, which means peace or wholeness. It is the song of the King in whom is wholeness.

Vol. II, pp. 458-459.

Constant Renewal

The perception that dawns on a person to see the world not as finished, but as in the process of continued becoming, ascending, developing—this changes him from being "under the sun" to being "above the sun," from the place where there is nothing new to the place where there is nothing old, where everything takes on new form. The joy of heaven and earth abides in him as on the day they were created.

In this luminous perspective one looks at all the worlds, at the general and the human development, at the destiny of each creature, at all the events of all times.

The time that is an uninterrupted Sabbath[10] on which eternal peace shines, is the day when, by the nature of its creation, there pulsates a continued thrust for newness. It needs no end, no termination. It is the choicest of days, an ornament of beauty, the source of all blessings.

Vol. II, p. 535.

---

9. The Hebrew name for Israel is a composite of the two Hebrew words *shir el*, the song of God. The identification of Solomon in the Song of Songs with God and the correspondence of God's four-letter name with the four levels of song is found in Zohar III 27b; Tikkune Zohar 10, 13; Shir Hashirim Rabbah 1:11; and in other sources.

10. An allusion to the messianic age.

ABRAHAM ISAAC KOOK

The Ascending Soul of All

Why shall we not compare the events of general existence to the events in the life of an individual person or any other creature?

Why shall we not see all existence as aspiring, hoping, ascending and descending, and then ascending again, in inner feeling, and overall enlightenment, that it grows according to its immense dimension as the person in his state and another creature in its state?

Why should not everything be presented to us as one comprehensive entity, and why should not the good element wherever it may be found illumine its own way, and that of the collective whole? Why should not the light of God be sought in every place, why should not joy penetrate to all parts of life, why should not the yearning for the good overpower every other kind of firmness and strength?

As these and similar questions are raised with greater resoluteness, with greater courage and sharpness, they answer the claims toward which they press, and elicit the conclusion sought.

It is logical that every spark of life has a soul, that it yearns to ascend, and that it ascends by divine grace, which is active at all times. Certainly it follows that every creature ascends, in whatever dimension of existence it has its being, whether in the form of an active force within the body or outside the body, and every species of the differentiated order of species and their particularizations. This is, above all, true of people and families of nations and tongues.

Every general concept has a soul that continues to ascend, and surely whole worlds continue to rise, continue to ascend.[11] They live in their functional bodies until the time

---

11. Rabbi Kook regards every concept as an embodiment of some element from the abstract world of ideas, and this is its soul. It seeks to rise above its fragmented form to rejoin the unfragmented ideational world whence it derives. This idea seems close to the Platonic world of ideas from which all finite forms take their sustaining essence.

when their souls are perfected, and then all the spiritual essence they embody rises, joining the general treasure of higher life from the confinements of the corporate and spatial world, with all their general and particular potency.

When we realize how many numberless worlds existed before us we know therefrom how much delight and spiritual illumination has emanated from their general spiritual essence, in all their particulars. This delight-bearing illumination in some form is joined to all of us in togetherness.
Vol. II, pp. 537-538.

The Concept of Evolution in Relation to the Future

The concept of evolution of existence, of all that has being, lowers man's spirit and elevates him. A life-enhancing and a life-negating principle are embodied in it. When a person looks backward and sees the lowly state in his past, and considers his own present moral, intellectual and physiological condition, so fortunate, so happily in contrast to the past, his mind becomes disoriented on the one hand. His moral discipline is weakened. Whatever moral sensibility he may feel in himself when the evil inclination of some lust should assail him he will say that it is too much for a creature like himself, whose origin is from dumb beasts and crude savagery.

In contrast to this the concept of evolution in relation to the future elevates man to the moral height that one envisions in the account of man's greatness at the time of his creation, when he dwelt with God, before his banishment from the Garden of Eden.

As a person rises in knowledge and understanding, in the study of Torah and in the cultivation of good attributes, in his intellectual and moral propensities, he marches forward toward the future. Automatically the doctrine of evolution works on him to set him on the right course and to strengthen his moral senses, until he will enter the domains of holiness and purity with a higher vigor full of the strength of the Lord. The concept of the past will inspire him with fear, as he will reflect on the frightful lowliness of the past and feel that by corrupting his ways he may fall to that dark, lowly state. By contrast, by perfecting his ways and actions, personal and social, there is open to him a great light that directs him to endless progress.

Vol. II, p. 561.

The Principle of Universality

A person must liberate himself from confinement within his private concerns. This pervades his whole being so that all his thoughts focus only on his own destiny. It reduces him to the worst kind of smallness, and brings upon him endless physical and spiritual distress. It is necessary to raise a person's thought and will and his basic preoccupations toward universality, to the inclusion of all, to the whole world, to man, to the Jewish people, to all existence. This will result in establishing even his private self on a proper basis.

The firmer a person's vision of universality, the greater the joy he will experience, and the more he will merit the grace of divine illumination. The reality of God's providence[12] is discernible when the world is seen in its totality. God's presence is not manifest in anything defective. Since He does not abide where there is deficiency, how can He abide where everything is lacking, where all we have is the weak and puny entity, only the particularity of the ego?

This call to be committed always to the principle of universality, to the divine ensemble, where all things have their being, is the essence of the soul of the *zaddikim*, who walk

---

12. Lit., "God's full name."

before God and whose delight is in the Lord.
Vol. III, p. 147.

Withdrawal and the Revelation of the Soul

The greater the person, the more he must seek to discover himself. The deep levels of his soul remain concealed from him so that he needs to be alone frequently, to elevate his imagination, to deepen his thought, to liberate his mind. Finally his soul will reveal itself to him by radiating some of its light upon him.

Then he will find his happiness. He will rise above all lowliness. He will elevate himself above the flux of events by submitting to and uniting himself with the events. He will humble himself to the level of the lowest, to a point of nullifying his ego, of being able to say, "I am a worm and not a man" (Ps. 22:7). He will nullify his own particularity by entering the depths of his own being, like Moses who said: "And we—what are we?" (Exod. 16:7). Then will a person recognize every spark of truth, every spark of equity, wherever it makes its appearance in the world.

And all will be drawn to him, without hostility, jealousy and rivalry. Peace and courage will dawn on him, compassion and love will shine in him. A zeal for accomplishment and work, a desire for action and creation, a yearning for silence and inner contemplation will join together in his spirit. He will become holy.
Vol. III, p. 270.

Withdrawal and Sociability

The person with a radiant soul must withdraw into privacy frequently. The constant company of other people, who are, for the most part, crude in comparison with him, even in their spirituality, dims the clear light of his higher soul. As a result his important work will diminish. He might have been able to benefit the people, his society, by frequent with-drawals, without terminating his relationship with them even then. He would have kept the needs of his generation before him, to pray for them, to delineate their virtues, the treasure of goodness that is in them. But they will suffer decline through his decline, through reducing his spiritual potency as a result of their distracting closeness to him.

It is very difficult to suffer the company of people, the encounter with persons who are totally immersed in a differ-ent world with which a person who is given to spiritually sensitive concerns, to lofty moral aspiration, has no contact. Nevertheless, it is this very sufferance that ennobles a person and elevates him. The spiritual influence that a person of higher stature exerts on the environment, which comes about through the constant encounter, purifies the environment. It lends the graces of holiness and freedom on all who come in contact with him.

And this nobility of a holy grace returns after a while with stronger force and acts on the person himself who exerted the influence, and he becomes sociable, abounding in spiritu-ality and holiness. This is a higher attribute than the holiness in a state of withdrawal, which is the normal fate of the person to whom the higher spiritual concerns are the foundation of his life.
Vol. III, pp. 271-272.

A Genius for Compassion

In every expression of genius the perceptive eye, which penetrates to the inner essence behind the action, can discern the grandeur of the spirit of genius itself, in its full potency, in its majestic beauty.

In the genius of compassion of a great philanthropist, to whom acts of compassion and goodness are his soul's commitment and the ornament of his life, the inner probing will recognize the splendor of compassion in itself, which is more precious and exalted than all the deeds of compassion and goodness that are carried out in action.

Fortunate are we all if the light of compassion shines in us. Fortunate is the world, fortunate is humanity and fortunate is the nation when a vision of philanthropic genius appears in one of its children. The holy spirit of philanthropy is life's treasure. It treats all with an impressive equality. It breathes life into every individual soul in the nation, and adorns it collectively with abiding beauty.

This genius of compassion sometimes appears among the poor, except that the majestic holiness of a compassionate life always remains in their hearts, only occasionally expressing itself in philanthropic acts. When the predisposition to philanthropy should come upon the opportunity to act, this spirit will be even more wonderful. But those who judge life on the basis of its true meaning, those who meditate on ideas in their purity, will recognize the nobility of compassion even when it is covered up with many veils because of an inability to manifest itself.

Vol. III, p. 313.

Good to All

When the longing to be good to all is intensified in a person, then he knows that an illumination from the higher realm has reached him. Praised be he if he prepares a proper place in his heart, his mind and his actions and in all his feelings to receive this noble light, which is the most precious asset on earth. Let him hold on to it and not let it go.

Let him not allow any impediment, physical or spiritual, to keep him from welcoming this holy thought into his inner being. Let him battle against all of them, and remain resolute. Let him draw his knowledge from afar,[13] emulating the attributes of God, who is good to all and whose mercies are over all His works.

Vol. III, p. 316.

The Divine Eye

It is an art of great enlightenment to purge anger from the heart entirely, to look at all with a benevolent eye, with compassionate concern, without reservation. It is to emulate the eye of God that focuses only on the good. This should also include the works wrought by the wicked, even on those most thoroughly immersed in wickedness. It means to pity them for being sunk in the mire of wickedness, to find their good aspects and to minimize the scope of their guilt. It involves stressing the positive side even of seducers to idolatry whom we have been admonished not to pity and not to spare (Deut. 13:9). The admonition applies only to a legal trial that has to do with action, but on the theoretical side there is much to contemplate, to discern the good intention that may be hidden even in the act of seduction. On finding this aspect there is removed the poisonous element in the seduction, and its destructive aspect diminishes. In the end such wicked persons are also due to be mended.

When we reflect on the *aggadah* that states that the descendents of Sisera taught Torah in Jerusalem, and the descendents of Haman taught Torah in Bene Berak (Gittin 37b)[14] we reach the depth of compassion, which calls on us not to be caught up in the stream of hatred even of the fiercest enemy. This surely suggests the inference as to what attitude to adopt toward those who cause us to suffer pain by their

---

13. Cf. Job 36:3 and commentary of Ibn Ezra.

14. Sisera was a Canaanite general who oppressed the children of Israel (Judges 4:2,3). Haman's enmity is, of course, well known.

views and their destructiveness, inspired by noble motives, according to their opinion. This is surely the case when the good intentions, on being realized in action, effect good results, even if together with the good there is also some evil and damage. The evil does not nullify the good.

It is for people of integrity, who concern themselves with holy pursuits in truth and in uprightness, to refine all concepts that are active in life, from their dross, and to establish them on their clearest basis. It is precisely through the refinement of thoughts in which there is an admixture of evil and impurity that there will emerge great life-renewing light, exceeding in importance the conventional positions. These will express an authentic content, clearer and more potent, more vital for the spirit and more edifying and fructifying life.

Whoever reflects on divine ideas in their purity cannot hate or despise any creature or talent in the world, since everything manifests the grandeur and might of the action of God. At times he may sense a certain strangeness in some aspect of it, that more of the negative is represented in it, that is, an aspect that severs him from the light and life in the source of everything.

It thus turns out that the hostility and disparagement are to be directed not at what is present in any movement or culture, but at what is absent in it. In other words they are to be directed at the fact that these have not yet completed the process of clarification and unfolding of content to a point of being linked with the higher sweep and the penetrating perception of the sublime idea, of the absolute reality of God, in its majestic significance.
Vol. III, pp. 326-327.

The Holiness That Abounds with Love for All

The higher holiness abounds with love, compassion and tolerance, as the mark of its most radiant perfection.

Hatred, sternness and irritability result from forgetting God, and the extinguishing of the light of holiness.

The more intense the quest for God is in a person's heart, the more the love for all people will grow in him. He will also love the wicked and the heretics and desire to correct them, as he indeed corrects them by his great faith.

However, a person is unable openly to show love except to someone in whom he finds a good element. He will thus be able to direct his love to the dimension of the good. He will not be hurt by the evil side in those people to whom he will extend love in meeting his commitment to love people, which involves being good and extending good to the wicked as well as to the good.

Vol. III, p. 317.

The Love for People from the Source of Compassion

The love for people must break out from the source of compassion; it must come to us not as a prescribed statute. Otherwise it will lose its most luminous element. It must come as a spontaneous movement of an inner soul force. It will have to withstand many difficult tests, to overcome many contradictions that are diffused like stumbling blocks in diverse statements of sages, in the superficial aspect of many *halakhot* [laws], and in a multitude of views that result from the narrowing of the literal part of the Torah and the national system of morals.

But it is clear that once the love detaches itself from its divine source, its flower withers away. The divine source, then, radiates its light through the channels of the Torah and prescribed action, and through a confinement into distinctive national forms.

This results in spiritual labor of immense scope: how to preserve all these channels and yet to draw the waters of

compassion in their original purity and breadth. Many times one is forced to descend to deep, dark regions, in order to find there the greatest, noblest and freest light.
Vol. III, p. 318.

Essays

A Note on the Text

The ten essays here included are a good summation of Rabbi Kook's religious philosophy. They are not a systematic exposition of his thought. Each expounds an independent theme, and is complete in itself, but together they clarify some of the basic elements in his thinking. The first eight essays appeared in 1914 under the general title "Zironim" (A Row of Plants) in a periodical *Hatarbut Hayisraelit* (Jewish Culture), and were reprinted under the same title in volume *Orot*, one of the volumes of Rabbi Kook's collected writings, which was published in 1963.

The first essay, "A Thirst for the Living God," is a probing of the dialectical process by which the soul seeks its moorings in God. The source of the quest is the inner nature of the soul, which cannot find rest in a secular ideology. But where can it find its religious anchoring? The study of the phenomenology of the world discloses a divine dimension and he who seeks with sensitivity will find that the world points to a reality transcending it. But this is only the antechamber. When his quest, on this level, has proceeded far enough, a person discovers light from another source—from within the soul itself, which bears the most authentic testimony to God's presence.

The relation of tradition to faith as an inner experience is touched on in the second essay, "The Sage is More Important Than the Prophet." Here he interprets prophecy itself as an experience of illumination, reaching man through the imaginative faculty; and he places it in the same category as poetry and other expressions of creative inspiration. This view is very similar to the view of Maimonides as expounded in the *Guide of the Perplexed* (I,36; II,45). But the efficacy of this type of illumination is confined to declarations of general principles, whose implementation calls for a special talent in dealing with particulars; and this is the work of sages. Rabbi Kook regards the widespread revolt against the *halakhic* discipline as a reaction against the overconcentration on the *halakhah* to the neglect of the inspirational prophetic aspect of Judaism.

The third essay, "Souls of Chaos," will be best understood as a plea for a sympathetic understanding of the rebellious Jewish youth that were drawn to Zionism or Marxism. They often broke with the sanctities of Jewish life, and the leaders of the established Jewish community saw in them nothing but a destructive force. Rabbi Kook used sharp words in rebuking the protagonists of the established order who were thrown into panic by these young rebels. He called those champions of traditionalism "sinners, weak in spirit and hypocrites."

Rabbi Kook realized that these rebels frequently carried their rebellion to excessive dimensions, but he felt that the spirit of rebellion, as such, had a place in the economy of God's providence. These rebel spirits were reacting against the stifling inadequacies in the established pattern of Jewish community life. They were the visionaries and protagonists of new possibilities. They waged war against the old to make room for the new. They were thus serving as an instrument of the divine movement for the perfection of life. In the imagery employed in this essay, the realm of possibility is equated with the realm of chaos out of which God is forever forging new life. These souls drawn to the realm of chaos are, in other words, souls yearning for perfection and should not be rejected. Rabbi Kook hoped for the emergence of the truly righteous who would make the cause of those rebels their own, and lead in the struggle for change, effecting the birth of the new life forces without jeopardizing the good inherent in the old order.

The essay "The Works of Creation" touches on one of

Rabbi Kook's favorite themes, without delving deeply into it: that the true essence of reality cannot be disclosed in the surface probing of any phenomenon. The Torah and commandments embody a meaning that even a rational explanation will not disclose altogether. This mystical meaning, immanent in text and rite, deposits a potency in the soul even when we are not conscious of it, on which we draw in times of need. Similarly the particularities of the rebuilding taking place in Palestine were for him charged with a meaning transcending the conscious motivation of the builders. He felt that they were, without their knowing it, restoring Jewish identity to its historic authenticity.

In the essay "The Pangs of Cleansing" Rabbi Kook discusses the phenomenon of atheism. He refuses to dismiss atheism as wholly detrimental or even sterile as a cultural force. All phenomena—this is a basic assumption for him—must embody some good or they never would have arisen. Atheism, as he sees it, has a positive role in the dialectic by which religion is enabled to meet the challenge toward its own progressive unfolding.

Atheism is a negative force whose providential role is to challenge religion to purge itself of its dross. It is in a sense an instance of man's stirring to penitence in order to free himself of his deficiencies. "Atheism has a temporary legitimacy, for it is needed to purge away the aberrations that attached themselves to religious faith because of a deficiency in perception and in the divine service." But man never knows the precise boundary within which his ideologies serve their legitimate good, and he often allows them to proliferate to various excesses. Thus atheism, by proclaiming itself as a self-sufficient philosophy, poses its own problem for the world. For atheism is essentially sterile; it is devoid of a positive ideal, which emanates only from the divine mystery behind and beyond all being. The conflict between traditional religion and atheism is the dialectic at work to raise religion toward greater heights.

"Out of the clash of these two opposites will mankind be aided greatly to reach an enlightened knowledge of God, which will bring near its temporal and eternal happiness."

In the essay "Concerning the Conflict of Opinions and Beliefs" Rabbi Kook develops his philosophy of religious tolerance. The conventional defense of tolerance is based on the legitimization of pluralism and eclecticism, on a basic agnosticism, which allows many formulations of truth because truth as such is really beyond our discerning. For him truth rests on the belief in divine universality, which regards all being as the fruition of the divine ferment. Since all that exists is made possible by the action of God, there must be some validity in all of it. Its particularity of expression robes this valid essence in a finite shell that begets exaggeration and distortion, but it cannot annihilate the essence. Human versions of truth may thus differ in degrees, but none are totally true or totally false. In all ideologies and in all religions there must therefore be a core of validity that must be treated with respect and sympathetic consideration in our own quest for truth.

The ninth essay, entitled "The Road to Renewal," first appeared in 1909 under the Hebrew title "Derekh Hathiah" in the short-lived periodical *Hanir,* and it offers one of the most comprehensive statements of Rabbi Kook's philosophy of Judaism.

The force that directs the world toward the absolute good that pulsates throughout existence, declared Rabbi Kook in this essay, is a spiritual illumination from the divine source of all existence; it is what we commonly call a mystical experience, though Rabbi Kook does not use this term. This illumination is initially experienced by certain properly qualified individuals and they channel it to society where it functions as an imperative "for the perfection of the moral, social, intellectual and practical world." But Rabbi Kook warns that this inflow of psychic and spiritual energy may, in fact, be distorted and become a source of idolatrous aberrations. The decisive factor is a moral and rational refinement that must precede in the medium where the illumination is to act. Only where such refinement has preceded will the illumination be grasped in its full authenticity and evoke as its response the passion to perfect all life.

The Jewish people has experienced this illumination in its greatest authenticity, because Jewish life had felt the refining impact of an ancestral heritage of profound spiritual sensibility and because of the purging effected by slavery in Egypt. And it is the vocation of the Jew, Rabbi Kook further affirmed, to bear witness to his vision in all its rational and ethical implications, thereby to help the world free itself of idolatry and allow the light from the divine source to guide it toward the perfection of life, including all its corporate constituencies.

But the light has often been blunted in Judaism itself. One of the factors responsible for this has been the misuse of an institution that in its essence was meant to aid the quest for the good: the emergence of a Torahitic tradition expressed in written documents. These are meant to aid the channeling and shaping of the new light that ever continues to radiate from its divine source. But often the study of texts and the concern with the prescribed code of religious discipline, the crystallizations of past achievements, became the sole expression of Jewish religious life; and vision, and illumination, atrophied. The peril in such atrophy was dramatized by the reaction it stimulated: the rise of Christianity and of the false messiahs, Shabbetai Zevi and Jacob Frank. Hasidism was a force for spiritual rejuvenation, but the full renewal needed, Rabbi Kook felt, would come with the restoration of the Jewish people in the Holy Land, when it rises above the morass of secular nationalism and reaches a full affirmation of spiritual authenticity.

The renaissance in Eretz Yisrael, Rabbi Kook warns,

cannot be a fulfillment of Jewish hopes for renewal on the plane of secular nationalism. It must involve also a religious renaissance. But those who will lead such a religious renaissance cannot be merely the masters in the study of traditional Torah texts. They must be men who will go beyond this. They must be deeply spiritual personalities for whom contact with the divine spirit is a living experience and who will bring new light and quickening vitality to the entire fabric of Jewish life. This will enable Jews to realize the ancient dream of self-renewal in its fullest scope, and it will enable the Jewish people to meet its commitment for larger world service.

The last essay, "Fragments of Light," appeared in 1910 in the journal *Takhemoni*, which was published in Bern, Switzerland. It foreshadows many of the unique positions that Rabbi Kook formulated in the later developments of his philosophy. It is primarily an attempt to explain the reasons for the commandments. In their initial role they defined the uniqueness of Jewish identity, but they also served in their basic goal as a channel for human unity, for the integration of the Jewish people with the rest of humanity. This is indeed the vocation of the Jew, to bear the vision of universalism that summons all people to rise out of their ideological and national parochialism and embrace the principle that all existence is in its essence harmoniously interrelated, that all seeming incompatibilities are only the result of fragmentation and exaggeration that recede as we rise to the higher wisdom of life's unity.

Three striking positions are developed in the course of this exposition. He sees all human values under four basic categories, the divine, the moral, the religious and the national. The religious, by which he refers to organized religion, is the third level of value. Its viability depends on the extent to which the divine and moral sensibilities are channeled into it. The highest level of value is associated with the yearning for the direct encounter of God, presumably in a mystical experience.

The second position that is noteworthy is his concept of religious integration. He sees legitimacy in all religious systems. Their fragmentation is the result of unique historic developments of those espousing them. They are meant to join in harmonious interrelations, which would then reveal the full richness of the religious component in the world's cultural evolution.

The third noteworthy element is his position on the inclusion of animals in the fullest unfolding of morality. The universal man of the future, he believed, would abandon the eating of meat and return to a vegetarian diet, to which he had been confined before Adam's disobedience in eating the forbidden fruit. The permission to eat meat was a concession to man's moral weakness, but he would rise out of it when his spiritual development reached the level of true universality.

A THIRST FOR THE LIVING GOD

The spirit cannot find its stability except in a life oriented toward God. Knowledge, feeling, the imagination and the will, in their inner and outer manifestations, all condition people to center their lives in God. Then will they be able to find their fulfillment, their equitable and satisfying state. If a person should seek for himself less than this exalted state, he will at once become like a ship tossed about at sea. Stormy waves, raging in opposite directions, will continually rob him of peace. He will be thrown from wave to wave, and he will be unable to find himself. If he should be able to immerse himself in some crude and vulgar preoccupation, he may succeed for a time in reducing the perspective of his life, and it will seem to him that he has finally found peace. But it will not take long, and the spirit will break out of its imprisonment and the maddening agitation will begin to act in all its fury.

The place where we may find peace is only in God. God, however, transcends the existing world, making it impossible for us to grasp any aspect of Him in feeling or thought. This makes Him, as far as we are concerned, nonexistent, and the spirit cannot find contentment in what does not exist. It is for this reason that wise men who devote themselves to the quest for God are, for the most part, spiritually weary. When the soul aspires to the most luminous light it cannot be content with that light which shines in the quality of justice in the best of good deeds, or in the measure of truth in the most precise body of knowledge or in the attribute of beauty in the most exalted of visions. It then sees the world as trivialized. The soul has become so ascendent that the entire world, its material as well as its spiritual manifestations, appears to it as an imprisonment, gripping us in its choking atmosphere. Such men seek what is beyond their reach, what, in their condition, does not appear to exist, and to change the nonexistent to an existent is even beyond the will to entertain. It is for this reason that there is often a weakening of the will as well as of the other life-forces among people whose inner disposition is directed toward the quest for God.

It is necessary to show how one may enter the palace: by the way of the gate. The gate is the divine dimension disclosed in the world, in all its phenomena of beauty and grandeur, as manifested in every living thing, in every insect, in every blooming plant and flower, in every nation and state, in the sea with its turbulent waves, in the panorama of the skies, in the talents of all creatures, in the thoughts of writers, the imagination of poets and the ideas of thinkers, in the feelings of every sensitive spirit and in the heroic deeds of every person of valor.

The highest domain of divinity toward which we aspire—to be absorbed in it, to be included in its radiance—but which eludes all our longing, descends for us into the world, and we encounter it and delight in its love, and find peace in its tranquillity. At times, moreover, we are privileged with a flash emanating from the higher radiance, from that higher light which transcends all thought. The heavens open for us and we see a vision of God.

But we know that this is only a temporary state, the flash will pass and we will descend to dwell once again not inside the palace, but only in the courts of the Lord.

When the longing for the light reaches its highest point, it begins to draw a great profusion of light from the hidden radiance in our own soul through which is revealed the great truth, that all the worlds with all that is in them only appear to us particular effulgences but they are in truth manifestations of the higher light, and, seen in their essence, they make up one whole, a unitary manifestation in which is included all beauty, all light, all truth and all good. These manifestations continually emerge and develop, they show themselves increasingly as in truth individual expressions of the all-good. The bounty that streams through all the good, that raises the soul to its highest, that, on the one hand, shrinks for us the significance of the existential world, the physical as well as the spiritual, in all its splendor and magnificence—this very bounty now renews for us all the worlds and all creatures, endowing them with a new image, and every sign of life stirs joy, and every good deed delights the heart and every discipline of study broadens the mind. The narrow boundaries of all these no longer oppress the soul, which at once realizes that all these tiny sparks continually ascend and become integrated into the comprehensive unity of all life.

THE SAGE IS MORE IMPORTANT THAN THE PROPHET

As a rule poets know how to portray the nobler side of life, its beauty, its dynamism and vitality. They also know how to describe the evils of life and to protest against them vigorously. But it is outside the competence of the imaginative faculty to probe the particular conditions that preserve life and safeguard it from even the most minor defects that are due to generate very destructive consequences. This falls within the competence of a body of knowledge that deals with particulars. Here begins the work of physicians, economists, engineers, judges and all those who pursue practical wisdom.

This distinction has even wider application. Prophecy saw the great evil of idolatry in ancient Israel, and protested against it with all its might; it envisioned the majesty and delight associated with the belief in one God, and portrayed it in all its radiance. It saw the corruption in moral depravity, the oppression of the poor, murder, adultery and robbery, and it was infused with the spirit of God to offer help and to rectify these conditions through lofty and holy exhortations.

But the little lapses out of which was forged the gross body of sin—these remained hidden from the eye of every prophet and seer. Similarly it was not within the sphere of prophecy to grasp how the habituated performance and the study of commandments will, after a span of time, release their hidden inner graces, and a wholly divine influence will decisively vanquish the darkness of idolatry. Nor could it grasp how the slow negligence, which disparages the performance of the commandments, with their inferences and elaborations, will start a process of erosion, destroying the vessels in which is stored the exalted spirit, causing the human passions, the straying imagaination, which abounds in beautiful shoots outside but in poisonous elements within, to become automatically ever more potent.

It is true that this perception was granted to the prophecy of Moses, of which God is quoted as saying that He revealed it to him "from mouth to mouth" (Num. 12:8), the prophecy of undimmed clarity that discerned simultaneously the claims of general principles as well as of the exacting demands of the particulars. But there never arose another like Moses, as we are told, "There never arose another prophet like Moses whom the Lord knew face to face" (Deut. 34:11). It was, therefore, necessary to assign the enunciation of general principles to the prophets and of the particulars to the sages; and, as the Talmud declares, "the sage is more important than the prophet" (Baba Batra 12a). And what prophecy with its impassioned and fiery exhortations could not accomplish in purging the Jewish people of idolatry and in uprooting the basic causes of the most degrading forms of oppression and violence, of murder, sexual perversity and bribery, was accomplished by the sages through the expanded development of the Torah, by raising many disciples and by the assiduous study of the particular laws and their derivative applications. " 'The eternal paths lead to Him' (Hab. 3:6);—the term of 'paths,' *halikot*, may also be read as *halakhot*, and the text would then mean that the laws lead to Him" (Niddah 73a).

In the course of time the concern with the work of the sages predominated over the work of the prophets and the institution of prophecy ceased altogether; after some time the general principles declined, they were immanent in the particulars but were not readily apparent. At the end of the present epoch, when the light of prophecy will begin to have its revival, as we are promised, "I shall pour out My spirit on all flesh" (Joel 3:1), there will develop a reaction, a pronounced disdain for the particulars. This is alluded to in the

Talmudic statement that at the dawn of the messianic age "the wisdom of the sages will become unsavory and those who live on the boundary [that is the sages who define limits in the law] will turn from city to city without finding grace" (Sotah 49b).

This will continue until the radiance of prophecy will reemerge from its hiding and reveal itself not as an unripe fruit, but as the first fruits full of vitality and life, and prophecy itself will acknowledge the great efficacy in the work of the sages, and in righteous humility exclaim: "The sage is more important than the prophet." This transcending of one-sidedness will vindicate the vision of unity expressed by the psalmist: "Mercy and truth have met, justice and peace have kissed, truth will rise out of the earth and mercy will show itself from heaven; the Lord will also bestow what is good and our earth will bring forth its bounty" (Ps. 85:11). The soul of Moses will then reappear in the world.

SOULS OF CHAOS

The conventional pattern of living, based on propriety, on the requisites of good character and conformity to law — this corresponds to the way of the world of order. Every rebellion against this, whether inspired by levity or by the stirring of a higher spirit, reflects the world of chaos. But there is a vast difference in the particular expressions of the world of chaos, whether they incline to the right or the left [positive or negative in motivation]. The great idealists seek an order so noble, so firm and pure, beyond what may be found in the world of reality, and thus they destroy what has been fashioned in conformity to the norms of the world. The best among them also know how to rebuild the world that has thus been destroyed, but those of lesser stature, who have been touched only slightly by the inclination to idealism — they are only destroyers, and they are rooted in the realm of chaos, on its lowest level.

The souls inspired by the realm of chaos are greater than the souls whose affinity is with the established order. They are very great; they seek too much from existence, what is beyond their own faculties to assimilate. They seek a very great light. They cannot bear what is limited, whatever is confined within a prescribed measure. They descended from their divine abode in accordance with the nature of existence to generate new life; they soared on high like a flame and were thrust down. Their endless striving knows no bounds; they robe themselves in various forms, aspiring constantly to what is beyond the measure of the possible. They aspire and they fall, realizing that they are confined in rules, in limiting conditions that forbid expansion toward the unlimited horizons, and they fall in sorrow, in despair, in anger, and anger leads to—wickedness, defiance, destruction and every other evil. Their unrest does not cease—they are represented by the impudent in our generation, wicked men who are dedicated to high principles, those who transgress conventional norms defiantly rather than because of some lust. Their souls are of very high stature; they are illumined by the light that shines from the realm of chaos. They chose destruction and they are engaged in destroying, the world is undermined by them, and they with it. But the essence of their aspiration is a dimension of holiness, that which in souls content with measured progress would yield the vigor of life.

The souls inspired by a destructive zeal reveal themselves especially at the end of days, before the great cataclysm that precedes the emergence of a new and more wondrous level of existence, when the old boundaries expand, just prior to the birth of a norm above the existing norms. In times of redemption insolence is on the increase. A fierce storm rages, more breaches appear, acts of insolence mount continually because they can find no satisfaction in the beneficence offered by the limited light. It does not satisfy all their yearnings, nor does it unravel for them the mystery of existence. They rebel against everything, including also the dimension of the good that could lead them to a great peace and help them rise to great heights. They rebel and they are indignant, they break and they discard; they seek their nourishment in alien pastures, embracing alien ideals and desecrating everything hallowed, but without finding peace.

These passionate souls reveal their strength so that no fence can hold them back; and the weaklings of the established order, who are guided by balance and propriety, are too terrified to tolerate them. Their mood is expressed in Isaiah (33:14): "Who among us can dwell with the devouring fire? Who among us can dwell with those who destroy the world?" But in truth there is no need to be terrified. Only sinners, those weak in spirit and hypocrites, are frightened and seized by terror. Truly heroic spirits know that this force is one of the phenomena needed for the perfection of the world, for strengthening the power of the nation, of man and of the world. Initially this force represents the realm of the chaotic, but in the end it will be taken from the wicked and turned over to the hands of the righteous who will show the truth about perfection and construction, in a great resoluteness, inspired by clear perception and a steady and undimmed sense of the practical.

These storms will bring fructifying rain, these dark clouds will pave the way for great light, as the prophet envisioned it: "And the eyes of the blind shall see out of obscurity and out of darkness" (Isa. 29:18).

THE WORKS OF CREATION

A force for life and good, for creativity and bravery, is given to the individual and the group through the beauty and goodness, the strength and perseverance, hidden in the mystical meanings of the commandments when they are kept in faith, for the sake of God. Whoever neglects the teachings of the Torah, even the slightest of the commandments, will lack the strength to persevere in a time of trouble. Whoever keeps all the commandments and is steadfast in his loyalty to the Torah, without wavering, will be strengthened by the life force immanent in the basic meaning of the Torah, although at the time when he keeps or studies the Torah he may not feel in himself any accretion of physical or spiritual strength. And whenever the occasion should arise when strength is needed there will emerge a hidden life-force, stored up in the Torah and the commandments, that warms the heart and illumines the soul.

We can take to heart the higher meaning immanent in the commandments by explaining them in rational terms prevalent in current thought. But we must not err in assuming, when dealing in these lofty subjects, the divine objectives, that if they have been explained to us, we may already define all their significance. But this we know — we have here what exalts the heart and what gives life the basis of free commitment, full of delight.

From a distance we see the people of Israel, adorned in all its glory, as we dream of it, and look forward to seeing it. We see it marching majestically to establish its identity on a sound basis, so that it may be complete in all its faculties, for its own sake and for the sake of the world. Its evolution did not begin with its way of life and then rise to its ideology but the other way around, from the top downward; from its conception of itself and of the world it moved to its pattern of behavior, and it finds its peace, its dignity and self-esteem when it realizes its spiritual essence in its way of life, that of its constituent individuals and that of the people.

This is the secret of penitence that will bring on the redemption. In the future the edifice of redemption will begin inwardly; from the center point of Zion it will spread out to the streets of Jerusalem, to the boundaries of the land of Israel. "Do good in Your favor to Zion, build the walls of Jerusalem" (Ps. 51:20).

The future approaches, it comes closer to us. Let us raise ourselves a little, let us cleanse our feelings and our minds, and we are near it. We see its rays of light covered over by a veil, whose thinness or thickness depends on our individual assessment, and each one finds what his thoughts prompt him to find. Happy is he who has filled his heart with life's hope, and with the anticipation of redemption. He can see already the light of deliverance, as it sends forth its beams.

In the revealed Torah, in all its branches, there breaks through the flow from these secret springs, streaming from the depths of the supernal thoughts, that sustain the eternity of Israel. "The Eternal One of Israel will not lie nor change His mind, for He is not a man to change His mind" (I Sam. 15:29).

The visible developments taking place before us here are set in a humble format, replete with material and spiritual poverty. Eretz Yisrael is returning to life through modest efforts, directed by confused thinking, notions shot through with ignorance and despair, soiled with religious nihilism and an inclination to evil. In all of these there is hiding the presence of the living God. "How great are Your works, O Lord, Your thoughts are very deep" (Ps. 92:6).

THE PANGS OF CLEANSING

All the ideological controversies among people and all the inner conflicts that every individual suffers in his world outlook are caused by the confusion in the conception of God. This is an endlessly profound realm and all thoughts, whether practical or theoretical, are centered in it.

One must always cleanse one's thoughts about God to make sure they are free of the dross of deceptive fantasies, of groundless fear, of evil inclinations, of wants and deficiencies. Faith in God enhances human happiness only to the extent that the greatness of God is probed and studied by the elite elements of the human race, who are equal to it. Then is the soul illumined by the divine light, through cleaving in love and full understanding to Him who is the life of all life, and all feelings, all ideas and all actions, thus become refined. The attachment to God in feeling will have its effect in directing life on an upright path to the extent that this basic principle is operative in the soul, in a state of purity.

The foundation of religious faith is rooted in the recognition of the greatness and perfection of the Infinite. Whatever we conceive of it is insignificant in comparison with what by right we should conceive of it, and what we should conceive of it is not much more significant in comparison to what it really is. Whatever we may say of the good, of mercy, justice, might, beauty, of life and the beauty of life, or of religious faith, or of the divine—what the soul in its authenticity aspires for is above all these. All the divine names, whether in Hebrew or in any other language, give us only a tiny and dull spark of the hidden light to which the soul aspires when it utters the word "God." Every definition of God brings about heresy, every definition is spiritual idolatry; even attributing to Him intellect and will, even the term *divine*, the term *God*, suffers from the limitations of definition. Except for the keen awareness that all these are but sparkling flashes of what cannot be defined—these, too, would engender heresy. Among people who have lost this basic awareness they have indeed engendered gross heresy. If we become alienated from this basic perception, our faith will be improverished and become valueless. There is no other alternative if our faith is to shine in a living light, but that it be linked to a level of enlightenment that transcends all particular values; and thus it will assure stability to all values. All teachings beyond this perception of the greatness of the Infinite are only explanatory aids to reach the essence of religious faith—they are in the category of "the limbs of the King" and some are in the category of "the garments of the King."* One who is disdainful of the garments of the King is also guilty of irreverence. One must, however, draw a distinction between the essence of faith and the explanatory aids, as well as the different levels among the explanatory aids themselves.

The confusion of thought born of deficiencies in study and knowledge leads a person to focus his thought on the divine *essence*. The more he will immerse himself in the folly of this insolent and absurd preoccupation, the more he will think that he is thereby drawing closer to the exalted knowledge of God, to which he had heard that the world's leading spirits have always aspired. When this habit pattern is established over many generations various false notions are engendered, which lead to many tragic consequences. They beget a state of confusion that undermines the individual's material and spiritual vitality. The greatest impediment to the human spirit, on reaching maturity, results from the fact that the conception of God is crystallized among people in a particular form, going back to childish habit and imagination. This is an aspect of the

*The Zohar, II 85a and III 110a, identifies the two as referring respectively to a higher and lower level of prophecy, or to the written and oral Torah.

offense of making a graven image or a likeness of God, against which we must always beware, particularly in an epoch of greater intellectual enlightenment.

All the troubles of the world, especially the spiritual, such as grief, impatience, disillusionment, despair, the truly basic troubles of man—they came about only because of the failure to view clearly the majesty of God. It is natural for a particular creature to feel insignificant before the whole, especially before the source of all existence, in which one senses infinite transcendence of the whole. There is no anguish or depression in such lowliness, but pleasure and pride, a sense of inner power adorned by every kind of beauty. When this perception of God's majesty develops in the soul, in all its dimensions, it reconciles life to its natural subjugation. It fills life with peace to the extent that the individual recognizes the greatness of the whole and the majesty of its source. As the soul diminishes itself before its Creator, the phenomena of existence ascend in power and beauty and become permeated with the touch of universality. This natural diminishing engenders greatness and dignity, distilling in the soul endless delight in its very being, and in its ever-widening role, reaching out to the Infinite beyond. But when is it natural? It is when the greatness of the divine is well perceived in the soul, in a pure conception, above considerations of the divine *essence*, but oriented toward the vision of the goodness of life. Then does the claim for self-diminishing emanate from every aspect of the soul, its universal as well as its particular dimensions.

The general failure of the spiritual disciplines to focus on studies pertaining to God has dimmed the conception of God; there is no rational service of God sustained by refined feelings. The outward fear, the natural faith and the feeling of lowliness remain in many hearts as an inheritance from earlier epochs when the divine perception and feeling were prevalent in an enlightened state in full force, when, because of their greatness, they naturally evoked humility from people. Since the thoughts concerning God in their basic elements are unclear, God's being, as conceived by the multitude and even by individuals who should be their leaders, is that of a ruthless power from whom there is no escape and to whom one must necessarily be subservient.

When one submits to a service of God on this empty basis, according to the confused notions that are engendered in the soul when one thinks about God without enlightenment and without Torah, we have here a lower form of piety severed from its source, which is the higher piety. The person increasingly loses the splendor of his world by orienting himself to a lower level of intellectual life. No grandeur of God is then manifest in the soul, but only the lowliness of wild imaginings, that conjure up a form of some deceptive, vague, angry deity that is dissociated from reality. It confuses everyone who believes in it, depresses his spirit, blunts his feelings, inhibits the assertion of his sensibilities, and uproots the divine glory in his soul. If such a person should repeat all day that this faith is the faith in the unity of God, his statement would be empty, and it would register nothing in his soul. Every sensitive spirit must turn his mind away from this. And this is the atheism which is due to arise prior to the messianic liberation, when the knowledge of God is due to run dry in the household of Israel—and in the entire world.

The tendency of unrefined people to see the divine *essence* as embodied in the words and in the letters alone is a source of embarrassment to humanity, and atheism arises as a pained outcry to liberate man from this narrow and alien pit, to raise him from the darkness of focusing on letters and expressions, to the light of thought and feeling, finally to place his primary focus on the realm of morals. Atheism has a temporary legitimacy, for it is needed to purge away the aberrations that attached themselves to religious faith because of a deficiency in perception and in the divine service. This is its sole function in existence—to remove the *particular* images from the speculations concerning Him who is the *essence* of all life and the source of all thought. When this condition persists for a period of several generations, atheism necessarily presents itself as a specific cultural expression, to uproot the remembrance of God and all institutions of divine service. But to what uprooting did divine providence intend? To uproot the dross that separates man from the truly divine light, and in the ruins wrought by atheism will the higher knowledge of God erect her Temple. To cleanse the air of the arrogant and evil aberration of focusing thought on the divine *essence*—a preoccupation that leads to idolatry—a thoroughgoing atheism arises, in itself no better than the former but opposed to it in absolute terms. Out of the clash of these two opposites will mankind be aided greatly to reach an enlightened knowledge of God, which will bring near its temporal and eternal happiness. In place of the presumptuous and vain preoccupation with the divine *essence*, the human heart will be oriented to concern itself with pure morality, and the heroism for higher things, which emanate as flashes from the divine light and are at all times connected with its source, showing man the way of life and placing him in the light of God. The mighty wind will come from the four corners and will raise in its surge, against their will, the anguished victims of the conception of God contrived by the sick imagination. "And you will know that I am the Lord when I have opened your graves." "And I will bring you up from your graves, O my people, and bring you to the land of Israel" (Ezek. 37:13, 12). The violence of atheism will cleanse away the dross that accumulated in the lower levels of religious faith, and thereby will the heavens be cleared and the shining light of the higher faith will become visible, which is the song of the world and the truth of the world.

Whoever recognizes the essence of atheism from this perspective embraces the positive element in it and traces it back to its origin in holiness. He glimpses the awesome splendor in the ice-like formations upon the celestial horizon (Cf. Ezekiel 1:22).

When one discovers the stern protest embodied in rebellion and atheism, which seeks to repudiate the good of our ancestral inheritance in pursuit of some new vision, one finds the element of good inherent in it. It is in truth a general aspect of penitence stirring the heart. It is the kernel of repentance that seeks to redress everything lowly and defective, and as a result of it one also comes to redress the defect that is represented in its destructiveness. Then there will be a general return to God, and redemption will come to the world. The perfection of the world that will be effected by the influence of the Jewish people is found in the ideal of penitence. As long as a person orders his life on the basis of a fixed pattern he will not be able to escape his intellectual, moral and practical deficiencies, and how will he be able to mend himself? We must therefore not permit habit to be the primary factor in our social or personal life. The individual person as well as society at large must always seek to correct itself and to mend its spiritual and practical defects. All reformations of life and all revolutionary proposals that aim to change the order of things so as to improve it are all paths of repentance. Repentance must always be at the summit of all efforts to improve the world.

From time to time there is exposed the admixture of the pure belief in one God with the obfuscation of ascribing corporeality to Him, and whenever an aspect of anthropomorphism falls away, it appears as though religion itself has fallen. Soon, however, it turns out that religion has not fallen, but has become clarified. In the recent turn of the human spirit toward pure faith the last subtle shell of anthropomorphism is giving way, which consists in ascribing the attribute of general *existence* to God, for truly whatever we ascribe to the term *existence* is immeasurably remote from the divine. This denial has the sound of atheism. It is, however, the highest expression of religion when it becomes well clarified, and the human spirit grows accustomed to hearing the message of religion in terms of actions and influences, the phenomena of existence and the phenomena of the Torah and of morals—the recognition that *the divine is the activating influence on existence and is, therefore, obviously above existence.* What looks like atheism, cleansed of its defilement, thus returns to the highest realms of pure religion. But this denial of *existence* [in God], which is a return to the vision of God as the source of all existence and to the most ultimate essence of the majesty of all existence, requires the most scrupulous understanding. Each day it must be traced back to its authentic purity.

Religion is corrupted through the decline of the higher Torah, through which one gains the recognition of the greatness of God, the higher perfection that is infinite and beyond assessment. Thus our religion does not yield the noble fruit it ought to yield, it does not raise the souls from their lowly state and the numbers of those who dishonor it and desecrate it increase. However, the Jewish religion is rooted in the Infinite, which transcends every particular content of religion, and for this reason the Jewish religion may truly be considered as the ideal of religion, the religion of the future, the "I shall be what I shall be" (Exod. 3:14), what is immeasurably higher than the content of religion in the present. The ideal essence descends many levels to become the Jewish religion as a corporate religious establishment rather than the ideal essence of religion. The aberration of atheism arises against religion as an established institution, but atheism does not affect the ideal essence of religion, which is beyond atheism as it is beyond institutional religion. Atheism is without a true ideal; as the Zohar put it (Mishpatim, II, 103a), "The alien deity is sterile, it bears no fruit." Despair and chaos contribute nothing, and therefore there is no place for an ideal contrary to the religious ideal. Though there is a conception [in the Cabbalah] of a negative counterforce paralleling institutional religion, the ideal essence of religion, which corresponds to what the Talmud calls the "fiftieth level of understanding" that was not revealed to Moses (Rosh Hashanah 21b), has no counterpart in the realm of the negative. The influence of this fiftieth level of understanding, the ideal essence of religion, infuses life to all other levels and subdues the negative aspect of atheism, which is devoid of an ideal, before the holiness of religion, which remains attached to an eternal ideal. "With You is the source of life" (Ps. 36:14).

On seeing such convulsions people believe that religion is dying, that the world is being overturned. In truth, however, the shadows are stirring, they are in flight in order to make room for the light. If religious faith is to be revitalized, a great effort is needed to deepen the knowledge of God, to follow the most subtle paths of mystical thinking through which one rises above every kind of limitation in God. As it is a case of folly and weakness to ignore "revealed" knowledge, the beauty and might exemplified in empirical existence, so is it foolish to detach our minds from the inclination to pursue the promptings hidden in the depths of the soul, without which one cannot discern anything sublime that transcends our dull senses, which have been dulled by much defilement and affliction. It is only thus that the soul can be filled with knowledge and sensibility, and it is only through such subtlety of thought that the world will be filled with the light and the dew of revival, that the dormant will be awakened and the dead return to life. The best among the *zaddikim*, the sages most informed in the knowledge of God, must bestir themselves greatly to stimulate the interest in studying the greatness of God through all methods, the rational and the ethical. Then will religion regain its strength, it will rise out of its darkness toward a great light, and it will become the life-giving force to the highest and the most sensitive of souls, even as it is in its authentic nature. Thus will it necessarily regain its respect among all sections of humanity. For the Jews this is the anchor of the nation's rescue in this epoch—to restore to it the preciousness of religious faith in its purity, which is the entire basis of their existence.

But it is precisely when the lights are in convulsion, and the vessels that have housed them seem about to break, that there is need to proclaim that indeed the letters, the words, the actions, are not the essence of the light, but they are vessels, the organs of a living body, which bears within itself a soul. But alas for anyone who denies them even the role of vessels. Whoever denies the holiness of the letters, the words, the actions and the forms within their own domain, will render himself speechless, without utterance, without any inner conceptual image, and altogether without the power to act, flooded by various forces that will disturb him altogether, body and soul.

Raise up religion, elevate thought, acclaim the real life, lived according to the conceptual forms and the practical actions in which the imagination has robed the higher light. It is a divine service through life, through the Torah and through the commandments.

כי"ק הרב. קובץ א׳. דף נ"ח
אורות הקודש, עמוד פ"ב-פ"ד

This manuscript page corresponds to page 207 of the text.

CONCERNING THE CONFLICT OF OPINIONS AND BELIEFS

Thought has become impotent because of the influx of strange ideas, especially the strange ideas of idolatry. They stream into our midst and they have trapped many hearts, they have perverted the paths and have turned many of our youths from the way of life to the way of death. Those who defend the concepts of Judaism have raised an outcry, they refute the wrong opinions, exposing their falsehood by defining the concepts of Judaism. But it is very doubtful if it will be possible through this strategy to defeat what has erupted with the force of an earthquake.

Particularly mistaken are those who seek to formulate specific definitions of Judaism from the aspect of its soul and its spiritual essence, though it may be possible to define it from the point of view of its objective manifestation as a historic phenomenon. Everything is embraced in its soul, it includes all spiritual inclinations, the open and the hidden, in a higher generalization, just as everything is included in the absolute reality of the divine. Every such definition in Judaism is heresy and is analogous to establishing an idol or a molten image to explain the character of God. The status of the Jewish people, the bearer of Judaism, among the nations, resembles the status of the person among other beings. Many beings have attributes of excellence surpassing those of man, but the combinations of qualities and the spiritual advantage they facilitate to exercise intelligence in directing his potentialities make the person a higher being in the world. Similarly there are many peoples who excel the Jewish people in certain talents, but the Jewish people as the microcosm of all humanity integrates within itself the unique qualities of all peoples, in an ideal, holy form, in an exalted form of unity.

We need a penetrating grasp of these events, an all-embracing overview, together with a penetrating probe of all the ideas and the religious concepts in the world.

Every universal theory carries with it certainty to the extent of its universality, and together with its certainty, which rules out the possibility of doubt, there goes a refusal to share with others in any collaborative pluralism. The certainty that goes with universality and the principle of singularity go together. To illustrate, the old theories of astronomy, which were particular expressions applicable only to the area of astronomy, carried an element of doubt within them, so that there was a common adage among astronomers that the objective of the astronomical theories was only to find a solution to account for the different motions of the heavenly bodies, and that another solution was also conceivable. But since the theory of gravitation began to explain the astronomical problems, because it is a universal, cosmological theory, the element of doubt has been discarded. This also led to the second consequence: The old astronomical theories could be joined to each other, something that is ruled out under the new astronomy. Being universal and certain, it is intolerant and no one can try to account for some astronomical phenomena by the theory of gravitation and other planetary movements according to the old astronomical hypotheses.

It is similar in the realm of the spirit. Idolatry was tolerant, while the belief in the unity of God is intolerant; being universal and not particular, certain and not beset by doubt, it is singular and not pluralistic. The principle of universality is not tolerant according to the superficial conception of tolerance, but in its very intolerance is contained the essential basis of tolerance. The wrong kind of tolerance, which weakens life, is invoked on the discovery of particulars that cannot be included in their general category, and the perverse kind of tolerance comes presumptuously to regard particular notions as though they were universal principles. Because they are particular concepts they cannot animate the diverse expressions of the spirit outside their own domain, and in their disdain for other concepts that they cannot incorporate in themselves, they only shrink the unfolding of life and diminish the manifestation of the spirit.

The concept of higher comprehensiveness, however, through its breadth and certainty, offers us an ideal system in stressing the principle of singularity, which brings with it a noble zealousness that engenders grandeur of spirit and removes every weakness of limited particularisms, all doubt and all eclecticism. "The Lord alone will lead them, and there is no other god with Him" (Deut. 32:12). Because it is universal, because everything is included in it, it cannot by nature exclude anything from its domain, it finds a place for everything. In doing this it only increases our perception of the light in all life-styles and in all expressions of the spirit. The basic thrust of its kind of tolerance is to find a place for every form of illumination, of life and of spiritual expression.

This concept of tolerance is aware that there is a spark of divine light in all things, that the inner spark of divine light shines in all the different religions, as so many different pedagogics for the culture of humanity, to improve the spiritual and material existence, the present and the future of the individual and of society. But they exist on different levels. Just as there is only one force of germination, and it is manifest in the cedar of Lebanon as well as in the foliage on the wall, except that in the first instance it appears in a rich and beautiful form and in the second instance in a poor and limited form, so does the spark of divine light appear in the more advanced religions in a form that is rich and exalted, while in the less advanced religions in a form that is blurred, poor and lowly. Human sin and ignorance have perverted man's general inclination, which aspires for the good, for truth, for spiritual happiness in the fullest sense of the term. But even in the crudest husks [that cover and blunt man's higher self] is hidden that spark of the good, the light of God, the supreme light that we cannot define and that cannot be robed in letters of any expression, nor of any kind of thought.

The world is continually progressing, sound thinking continues to make headway, healthy logic and the rich fund of experience are removing the roadblocks, error is diminishing, the entanglements of the imagination are being released. There remains within, in full force, the inner impulse that is pushing the good sparks to become manifest, and the good sparks, which are flashes of the light of the good emanating from the light of the God of truth, begin to be seen through the openings in the zone of darkness. It is for this reason that grains of truth and light diffused among the different religions have begun to sparkle. The source of this light is the only living fountain, whose source is always the light of Israel, the pure faith that is based on the foundation that gives it permanence and that will never decline.

Therefore, instead of rejecting every pattern of ideas from which the tiny elements of good have begun to sparkle and which in themselves have trapped souls to lead them to the depths of the abyss—the place where reigns the darkness that deadens the soul in its prime of vigor—a task that is bound to fail, it is for us to enhance the original light. It is for us to disclose the breadth and depth, the universality and eternity that is immanent in the light of the faith of Israel. It is for us to clarify how every spark of the good that is manifest in the world stems from its source and is linked with it in a natural bond. Then will all the sparks newly made manifest add light and life to the soul of the people mighty in its spiritual vitality, in its divine potency. Those thirsty for light will look and be enlightened, and will no longer go to feed in alien pastures even for nourishment they had begun to think could be found only in those places.

This type of tolerance is bound to spread so that the human spirit will be able to find the divine spark hidden in everything, and automatically discard every dross. "And I will take away his blood out of his mouth, and his abominations from between his teeth, and he also shall be a remnant for our God" (Zech. 9:7). All the sparks will be joined into the most august torch, and all nations will acquire a clear language to call in the name of the Lord. "Take away the dross from the silver and there will emerge a refined vessel" (Prov. 25:4).

ABRAHAM ISAAC KOOK

THE SOUL OF NATIONHOOD
AND ITS BODY

There must necessarily be a gap between the abstract, ideal content of the universal objective and its expression in reality, between the good intention that inspires a person at the heights of his spiritual life and the spirit that is with him always, to guide his way and his behavior. Were it not for this difference in gradation the pattern of behavior would become blurred, existence could not retain its stability, there would be no fixed rules or boundaries. The particular programs and goals that are the foundation of the world and the fullness therefore could not exist.

When the lofty ideals that have their being in a state of nondetermination, in the roots of the soul and its basic aspirations, become confined within a particular boundary, they at once lose their ardor and descend from the heights of their potency. They gain a practical advantage and become accessible to effectuation through their limitation, but they lose the higher purity they had before their incarnation within their assigned form. Their light has dimmed; at times it loses much of its brightness, reaching a point of near darkness out of its functional necessity. Then the ideals carry this mission: after they have entered the practical world, to return to that level of loftiness and purity and to that majesty of scope and quality which they had while they were being shaped in the realm of the imagination. The success of this process will depend on the extent of the light's materialization. If it has not been overly materialized and if it has not descended too far from its lofty heights, then the road of the higher penitence will be open, and the ideals will readily find a clear pathway leading back to their spiritual essence.

But even if the extent of materialization is only minor,

everything may yet turn to naught through an overpowering desire for the heights, which may stir within the limited boundaries. In a great effort to ascend to their conceptual roots, these "materialized" ideals may lose their practical attributes, which would contravene the planned order of materialization. If this desire should be so strong as to break the confinements, and thereby effect a wide separation between the ideals in their essence and their incorporation in the special world of action and limitation, then the light will of necessity be diminished in order to contain this excessive desire.

The light will then release its rays in delimited measure, and they will make their way at a slow pace. They will send flashes across the boundaries and they will release sparks time after time from the original exalted light of eternity. From the abstract goals there will reach out channels to carry the dew of a higher life within the boundaries, the particularized forms, and this dew is the dew of light and it will banish the darkness and illumine life.

Then will the world be built anew, heaven and earth will kiss, and the joy of creation will become manifest. This process is at work in the case of the individual, the nation, the world and all existence.

The love for the nation, or, more broadly, for humanity, is adorned at its source with the purest ideals, which reflect humanity and nationhood in their noblest light. In the conceptual world these are entities full of majesty and beauty, delight and life, mercy and truth, justice and humility, valor and joy, intelligence and feeling. They are in a state of continuing progress, which brings joy to every noble heart. This is how they appear in the conceptual world. But when they enter the world of action, and are set within boundaries, at once some elements of the higher light disappear. The large *aleph* becomes a small *aleph.* * The obstructions of life multi-

---

*The Hebrew permits the designation of special importance in an utterance by enlarging a letter.

ply. The agitation of anger and fear, of hostilities and arrogance, grow and fill the atmosphere. Humanity, on the practical level, robes itself in soiled garments; its many lights fall into hard shells in which it is wrapped. The one who loves it as it is will be unable to rise toward a higher life. He is rather likely to absorb into himself the filth accumulated within it than the holy sparks hidden in its secret places.

The same applies to the status of a particular nationalism, which includes also our own nation.

Inestimably beautiful is the ideal of establishing a chosen people, a kingdom of priests and a holy nation, out of a people sunk in frightful servitude, the brilliance of whose patriarchal origin shall illumine its darkness. In the divine heights this ideal abides in the secret hiding place in its purity. But it must be materialized, set within a particular boundary, among people with good and also evil passions, in communities in need of sustenance, of gaining a foothold on the land, of governmental authority. The collective life must allow room for everybody, from the heights of people of pure spirit and refined souls to the lowland of inferior people who are bound to pursue the lower aspects of existence. Mortal eyes, bleary, lose all their brightness, the spiritual dimension becomes enslaved and darkened in the darkness of life, which abounds with filth and refuse. Humanity in its limited form, which is pervaded with abominations more than with refinement and light, is therefore likely to influence its devotees with evil and gross darkness. This is the source of the evil in liberalism. And when the particular nationalisms robed themselves in the thick garments of worldliness, humanity, too, descended from its heights. The nationhood of the Jewish people was broken so that it ceased functioning, and what is left is only the highest dimension of its basic conception, hidden in the ideal of reviving the nation in the highest dimension of its purity.

Streams of light can descend from this august position to

ifice of the nation to its original scope, its scope at
ng of its existence. By drawing on this higher,
ence, the nation's worldly garments can also be
t if a person should wish to embrace the nation in
condition, in its coarser aspects, without inner
from its ancient, higher light, he will soon take
filth and lowliness and elements of evil that will
erness in a short span of history of but a few
This is the vision of the evil kind of nationalism
unter.
the end the general love of humanity will over-
il surrounding it, and the basic love of nation-
community of Israel, will destroy all its thorny
d she will draw from the divine source, as in her
She will be planted again in the place that has
ne, with a great wealth of her authentic charac-
practical self-limitation, and of many marks and
will enrich her image. Her broken vessels will
the sparks of purity that have been scattered will
together, one by one. From the general ideal
tence will the light of Israel again be manifest,
urity and might, restore the purity of the human
se of Sharon,* rooted in eternal righteousness,
, and shed its light and splendor to all sides.
ine spirit exists in the community of Israel in the
oncealment, in the holy of holies, in the dark
faith in God is hidden, robed in the garment of
ligion. The delusion of centering our religion on
its outer forms, which, because of its weakness of perception,
despises all the wealth in the mystical realm, has darkened the
eyes and reduced our spiritual vision by building a wall of
dross for the free spirit. It has created a filthy atmosphere for
the rise of the crude heresy in its despicable form in which we

---

*A metaphor for the Jewish people.

encounter it in our time. When this outlook is applied to nationalism, it chooses precisely its worst elements, those likely to corrupt everything noble in the image of the individual, whose path is meant to point toward God. Without the dew of life in the love of God, of a noble reverence abounding with discernment and knowledge, and a life-faith pulsating with freedom, nationalism must take its path to pick grains from the animal dung of an inferior nation. In a gloomy spirit, full of anger and sickness, it will pride itself in the outwardness of a language whose mighty holiness it does not recognize, of a land from whose wondrous qualities it is alienated, of nostalgic yearnings from which it has discarded every element that can nourish and vitalize. The adherents of such a nationalism will be disdainful of a nationalism the nobler and the more spiritual it is at its source, and they will contaminate it with the filth of their own impurity. There is no faith, there is no fear of God, there is no moral grandeur and no heroism of spirit—and what life can be revived by it?

This is the narrow state to which the community of Israel will descend prior to an awakening to the true revival. On awakening she will thrust aside with decided indignation all her dross, and with a divine resoluteness she will gather to herself all her good. From the holy heights she will restore to life all her treasures, and all her precious possessions will shine with a higher illumination. The sounds of song, the majesty of the holy tongue, the beauty of our precious land, which was chosen by God, the ecstasy of heroism and holiness, will return to the mountains of Zion. With the cleansing potency of the original soul of our people, with hidden divine influences and with the light of mercy and a higher pleasure hidden within it, will they come and also cleanse all the outer garments in which the soul and spirit of the nation robed itself. From the source of higher delight will flow many spices to remove the filthy smell that was absorbed by the crude nationalism enclosed in its materialism. And as smoke fades away so will fade away all the destructive winds that have filled the land, the language, the history, and the literature. "I will take you from among the nations and gather you out of all the countries and bring you into your own land. I will sprinkle on you clean water and you will be clean from all your defilements; from all your abominations will I cleanse you. I will give you a new heart, and I will place in you a new spirit; and I will remove the heart of stone from your flesh, and I will give you a heart of flesh. I will put My spirit within you, and I will cause you to walk in My statutes, and you will keep My laws and do them. And you will dwell in the land I gave to your ancestors, and you will be My people and I will be your God" (Ezek. 36:24-29).

THE SIGNIFICANCE OF THE REVIVAL

To be attached to God is the most natural aspiration of a person. What is throughout all existence in a state of dumbness and deafness, in a form of potentiality, is developed in man in a conceptual and experiential form. There can be no substitute in existence for the longing to be absolutely linked with the living God, with the infinite light. As we are under a compulsion to live, to be nourished, to grow, so are we under a compulsion to cleave to God. This cleaving to God, to which we are summoned with all our soul, must necessarily develop in us. It must grow in our feeling, it must become more clarified in our understanding. Under no circumstances can humanity and all existence dispense with the quest for divine cleaving, which is present within her, even if in a hidden form.

The primitive stage of humanity, the epoch of gross darkness, left in the world forms of life that impeded the full manifestation of the divine cleaving. It is impossible to assess the pain of the general world soul and the pain of the soul in every living creature and every person as a result of the spiritual oppression, the denial of its hidden good that was to offer so much light, so much joy, that can engender a life of breadth, of endurance, of higher vistas and strength. A person needs such a life; it is of the essence of his nature and existence. But human weakness intervened and fashioned dumb idols, gross, materialistic, vulgar, limited and defective divinities, and the light was shut out.

We can imagine the suffering of the great soul of the spiritual giant, the soul of Abraham, with all its aspirations, with its mighty longing for freedom and light, over the world's disgrace. How embittered it is on realizing the happiness, the light intended for all, for every living being, for every soul. Abraham heard the vast realm of the divine calling to existence: Be illumined; calling to every particular being: Fill yourself with happiness, greatness, loftiness, peace, good, strength, love and delight. But the wells have been shut, the "Philistines shut them and filled them with earth" (Gen. 26:18). How this lion of a man breaks out of his confinement, how angrily he takes his staff in hand, breaks the idols and calls with a loud voice for the light, for one God, the God of the universe.

The Jewish people took this aspiration as the basis of its national existence, as conditioned by its historic destiny. Thus, out of the free moral impulses—the universal moral system—were drawn the bases for the establishment of the faith of Israel, which is so vital to us and to the entire world. It is precisely when we imagine, invoke and focus on the name of the God of Israel that we give clarity to our inner visions, our profoundest experiences. Our peace of mind and our relaxation of soul, the conditioning of our lives in purity with firmness and holiness, are established through cleaving to God. Morality is not centered merely in good deeds on a societal level. Morality is primarily a refined, inner disposition within the soul to seek the good, the absolute good, to be good in oneself, to cleave to the good. This holy spirit can exist among us only within the context of an attachment to God, which is contributed to us by the faith of Israel, the practical and the ideational. Under this spiritual, this inner moral necessity, we must immerse ourselves in our people. From all its generations we have acquired the whole treasure of life, which is true life, the link to our true existence, to the life of our soul of souls. In this state of purity we love the name of God, the divine light that abides in us, that abides in the whole people; we love the Torah and the commandments, the precepts of God and the laws He gave to Israel. And out of a strong sense of our own authenticity, the conviction is growing in us, the fruitful, lofty vision full of the substance of life, to broaden our philosophy, to disseminate our concept over the entire world.

Our strong commitment to assure the continuity of Judaism, with its ideas and pattern of behavior, together with its corporate self on its own land, stems from the widespread recognition by our people that we still have a long distance to travel in order to complete what we began. We began to say something of immense importance among ourselves and to the world, but we have not yet completed it. We are in the midst of our discourse, and we do not wish—and we are unable—to stop. Under no circumstances will we abandon our distinctive way of life nor our universal aspirations, which transcend every particular party, both of which are interrelated, just as we shall not abandon our hope to return and be rebuilt, and exist as a nation in our historic homeland, as in ancient days. We cannot abandon all these. Even though one does not discern readily the place of ideals in vitalizing the life of a people, it is they that give life to all life, and when they recede the soul-animating life recedes. If we stammer so much in speaking of our mission, the fault is not in the clarity of the concept or in its truth. Our truth is strong enough, but it is so rich and so overpowering that we are still unable to explain it in clear language, and for this reason we shall not retreat. We shall speak and explain as much as our power of speech permits us. In our inwardness we understand our ideas, and in the course of time our speech will also emerge from its hard exile in which it is confined, and we shall be able to speak, to explain in clear terms what we seek with our full being. But until that golden age we shall not cease from our practical and spiritual efforts. Only a people that has finished what it started can descend from the stage of history, when its vision has already been fully disclosed to the world. To begin and not to finish—this is not in accordance with the rhythm in existence.

The soul of the eternal people ponders its thoughts, it weaves into one fabric all its meditations, and again as in a flash there pass before it generations and epochs, from its earliest youthful dreams, from the blossoming of its springtime, to its latter years, the time of fruition that began after the long decline. They are all intertwined in the chain of its thoughts, its meditation and its actions. It rouses itself as from sleep to renew its youth according to an old-new program, modest and weak, but held together with the mighty streams of the past flowing toward the future, to the accompaniment of ancient memories with residual strategies. Our work is like tiny growths of some mighty and majestic forest of Lebanon, which, after a holocaust of its beautiful cedar trees soaring toward the heights, has begun to renew its vitality and to bring forth tender, weak and impoverished plants, like pieces of foliage sprouting on a wall. But these are not pieces of foliage, they are mighty cedars at the beginning of their growth in a mighty forest.

Out of its inner depths the Jewish people will yet sound the same call that was issued by the rock from which it was hewn.* Out of its awareness of light and happiness, out of its profound compassion for every afflicted soul, for every confused creature, for the forms of national, social and moral life that proceed on paths full of entangling thorns, because of the absence of a source of light to reveal to them that yearning for which the soul of all existence cries out in its pain, it will sound the call: Seek me, search after me, and live. In dark paths some have fabricated imitations; with hearts full of hypocrisy and cowardice, they approach to portray the greatness of the King of kings, whose greatness and might they had heard about on the outside. Not so, the Jewish people; such service is inferior in its eyes, even though many individuals in its midst are drawn to it. Not so is the spirit of a mighty

---

*The reference is to father Abraham.

nation, an ancient people, a nation that seeks forcefully the light of God and the joy of life. It will release a fierce wind to destroy the imitation that invaded it from the other side of the boundary, and it will raise up against it an adversary in which the spirit of God will be embodied. With an ardent soul, full of life and enduring heroism, it will bestir itself and call out: Here is light, here is the voice of the living God calling to me from the depths of my being, here is the light of eternal freedom for all existence, that has come and shines from the light of God on Mount Zion, the place of the valley of vision, where the word of the living God has begun to be heard.

All the rebels of the world will yet hear, all the heretics of the world will understand, all who still have a spark of life will return, from the depths of the earth souls will ascend, the unfortunate ones will raise themselves from the bottom of the pit, "those lost in the land of Assyria and the forsaken ones in the land of Egypt will come and serve the Lord on the holy mountain in Jerusalem" (Isa. 27:13).

They will bow down and arise full of strength, they will be renewed, invigorated with light and strength, legions and legions of them, with firmness of heart they will arise and cry out: A people has arisen, has begun to be a nation, that will release a flow of divine life to all worlds, a mighty people that has made a way in the stormy sea, that has paved an eternal pathway for the vitality of life that is distilled by attachment to God. "The God of Israel gives strength and firmness to the people, praised be God" (Ps. 68:36).

THE ROAD TO RENEWAL

The nature of the spiritual reality cannot be discerned through scientific probing. Objective knowledge, rational analysis, philosophy—these disclose only the external phenomena of life. Even when they deal with the inner aspects of existence they are focusing only on the shadows cast by life's essence, but not on its inner content. The true achievement of rational demonstration is only to prepare a path for the spirit to reach the outer chamber of the spiritual domain. But as long as man is immersed in his senses and their narrow confinements he will not be able to know fully the spiritual dimension of life, only faint shadows thereof will be discernible through them. And if he should relate to these shadows as though they were the true reality, then these shadows will turn for him into a heavy burden and they will diminish both his physical and his spiritual vigor, so that he will seek to flee from them as something detrimental.

But the more a person will seek to flee this shadow, the shadow will pursue him; there is only one therapy to escape it, and this is to augment the light.

This augmenting of light can come about only through rising to the inner chambers of the spiritual domain, but for this man does not have any psychic faculty except the profound intuition of a faith in the divine. Through this faith we attain the climactic reach of knowledge and of feeling that links man's spiritual life, in its existential fuctioning, with the ultimate spiritual reality. Thus he merges his life with the higher realms of existence that transcend all limitation and are free of the weakness that clings to the physical.

The psychic life of the individual in its various expressions merges with the larger psychic life through bridges that link them—the heroic personalities of the spiritual life and the psychic treasures of the group. This merger determines the distinctive characteristics of communities, such as societies, families and nations, reaching out to the highest levels of being. The spiritual splendor then descends from the highest spiritual source to the particular units of existence, which are differentiated from the whole only through the limitations of subjectivity. These limitations give way as the morning clouds before the rising sun, through the perception of the universal aspect of existence in every soul and spirit.

The psychic reality at the heart of existence manifests itself in visions of what is as yet nonexistent by the great figures of history. They are the ones who effected profound changes in the world, who overcame long-established traditions and inaugurated new and better ones. Thus they transformed the character of humanity, or of a great part of it, and this part will in turn exert its influence on the whole.

The psychic reality of existence that radiates an abundance of psychic potency on life is manifested only in the heroic spirits of the world, who are girded with a divine strength, who are at home in the vast ocean of religious faith. This is quite different from the dimension of reality portrayed for us in the shadowy knowledge of scientific enlightenment, be it shallow or profound.

It is to be noted, however, that our scientifically oriented culture, based on inferential reasoning and sense perception and the natural moral sense deriving from them, prepares mankind to absorb the light emanating from the universal spiritual psyche. Then under the impact of this light will the direction of our culture with its roots in reason, instinct and the natural moral sense take on great vigor and an abiding divine stability. Not so if the emanation of light reaches us without the preparation of the cultivated path of the scientifically oriented culture and conventional morality; then this very light will beget only darkness.

The irruption of spiritual light from its divine source on uncultivated ground yields the perverse aspect of idolatry, and it has caused false notions and evil passions, and from these perverse accretions humanity has not yet purged itself to this day. Even today our culture has not yet reached the point when a divine sensitivity for the absolute good shall pervade the soul of collective groups. The result is that the divine, as they conceive it, is for them an alien deity that expresses itself in grotesque caricatures. And we discern among them even now signs of evil and brutality, and the moral sense continues to atrophy and fades from their hearts.

Humanity has one refuge from this predicament—it is the example of the religious community of Israel, which has the divine sensitivity at the core of its being. Our instinct testifies and our analysis confirms it, that the God of the universe, unique in His unity, is the absolute good, life, light, who is exalted beyond all exaltation and better than all good ("the Lord is good to all and His mercies extend to all creatures," Ps. 145:9), who sustains and preserves and effects deliverance to all. This divine sensitivity is found not only among individuals of the Jewish people, but in its collectivity. If at times Israel tended to forget her soul, her life's essence, the institution of prophecy appeared to remind her of her vocation. Her descent to exile corrected her sinister inclinations so that in the end the divine sensitivity toward the absolute good was destined to prevail.

It is a fundamental error for us to retreat from our distinctive excellence, to cease recognizing ourselves as chosen for a divine vocation. We are not only different from other nations, differentiated and set apart by a distinctive historic existence that is unlike that of all other nations, but we indeed surpass the other nations. If we shall know our greatness then we shall know ourselves, but if we forget it then we shall forget our own identity; and a people that forgets its own identity is indeed small and lowly.

The road our nation has traveled in its general interrelations with humanity is very long. We are a great people and we have also blundered greatly, and, therefore, have we suffered great tribulations; but great also is our consolation.

The people of Israel yearns to exert an influence with its psyche, to bring near the great day when the influence of the spiritual in its existential aspects will find ready and prepared ground to make possible the fulfillment of the prophecy (Zech. 8:22-23): "And many peoples and mighty nations shall come to seek the Lord of hosts in Jerusalem . . . and they shall take hold of the corner of the garment of a Jew, saying, Let us go with you, for we have heard that God is with you." It is this very influence, by breaking in upon life when it is not ready, sowing its seed on unfertile ground, that produces weeds that are detrimental to every good.

Then will humanity no longer be content with the dry grains of speculations by finite mortals whose enthusiasms only reflect the weak and erring instincts of creatures of flesh and blood. But it will make way for a mighty psychic influence in which there is the spirit of the living God, of whom it is said: "Mercy and justice are the foundation of His throne, kindness and truth go before Him" (Ps. 89:15).

A profound moral and rational refinement, effected by a tradition, must precede the illumination of a psychic force from the higher autonomous realm of the spiritual. It is only then that the individual or society will grasp the full and dominant demand of this illumination for the perfection of the moral, social, intellectual and practical world. Everything will then be raised through the psychic illumination above the artificial culture based on the contrivances and designs of mortal hearts and minds.

But the element of refinement is an important component in this phenomenon. One unrefined element in the area where the light from the source of existence is acting can create a world of confusion and inflict immense damage upon great multitudes for generations to come. Humor, satire, criticism, the drama, art and philosophy with all the skills at their disposal will be unable to remove the intoxication effected on a society by a single undisciplined element of psychic force that, emanating from the action of the spiritual domain, has the capacity to enslave with a great potency all the souls that come under its influence. And if individuals allow themselves to imagine that they have succeeded in liberating themselves from this influence, and they have succeeded in channeling their lives along free, rational paths, contrary to the psychic influence dominant in their circle, this freedom is only external, in the peripheral zones of their spiritual being. In their inner essence they will not escape its power, and the critical eye will always discern that their original disposition continues its hold on their thoughts.

The displacement of the pernicious impact of a spiritual influence that has become distorted through the deficiency in the cultural milieu on which it acted can come about only through a higher and more resolute spiritual force. In its higher substantive content it necessarily embraces all the moral and rational characteristics of a culture that prizes freedom, rationality and criticism.

The higher spiritual illumination comes only through a pure reverence for God, a mighty divine faith that is to be found precisely in the community of Israel. The people of Israel achieved this psychic disposition through a moral and rational refinement effected as a result of an ancestral heritage and the purging effect of slavery. These conditioned Israel's history so that she was prepared to absorb the full force of the divine influence on the life of the community, on its mores, its aspirations, giving it rootedness in the souls of individuals and in its collective conscience for future generations.

As a result of this moral and intellectual refinement, a preliminary conditioning for the actions of the higher spiritual influence, there developed in the Jewish people the inclination to pursue the study and cultivation of nature, the desire for free inquiry, for a clear and rational ethic. This became the heritage of Israel, which is to be found always among Jewish groups and individuals in each generation.

The strengthening of all aspects of our nation's life is dependent on the strengthening of its spiritual character. This, in turn, depends on the illumination from the spiritual realm, the universal psyche, that will bring the spirit of man and of the world in the messianic age to complete harmony. The inflow of the divine psyche that pervades heaven and earth and encompasses all the fluctuations of life from its inception to its final epoch, in time and circumstance, vitalizes all the dimensions of our people's life: its history, language, land, life-style—everything is endowed by it with delight, valor and richness.

The preparation of the spiritual character of our nation for union with the universal psyche is made possible through the higher "moral Torah" that is conveyed through the divine revelation of morality and wisdom, and of the *mitzvot* that were given as a means of human refinement. It cannot be effected by a prescriptive moral code alone, which may soon be corrupted by the mire thrown up by the ocean of the psyche. This must be supplemented by the inflow of original spiritual influences that express the divine good that pervades all existence and reaches down to every particular being. The thrust of the divine good is discernible in every part of this eternal Torah.

But when the components of the nation's life are remote from the spring of the divine, they absorb turbid and unrefined psychic elements that dull the splendor of absolute morality and cause them to lose the divine vigor that pulsates in them.

This affliction shows itself in an inner coldness and an enthusiasm for institutional conformity. Without the holy fire of genuine faith behind those institutional expressions, they become steadily weakened and they atrophy. Then they produce as a reaction an irritation over frustrated expectations, over a life of futility.

When this transpires, the nation will recall with longing her youthful days when she entered the covenant with God and, rising above her sophistication, she will turn back to the divine world she has abandoned. The divine psychic force hidden in her soul will be aroused, the refined spirit of wisdom and morality will come to life again; then will all her established institutions shine with an exalted light and a divine grace will fill them all. Every heart will then be pervaded with an inner love, tranquil and confident.

In every cultivated soul there will then be revealed the pulsating action of the universal divine psyche. It will express itself in vision, in song. Its impact will be felt everywhere. At first it will make itself felt among the people of Israel, and before long, it will also be felt throughout mankind. All that its general decadence erased will be inscribed again, all that has been forgotten will be recalled; and the joy of heaven and earth will return as in ancient days.

The illumination from the spiritual realm in all its fullness occurs in any society to the extent that it has been sensitized to the divinely oriented ideology that is concerned with the quest for the universal good, the absolute good that affects all existence. The illumination of the individual soul by the spiritual and moral force stirring in society is analogous to the movements of the particular beings in the planetary worlds, which are affected by the solar system of which they are a part. The illumination of the individual soul is affected by the movement of the universal good, which embraces in its laws the morality and justice at the heart of reality. The movement of the universal good represents of course a phenomenon of such immensity that the eye is blinded in looking at its light. It is for this reason that we can find no formula by which to define it.

The illumination from the spiritual realm is manifest in mighty waves in the souls of individuals of great spiritual vitality. But this power is perfected in them when their general roots, their national soul, is in a state of health; and conversely, when the national dimension of their being is defective, they too become inwardly damaged.

The psychic force of authentic spirituality, which transcends in its potency the spirituality gained by the study of texts, was manifested in the lives of individuals during the most enlightened moments of the nation's life, when it was at peace and at the peak of its creativity. These lives reflect the most luminous sparks from the full light embodied in the nation's inner essence, underscoring thereby the direction of its highest goals. This was the nature of Israelite prophecy.

The Jewish national psyche was in a state of health throughout the long period from the settlement in Canaan to the destruction of the first Temple, with but minor exceptions. A spiritual influence pervaded the national spirit and stirred it to a divine longing that needed to be shaped through the skills of wisdom and it inspired the prophetic vision among her best spirits. The mighty personality of the prophet was more dominant among the people than the devotion to the study of texts. It was dominant in the nation's psyche, the medium that actualizes the spiritual reality as a functioning force.

This force was dulled in the nation through the admittance of alien influences, which were also more in the nature of psychic experiences than the result of study. The psychic influence turned in the direction of the evil of idolatry, and the mighty soul of Israel, which was rooted in the living God, the holy God, was diverted from its purity. The collective aspects of the nation's life, like her politics, absorbed this psychic influence and it turned into a poison until she was broken altogether.

The decadence of the nation, her exile from her own land, effected an interruption of the psychic influence, which had formerly been at its height. Broken in body and spirit, the Jewish people returned from the brief exile in Babylonia and sought to rebuild its former station. But it no longer possessed the full force of its psychic illumination and instead of the inflow of spiritual influence there came to excessive focus the study of texts. Through study the people sought to redevelop within itself a cultural disposition faithful to its origins as well as to its existential needs and thereby to readapt itself to receive the illumination of the soul from the spiritual reality. The tradition was now conveyed through a new medium, after the former medium had become a source of stumbling.

The temptation to idolatry came to an end, but it was not altogether vanquished. Its voice was muted, but stealthily it remained alive and exerted an influence. It had to persist until it was to be totally overcome by the power of the nation, when a mighty surge of spiritual energy spreading great enlightenment would vanquish its darkness, including all the power in the primitive temptation to idolatry.

Then there appeared parties in the nation that had absorbed the external aspects of nationalism, together with its dross. Hatred for people grew, which is a distinctive effect of idolatry that always does its destructive work under the banner of nationalism. Though this hatred is ostensibly directed at other peoples and does not make one's own nation its target, in the course of time it turns to an internal disease and a hatred of brother against brother becomes sharpened, destroying the national welfare. Individuals still experienced the holy spirit. Illumined by the brightest light of holiness, they reached the highest level of spiritual sensitivity latent in the nation's soul, but these were only individuals. The pedagogy of studying texts proved too weak in the face of the pressures of life. The result was that the affairs of the nation, especially its political life, were entrusted into the hands of people who were remote from divine ideals, which are the essence of Israel's national soul.

The aspiration for self-revitalization, for an illumination of soul, as in earlier days, was at times felt in the nation. At times there arose illuminated spirits of great stature who sought by their psychic powers to stimulate a spiritual renewal among their people and to influence them to the recognition that study must be strengthened by the spiritual reality as it discloses itself in the course of its unfolding. But the times did not prove opportune for this.

In such an epoch of weakness arose Christianity and it wrought injury to the nation. Its founder was endowed with a remarkably charismatic personality, and he exerted great spiritual influence, but he had not escaped the defect of idolatry, which is an intensification of spiritual influence without the prior training in the existing moral and cultural disciplines. And he and his followers were so committed to the cultivation of the spiritual life that they lost their Jewish characteristics and they became alienated, in deed and spirit, from the source whence they had sprung.

But the concentration on a diet of study alone weakens the power of the nation unduly. The role of the individual as a source of spiritual enlightenment to the nation's life had to reemerge. Rabbi Akiba then came and declared: " 'The Lord (*et adonoy*) you shall revere' (Deut. 6:13)—the inclusion of the word *et* before *adonoy** suggests that we include the reverence due to the sages" (Baba Kamma 4lb). This mighty call gave recognition to the spiritual influence of the individual in the inner realm of Judaism. But the people were not altogether adjusted to this concept. The diffidence of Rabbi Simeon Imsoni, who had rejected the inference from the use of the word *et*, was hidden in the soul of the entire community of Israel.

---

*The term is superfluous but is often used to introduce a direct object.

Many generations passed and inspired individuals reinforced the spiritual efficacy of studying texts. A distinctive type of individual came to the foreground in the great *zaddikim* and holy sages, adding lustre to their practical achievements in the knowledge of textual learning. But the afflictions suffered by our people, the general decadence of life, caused a neglect of the soul force of direct spiritual influence and the aspect of study became dry and detached. Then there soon appeared rifts: undisciplined individuals, confused by false fantasies and mischievous inclinations, proclaimed visions, and, where there was a vacuum, they made headway and they brought bewilderment to the nation. These were the various false messiahs, who confused the world and caused great harm.

But amidst all the evil they caused, there was not lost the tiny element of good hidden in them. They exemplified a psychic renewal as opposed to the sole dependence on the one foundation, the study of texts, and indoctrination in the disciplined, practical performance of commandments. This served to remind the people of the healthy basis of the nation's earlier life, when the divine light had shone in her midst, and her prophets had seen divine visions.

Hasidism also arose from this claim for spiritual inspiration that had become dormant. After the unsuccessful attempt by the last false messiah Shabbetai Zevi, who had reduced the phenomenon of psychic inspiration to the level of madness and an evil intoxication, and its cessation after all the grotesqueness it had assumed in the last half-official false messiah Frank and his adherents—after all this there was the great peril that the nation might spurn altogether every vestige left it from the treasure of living spiritual inspiration. The result would have been sole dependence on a study of texts and the zealous performance of actions, the commandments and the customs. The people would have become bowed in body and crushed in spirit. In the end they would have been unable to survive from a lack of vitality and uplifting of spirit.

This was felt by that great personality, the father of Hasidism,* in whom the divine inspiration was a living soul force. But its form had been insufficiently grounded in textual study and it therefore could not be established firmly on graded Torahitic norms. This was needed to channel the spreading light so as not to go astray and result in harmful consequences.

Hasidism had an inner safeguard against the peril that had characterized the tendency to excessive inspiration in earlier movements. This was a remarkably deep-felt love for the nation, a love for the Jewish people as a whole and a love for individual Jews. This love stood as a mighty buttress in this inspirational movement of Hasidism against all destructive tendencies. But this in itself would not have been sufficient. Future generations might well have lost the blessings of revival in Hasidism had it not been purified by suffering as a result of the fiery opposition from the shining light of Israel's tradition of textual study centering in the practical disciplines of life. He himself had felt the living force of inspiration but for him this was peripheral to his primary concern, textual study. I am referring to the Torahitic psychology of Rabbi Elijah Gaon of Vilna. He fought the spread of the divine inspiration in the psychology of the Besht, which had not been sufficiently grounded in the textual study, thus creating the danger that it might become estranged from its roots in the Jewish tradition in the course of time.

This controversy for "the sake of heaven," through its two contending adversaries, had salutory results that were felt throughout the Jewish diaspora. It led to the formation of a group that established a base for the return to Eretz Yisrael and a renewal of practical work for the rebuilding of our ancestral homeland. This was the beginning of all the realistic movements that are aiding this phenomenon in our time.

---

*The reference is to Rabbi Israel ben Eliezer, commonly called the Baal Shem Tov, or, in abbreviation, the Besht.

These developments are themselves, incidentally, preparatory to a new surge of divine inspiration.

The psyche of the nation is showing signs of renewal. At first she tends to be drawn to the external trappings of the nation's life, without embracing the inner essence of the nation, her divine soul. At first she is content with the revival of the language, the land, the knowledge of history and an undefined nostalgia for the past. But without a divine light shining, the soul will grow troubled. Where is the love of truth? Where is the love for Zion and Jerusalem that had been, despite all inner weakness, so vital and stirring in the hearts of our ancestors, who had been exposed to so much wandering in exile? The mighty question that is bound to arise in due time will call the restored nation, her children who have come to build her anew, her youth and all who are anxious about her welfare, to return to her psychic source, the source of vision and prophecy. This vision comes as the fruit of a deep faith in God that dawns after all free probing and speculation, after a lapse of discipline and endless experiments in alluring and free life-styles. Resolute in body and spirit, and stirred by a deep and living passion, the young Israelite of the future in viewing the renaissance of his people and his land will speak proudly of the Holy Land, and glory in the God of Israel. A spiritual force of intense vitality will stir the dry bones that drew their sustenance from dry logic, lifeless metaphysics and the decadence of skepticism. Then will be fulfilled the prophecy: "And they will come and sing in the heights of Zion and they will be drawn to the blessing of the Lord, the wine, the oil, and the flocks of sheep, and they will be like a watered garden and they shall grieve no more" (Jer. 31:17). The spirit of the Lord latent in the nation will manifest itself in her with full force in a well-walked path, a path of heroism, of wisdom and piety, and of the splendor of redemption, which will inspire a new song among the people, and endow them with a new name, to be pronounced by the Lord.

The inspiration of an active spiritual influence exerts its

effect on practical life more than the method of studying texts. When free of external dross, of misleading fantasies and wicked goals, of pride and arrogance, the functioning of spiritual inspiration will restore to the nation its ancient honor by restoring the patriarchal dignity of Israel's princes, who were distinguished by a personal spiritual quality of a high order. The adherence to *zaddikim* with devotion and enthusiasm, through constant contact, raises the spiritual stature of the nation. The psychic fusion that is effected through the living contact of souls in the existential reality of life merges the inner light in the psyche of the higher person, the true man of God, with the other souls that are attached to him in love and faith. They experience the delight distilled by a great moral personality who constantly experiences divine influences of longing that the highest good be fostered in the world, and that the divine loving-kindness, in all its fullness, appear in every living soul.

The light of an active spiritual influence thus spreads to the souls of people who are spiritually impoverished, who are pursued by the pressures of the petty forces stirring in their narrow hearts. This merger ennobles those souls with a psychic beauty, it straightens what is crooked, it spreads a state of innocence, and wins forgiveness even for troubled sinners afflicted by the hostility of their gross natures that dominate their material existence.

This type of personal influence needs great safeguards, but it can be of great benefit. Its spiritual service cannot be measured according to the Torahitic knowledge and the educational aspects embodied in it. On the contrary, measured by this yardstick, the spiritual becomes a weak auxiliary to the practical. The rabbinate will then be judged according to the administrative role it plays and its educational function will be assessed according to the monetary value of the animals and the fowl, the pots and spoons and all other such petty items it has decreed as *kosher*, for it is only by such criteria that the practical sense of the multitude understands a service of usefulness. In the end such values are bound to decline and to sink ever lower, unless a mighty spiritual force should arise to support them according to their original inspiration that lifts all spiritual needs to their full stature.

This can be effected only by a personal influence that draws its inspiration from the domain of the spiritual in all its profusion, that represents a surviving remnant of prophecy.

Such remnants are to be found only in a state of decadence in the diaspora, because the nation itself is in a state of decadence while in exile. The nation longs to set root again in its homeland and to return to normalcy, as in ancient days. But to the extent of her readiness for the aspiration to greatness, she must, through her own initiative, discover a source of spiritual inspiration that shall act on all aspects of her life. She must discover a great personality from among her noblest spirits who are close to the source of her soul, who abound in vision and the song of holiness, and who yearn with the fullness of their being for light and deliverance, for her strength and her honor.

The enlightenment concerning the surface of things, with all its adornments, the surface study of the Torah, which is concerned directly with the practical aspects of life, will not endow such a personality with sufficient potency to aid in the renewal of the nation and the land.

This spiritual inspiration will appear from its hidden submergence in the realm of light. This realm of light continually discloses itself to humble spirits who are resolute in heart and anticipate deliverance, whose whole being is under the influence of the divine life pulsating in the soul of the collective life of the house of Israel. These mighty men of God will embrace in their being all the general and the particular forces needed for the nation's revival. They will integrate in themselves all the forces involved in the activist program and all the forces of feeling and thought. They will revitalize each soul through the influence of the living God, after they themselves will be adorned by the divine grace that is made manifest in the functioning spiritual essence of the living people, whose soul expresses the divine soul.

The breakdown of the boundaries that mark the separate spiritual domain of each soul will ennoble all souls. The deficiencies resulting from all the sinfulness in people will be overcome and a higher light drawing men "toward the blessing of the Lord" will break through, distilling endless delights for all those who have come to serve the renewal of the holy people on its homeland. The surge of literary creativity, when it is robed in the spirit of the people that has returned to life, will find new treasures that it had never expected to see. It will engage the best spirits of the world with a new vision of the divine psyche stirring in all its purity among this people that has awakened on the soil of its beginnings. Through the divine spirit pulsating in its being it will stir to life the spirit of all nations that have grown weary with the burden of life in its grossness that has become unbearably oppressive. "The vision is yet for the appointed time, and it declares of the end, and it does not lie. Though it tarry wait for it, because it will surely come, it will not delay. The soul of the one who is puffed up is not right, but the righteous shall live by his faith" (Hab. 2:3, 4).

FRAGMENTS OF LIGHT:
A VIEW AS TO THE REASONS FOR THE COMMANDMENTS

When we enter the vast domain of probing the reasons for the commandments, we cannot help being astonished at the meager attention paid to this important branch of literature, which, in the light of its subject matter, should have been of wider concern than any other branch of Torah study. In our generation we are more conscious of the lack of research into this important field of inquiry. The concern with strengthening Judaism, on the ideological and the practical levels, occupies the attention of our most talented spirits, who all are firmly committed to Judaism and ready to sacrifice their lives for it. On the face of it, it should be clear to us that Judaism's revival and revitalization, even its remaining firm in its present position, must be based on an inner light, on knowledge and feeling, which distill love and give firmness to the actions that derive from them. Toward this end, the most important task is a popularization of the study of the reasons for the commandments in depth and originality.

The first one to illumine our horizon by probing the reasons for the commandments was Maimonides in his *Guide for the Perplexed*. But how surprising it will be for us to assess the impression all his thoughts concerning the reasons for the commandments registered on the people generally and on individuals who investigate religious themes, from his own time to the latest generation! Less than any other conceptual theme in his writings did this subject, the reasons for the commandments, evoke any reaction. We know of almost no resultant stimulation and apparently no resultant emulation in response to his work. The facts indicate clearly that we have here a certain deficiency that needs to be mended, so that this beloved subject be pervaded by a new vitality and creativeness.

The connecting thread that links all the explanations for the commandments by Maimonides is: the uprooting of idolatry. We have here a noble cultural force of the past, which continues to release an idealistic spirit, the pride of our people in having been an important participant in building the spiritual and cultural world, but by its nature this is bound to weaken, since its brightest epoch is the *past*. In truth, however, the basic principle immanent in the reasons for the commandments points to the *future*. The past by itself, though it is very important, can, by itself, only bring to us values of archeological information that have no substantial contribution for ongoing life. The present alone surely will not suffice to radiate a light of idealism that can elevate the spirit with poetry and with an influence of holiness. It is only when the past flows on toward the great and progressively unfolding future that this branch of scientific knowledge can meet the conditions of life, both in establishing the worth of this noble branch of knowledge and in contributing to the revitalization of Judaism. Unless there is added to the past an influence that flows mightily from the farthest past, opening up with vitality to the present, and then reaching out with gathering strength and light toward a brighter future, abounding in idealistic anticipation for a higher life, it is in danger of presenting Judaism in the trappings of archeology. Indeed, we saw this development in western Europe where the Maimonidean influence became the most significant factor in the interpretation of Judaism. The respect for Judaism grew among individuals, and the historical value of the past occupied a major place in the literary efforts of the generations that were influenced by this spirit. But these works were not touched by the inner light of Maimonides in which the past merges with the present and the future. This is expressed not in the logical form of the past-oriented *Guide for the Perplexed*, but in the holy and simple piety of the *Mishneh Torah*, where refined feeling transcends the bounds of logical reasoning. Therefore did that logical approach suffice to stimulate enthusiasm for research into the antiquities of the Jewish people and for noting their spiritual treasures as an achievement of the past, which are indeed worthy of respect and love. But it did not suffice to establish Judaism as a fountain of life that fills all the recesses of heart and mind and engages the most creative powers of the intellect and of a vital love that knows no end.

When a spiritual phenomenon encounters another spiritual phenomenon that negates it, if it swerves from its course to avoid a confrontation, it will necessarily be damaged and weakened, even if it retains its original character and continues to hold its ground. But if it should respond by hewing a new path under the influence of the phenomenon opposing it, and with its aid, then the opposing force will stimulate it to greater strength, so that it will as a result rise to a higher and more enlightened state, emerging with fresh triumph in its basic goal and essence. After having turned the potency of the challenging phenomenon to its use, if it should desire to destroy it, it will be able to do so easily.

Although the inner dispositions of the sciences have changed in many important respects, with the changing times, their general characteristic continues to embrace all periods, in all their mutations. When Judaism had to defend itself as the champion of the basic idea of the divine, and then encountered the Greek conception of the eternity of the universe, Maimonides was very successful, not only in demonstrating a way of maintaining the divine idea on the basis of the belief in creation, but also by utilizing the ideology of the adversary. He spoke confidently about the conception of God, even on the basis of the theory of the eternalists. Then the results reached offered ample light on the well-trodden path of the belief in creation, with double vigor abounding in courage and life.

The relationship of the doctrine of evolution—in all its ramifications—to Judaism, and its fundamental concepts in our time, is similar to the ancient confrontation of the teaching about the eternity of the universe with Judaism in the time of the spiritual polemic with the Greeks. Here we need to follow resolutely the scientific method of Maimonides, although the methods of reasoning have changed with the changing times. With all the scientific defects in the theory of evolution, which is presently at the inception of its development and in its early stages, let us take courage to base the triumphant affirmation of Judaism on the basis of its assumptions, which, on the face it, seem so antagonistic to us. Obviously it is not the negative force of conflict in itself that releases the vitalizing energy of renewal engendered by the ferment of spiritual confrontation. It is rather that for victory in such a contest a strong intellectual effort is needed, and that the battle for spiritual survival, which calls for much planning, stimulates a great and very potent force for life. This force will become manifest in us when we shall endeavor to establish our spiritual position, not on the basis of any particular philosophy or on the basis of a commitment to some particular ideal, but through the fusion of all the idealistic forces, each now operative in isolation, integrating them into a comprehensive ensemble. This will be effected through the illumination of the core essence of our souls. This fusion carries the new light to its highest level of service to life and of eternal creativity. Through the graces of unending integration it gives us the faithful reassurance that even in the future, when "new" songs will be heard, and when our intellectual and cultural claims will take on new form, even then, a fountain of life will be open wide for us, to achieve great and new things, through the medium of clear understanding, which links together the multitude of its lights and always finds in them the fruitful creativity of the spirit.

On the face of it, an absolute moral system ought to be the most fundamental basis on which to establish eternal ideals, in which we would then have the thrust of the absolute dimension of life. By discovering that this is the considered objective of the commandments in their ramifications, in their general and particular specifications, we would at once be able to find the renewing element we seek. But we should not forget that one must not lean on a principle that is now under attack by forces seeking to destroy it. This principle is being undermined even before we are sufficiently fortified with respect to the dimension of the eternal that we are summoned to express.

Science is presently in revolt against absolutism in morals, which has heretofore been its beloved companion. Surely it will not prove to its credit in pursuing this course; it will no doubt change its position in one way or another, but it will always retain its independent way of looking at things. It is in rebellion against social morality in the name of individualism, which is also a moral claim. But we must in the end probe to the depths of this perception in its source in the psyche.

The assertion of individualism, which refuses to recognize subordination to any collective, forms the basis of the worst kind of anarchism. But it also stems from the highest scientific and moral sensibility, which does not see society as a composite with a constituency of those who serve and those who are served, of those who work and those for whom one works. Morality, in its highest level of nobility, does not wish to differentiate between individuals. It experiences equally every joy and every pain wherever it occurs in the endless realms of existence. Thus there is only the absolute individual. This feeling in itself, when it descends to a low level, is destructive of all positive morality, which is based on the relatedness to other individuals. The two extreme positions are only the marks of the boundary within which is explored the spirit of life and of knowledge. They will never be understood either from the lofty position that denies the particulars for the sake of the universal or from the lowly position that denies the universal for the sake of the realism of the particulars, which are close at hand and are subject to experience.

The definitive zone where the great vision ever beckons is built not of one particular perception, even if be as attractive and potent a concept as is that of absolute morality itself. It is built of general tendencies that in their organic orchestration present us with a universal overview, and offer us the basis for the affirmation of ideals, together with their practical and intellectual implementation. When we turn our attention to the wide horizon of the spiritual life, we see stretching before us an expanse embodying four components that embrace the totality of the cultural realm: the divine, the moral,* the religious and the national: (a) the spirit of God, in its general character that is free and absolute, transcending all knowledge and experience; it is precisely because it transcends all that it prepared the ground for the expansion of all branches of knowledge and of all the deepest and most general feelings that surround the spiritual condition of all existence; (b) the spirit of absolute morality, which develops in humanity as a result of divine prodding, stirring in the general soul of humanity, and which sometimes emerges as a potent, autonomous vision, unaware of its source; (c) the spirit of religious faith, in which are envisioned all the general theories emanating from the higher divine spirit and the spirit of absolute morality, but in a form pointing to action and to a way of life; (d) the national spirit, which defines the social boundary

---

*The category of the moral is missing in our text, clearly a printer's error, as may be seen from the context. Cf. Yeshayahu Hadari and Zvi Singer, *Perakim be Mishnato ha-Iyunit shel Harav Kook*, Vol. I, p. 48.

in its state of limited perfection and which includes within itself all spiritual forces in a manner adapted to its nature, and which also appropriates many elements from the three general expressions of culture [mentioned earlier] that transcend it in value and precede it in the order of genesis.

Obviously there are many expressions of life's vision and of lofty ideals, in each of which one may discern the particular spiritual trend from which they derive. However, the total strategy will be represented only through the influence of all the four components of the cultural world in their totality, especially in their organic integration and in their harmonious interrelatedness, in all the manifestations of life that continue to proliferate. Assimilation in the life of the spirit takes place in a wondrous manner. It is therefore truly impossible to find one pure tendency without some admixture from another. Despite this we always find aspirations that accentuate one component, without the other components being discernible. This at times results in a distortion of form—until a harmonious balance is reestablished that restores life to its proper form. From the perspective of holiness we see the two extreme attitudes toward the "ego" that inspire at the same time the highest kind of equity and the worst kind of anarchism that is bound to find redress from the depths of absolute destructiveness. Together they act to fuse the four limited cultural components that surround the world in all its fullness.

In whatever aspect of practical or spiritual life in which we encounter any deficiency, some lack of taste, or something that disgusts us, in action or in literature—it all derives from a lack of balance and harmonious relatedness between these general tendencies.

The community of Israel, which embraces all in its spirit—the living sanctuary dedicated to the great name of God who illumines the world with His glory—is stamped with the full influence of these four tendencies in their full characteristics. If one should gain ascendency and the other disappear, it would suffer a discernible weakening, which would also betoken as its cause a previous state of weakness. Even the inclination toward the divine in itself will not satisfy the Jewish people, which is universal in its disposition and aspires toward universality. They will automatically realize that the true aspiration for the divine is forever linked with the aspiration for morality, for religiosity and for nationhood in all their fullness. "God in His fullness for a world in its fullness." Certainly if either the moral, the religious or the national aspiration should reach out to detach itself from the "chariot" as a whole,* over which hovers the spirit of God, the defect will at once become apparent in the form of a "crisis," and it will necessarily return to its place and be reunited with the total ensemble in its fullness.

Peace in all realms of being is the concern of the heritage of the Jewish people. It derives explicitly from the vision of the prophets, to the extent that the prophetic illumination was able to preceive it, and it is interwoven with the most exalted thoughts in the depths of religion—but its first thrust must be to establish *internal peace.* The four basic cultural components, which register their impact on all humanity and whose glory fills the world, must necessarily act with individual autonomy to achieve their own perfection in the life of the individual person and of society as a whole. The sovereignty with which each important spiritual tendency addresses itself to the vision of life as a whole suggests to those who would effect unity on a shallow basis an image of divisiveness and opposition to another tendency and its resultant effects. This defect will be mended only with the full development, which will bring all into organic comprehensiveness, in which each will find its completion not by negating the other, but rather through the other's perfection and the enhancement of its authority. When

---

*An allusion to Ezekiel's vision of the chariot that bears the divine throne, here referring to the ensemble of the four levels of aspiration bearing the divine illumination.

this development, with its scientific expansion, embraces all these together, there will be revealed to us a new perspective in a very striking form to explain the reasons for the commandments, with sound historic validity directed also toward the future. Through the linking of all these tendencies there will become manifest for us the divine light, in such fullness and nobility as it is possible to disclose to us.

The divine, the moral, the religious and the national ideals, which are encountered in a state of separateness and conflict throughout the world, are in the Jewish perception in a state of integration so that much effort is needed to differentiate their particular influences on the practical aspect of Judaism.

If humanity is to find its happiness and perfection in all its aspects, it is essential that those sources of light shed their radiance in full togetherness in some appropriate organic form. Thus will be resolved all spiritual problems, of individuals and of nations, in a socio-spiritual form, in terms of that fullness and clarity which corresponds in breadth to the unity of God. This will parallel the far-visioned goal of socialism to solve the material problems of humanity. Conventional theology assumes that the different religions must necessarily oppose each other, that each one must by the very logic of its being negate the other. In dealing with the moral issue of tolerance, it is constrained to invoke the concept of doubt and uncertainty in the realm of religion. In doing so it resembles the immaturity in the personal and national, the economic and the social realms, which are in a state of opposition and competitiveness as long as human society is not yet fully developed.

On reaching full maturity the human spirit aspires to rise above all conflict and opposition. It will recognize all expressions of the spiritual life as an organic whole, in which differences in states will not be erased, in which there will remain a distinction between the primary and the peripheral, high and low, more holy and less holy, and between those two and the secular. But this will not be in a grievous form that inspires discord and hostility. It will be in a form similar to the division of organs in the body, and to the distinctive impulses in the fully developed spiritual life, each of which recognizes its place as well as that of its neighbor, whether it be below or above it.

When the light of Israel will emerge and make its appearance in the world, after purging itself with firmness and courage of the darkness and murkiness that attached themselves to it because of its lack of self-understanding, there will at once become manifest the precious vision of unity, which integrates all forces into one complete, comprehensive phenomenon, at the same time leaving intact the particular essence of each. The spiritual world in all its dimensions is patterned into one entity, so that even this area of religion that abounds in quarrels becomes filled with peace and light. There will remain a definite distinction in the levels of the different religions, in the values of one as against another, but through their general orchestration there will be made manifest automatically the central goal at the heart of the religions, which will then radiate light and the splendor of holiness upon the constituent individuals in the organic whole, each unit recognizing its value and its place.

This programmatic change, which bears within itself the assured beneficence of preparing the ground for the most perfect development, must necessarily be rooted in the graces of a national disposition in which the higher illumination of the sensibilities for the divine, the moral and the religious shall be well blended in essence, in an appropriate form, without conflict or inner contradiction. This precious grace we find in the impressive light of the reasons for the commandments, immanent in them in a manner that remains valid on all levels of life, as a dependable source for all the most advanced claims of a cultural, spiritual and practical nature. This harmonization,

312

fusing the four cultural dispositions into one full and abundant force for life through the medium of the commandments and their programmatic elaborations, channels into the practical aspect of religion the divine light that is above the conventional philosophizing in the study of religion. And those wondrous strategies that make up the expanse of Jewish history, that bear in them the fructifying element of the religious life in its greatest vitality, stand revealed to us in all their true authenticity.

The unity of existence, in its yearning to be included in the lofty, majestic and refined life of the divine, has its bastion in the community of Israel whose national spirit embraces all spiritual tendencies as its historic purpose. But it cannot allow the psychic life-force stirring in humanity to be separated from the cosmic life-force stirring existence generally. The peak idealism of humanity reaches its perfection through full identification with cosmic life in all its richness and majesty. The unity of the human spirit with the divine spirit, man's sovereignty over the world's lower creatures with an idealistic motivation inspired by the divine sensibility alive in him— this sovereignty began to be manifested in the miracles and wonders of the exodus from Egypt, which stamped the Jewish people with its historic character. The process of evolution that continues to move forward ceaselessly in all realms of existence also extends to the expanding spirit of humanity. It is only its insufficiently developed state that inhibits its spread to many different and conflicting areas to illumine them alike with the light of life.

It is only for a limited time that the rational soul will limit its concerns to the germination, growth and existence on the physiological plane. The general yearning for things that transcend those boundaries will in the end draw it toward the heights. When the spirit attains its climactic perfection, everything will shine together and at the same time. Just as the universal ["higher"] soul animates the divine *sefirot* [a term taken from the Cabbalah and signifying the ten immaterial divine forces released by God to engender and direct the material universe], so will it also animate "the dead." The spirit of the Jewish people, even in its latent state before its evolution as a separate national entity in all its fullness, when it was still part of the general life of ancient humanity, exerted an influence. The revelation of the Torah at a later date made this manifest for all the people in an act of "resurrection through the Torah."

The full scope of development in the human spirit cannot halt in the middle of the road and it will always pursue and attain its objective.

The very fact that national consciousness emerges before humanity consciousness, and the latter before cosmic consciousness, causes the vitalization of particular nations to precede the organic vitalization of humanity, of which all the prophets spoke. The latter must necessarily precede the vitalization of the constituent entities, which embraces everything, reaching down to include the vitalization of every individual, in all his splendor and glory, with which are associated reason and imagination, instinct and nature. The community of Israel does not grow weary in traveling on this eternal, long road. She treads on "the high places of the earth," ever aspiring toward "an unbounded inheritance" (Shabbat 118a) in which she will stand in one fellowship with "all His works and all His creatures."* All the awesome spreading out [lit., "thinning out"] of this aspiration does not blur the practical aspect of this aspiration of her national essence, which is sometimes effected by the pull of the powers of attraction. On the contrary, it endows it with greater force and clarity at the same time, for the full synthesis of all the life-forces in their togetherness is stored up in her treasure house. It is "the light of the universe in the treasure of life."

---

*An allusion to the High Holiday liturgy.

The coal releases such measure of heat as was stored up within it at the time of its formation. This principle of creation that ordains an equivalence between the potency imbibed by a subject at the time of creation and the influence exerted by it embraces also the life of the spirit, the diffusion of knowledge and morals. From this perspective the commandments are not associated with the reasons we find in them as artificially assigned tokens of remembrance, but as active subjects, synchronizing their role with the evolution of existence in a basic respect, which finds its clearest expression in the most mature portion of humanity—the community of Israel.

Love, the joy of life, which extends to the love of the sexes in its thrust toward the continuity of existence and the odyssey of its unfolding from generation to generation and from epoch to epoch, the divine yearning of elevating the meaning of existence, these are concentrated in all the high ideals that pervade life. The latter plant all the beautiful and fragrant flowers in the garden of the love between the sexes, which yields life innocence and happiness. The lower aspect of individualism deposited here its dross in a fierce, contemptible lust that manifested the shameful aspect of sex, in its psychological and pathological expressions.

The aspiration for practical and spiritual perfection, to condition the flesh and the spirit toward that love which endows all life with firmness and light, through the inner stirring of the longing to create life and to cultivate it toward its most ideal characteristic—this treasure of light is forever immanent, in all its splendor, in all its richness and goodness, in the stamp of the holy covenant of the commandment of circumcision.

The moral life cannot evolve to its highest development except through the influence of its divine source. The divine source will have its practical effect of preparing the way for a social culture only through a societal perfection that is first established in a stable and highly cultivated nation that is prepared to exist as a unique people. Its uniqueness is not enclosed in its particular nationality, which can stand competition with other nationalisms whose only purpose is confined in their own nationhood or in the social conditions they precipitate. The national content of this people can absorb what is glorious in all nations, the best of the idealism of fragmented humanity, and spread it later, in a more perfect and developed state, and in an appropriate and permanent form under the stamp of its own bold and luminous authenticity.

All the national commandments associated with Eretz Yisrael, and particularly with the Temple, the focusing of the divine service, out of all the broadest and most spiritual ideals, in this simple and natural framework that even a child can understand—this is one of the most basic expressions of the nature of life in its fullness, which links the lofty and the lowly. Thus it raises the lowly instincts and refines them, and lowers the lofty ideals that they may be merged with life.

This is the goal of the offering of sacrifices, which, in its development, must be concentrated particularly in one place, singled out from all humanity, where "many nations and kingdoms will gather to serve the Lord" (Ps. 102:23). With all the high flowering of culture, its natural base must be preserved in a "healthy state" (Ps. 73:4). The period of the world's infancy with its apparent wildness only adds a luxuriant wreath on the mature head of humanity, which is pervaded by eternal wisdom.

The stream of time changes its appearance but the thread of life is the same and it pervades all. The differentiation between the Jewish people and the other nations in the formative period of history was based on remembering the exodus from Egypt, which distinguished it "from all the people on the face of the earth" (Exod. 33:16). Historical culture continued to grow in enlightenment. The seeds sown by the concentration of the divine service had their effect, directly or indirectly, on all life. The hidden reverberations that are engendered in humanity when an important part of it is openly agitated by some movement constitute a force of very great potency. The renewal of the Jewish people in its thrust toward the future is directed with all its resources in a veritably opposite direction from that of the exodus from Egypt. It moves toward unification with all humanity in an organic way, after all its organs have been prepared for the influence toward perfection. *The flow of moral strategies becomes during the period of differentiation the preparatory channel for organic unification.*

The free movement of the moral impulse to establish justice for animals generally and the claim of their rights from mankind are hidden in a natural psychic sensibility in the deeper layers of the Torah. In the ancient value system of humanity, while the spiritual illumination (which later found its bastion in Israel) was diffused among individuals without involvement in a national framework, before nations were differentiated into distinct speech forms, the moral sense had risen to a point of demanding justice for animals. "The first man had not been allowed to eat meat" (Sanhed. 59b), as is implied in God's instruction to Adam: "I have given you every herb yielding seed which is on the face of all the earth, and every tree in which is the fruit of a tree yielding seed—it shall be to you for food" (Gen. 1:29). But when humanity, in the course of its development, suffered a setback and was unable to bear the great light of its illumination, its receptive capacity being impaired, it was withdrawn from the fellowship with other creatures, whom it excelled with firm spiritual superiority. Now it became necessary to confine the concern with justice and equity to mankind, so that divine fire, burning with a very dim light, might be able to warm the heart of man, which had cooled off as a result of the many pressures of life. The changes in thought and disposition, in the ways of

317

particularized developments, required that moral duty be concentrated on the plane of humanity alone. But the thrust of the ideals in the course of their development will not always remain confined. Just as the democratic aspiration will reach outward through the general intellectual and moral perfection, "when man shall no longer teach his brother to know the Lord, for they will all know Me, small and great alike" (Jer. 31:34), so will the hidden yearning to act justly toward animals emerge at the proper time. What prepares the ground for this state is the commandments, those intended specifically for this area of concern.

There is indeed a hidden reprimand between the lines of the Torah in the sanction to eat meat, for it is only after "you will say, I will eat meat, because you lust after eating meat— then you may slaughter and eat" (Deut. 12:20, 12:15). The only way you would be able to overcome your inclination would be through a moral struggle, but the time for this conquest is not yet. It is necessary for you to wage it in areas closer to yourself. The long road of development, after man's fall, also needs physical exertion, which will at times require a meat diet, which is a tax for passage to a more enlightened epoch, from which animals are not exempt. Human beings also acted thus in their most justified wars, which were incumbent on them as a transition to a higher general state.

This is the advantage of the moral sense when it is linked to its divine source. It knows the proper timing for each objective, and it will sometimes suppress its flow in order to gather up its strength for future epochs, something that the impatient kind of morality that is detached from its source would be unable to tolerate. When the animal lust for meat became overpowering, if the flesh of all living beings had been forbidden, then the moral destructiveness, which will always appear at such times, would not have differentiated between man and animal, beast and fowl and every creeping thing on the earth. The knife, the axe, the guillotine, the electric current, would have felled them all alike in order to satisfy the vulgar craving of so-called cultured humanity.

The commandments, therefore, came to regulate the eating of meat, in steps that will take us to the higher purpose. The living beings we are permitted to eat are limited to those that are most suitable to the nature of man. The commandment to cover the blood of an animal or bird captured while hunting focuses on a most apparent and conspicuous inequity. These creatures are not fed by man, they impose no burden on him to raise them and develop them. The verse "If anyone . . . captures by hunting any beast or bird that may be eaten, he must pour out its blood, covering it with earth" (Lev. 17:13) involves an acknowledgement of a shameful act. This is the beginning of moral therapy, as is suggested in the verse, ". . . that you may remember and be ashamed . . . when I forgive you" (Ezek. 16:63). It means: Cover the blood! Hide your shame! These efforts will bear fruit, in the course of time people will be educated. The silent protest will in time be transformed into a mighty shout and it will triumph in its objective. The regulations of slaughter, in special prescriptions, to reduce the pain of the animal registers a reminder that we are not dealing with things outside the law, that they are not automatons devoid of life, but with living things. What is inscribed in such letters on rolls of parchment will be read in the future, when the human heart will be conditioned for it. The feelings of the animal, the sensitivity to its family attachment implied in the role not to slaughter an ox or a sheep "with its young on the same day" (Lev. 22:28), and, on the other hand, the caution against callous violation of the moral sense in an act of cruelty shown particularly in the breakup of the family implied in the directive concerning a bird's nest, to let the mother bird go before taking the young (Deut. 22:26-27)—all these join in a mighty demonstration against the general inequity that stirs every heart, and renews vitality even to souls that have strayed, whose hearts have

ABRAHAM ISAAC KOOK

grown dull because of sickness and anger. The divine protest
could not extend to man's right over the animal raised by him,
until a much later time. Then concern will even be shown for
the taste of the food eaten by the tilling animal, expressing a
permanent spirit of compassion and an explicit sense of justice. "Oxen and asses that till the soil will eat their fodder
savored with spices, and winnowed with shovel and fan to
remove the chaff" (Isa. 30:24).

The prohibition of eating the fat comes to us, on the
other hand, in a subdued call. If, by necessity, to strengthen
your prowess, you slaughter the animal, which you raised by
your exertion, do not indulge in this to satisfy the vulgar
craving that lusts for fat, especially in the primitive stages of
man. When the savage luxury of eating fat and blood—one
can always find room for a delicacy—is forbidden, it takes
away the worst element of this cruel gluttony. The impact of
this provision will become apparent in the full maturing of
culture that is due to come in the future.

The legal inequity in the ownership of property is registered in the prohibition of wearing a mixed garment of wool
and linen. We are inhibited from the free mixing of wool,
which was taken by robbery from the innocent sheep, with
flax, which was acquired by equitable, pleasant and cultured
labor. The animal will yet rise in cultural status through the
control of a higher moral sense, so that its readiness for
idealistic participation with man will not be strange or far
away. Therefore we are directed to add to the fringe on a
linen garment a woolen thread of blue,* and similarly to mix
freely a mixture of wool and linen in the garment of the priests
(Exod. 28:5, 8).**

The mixing of meat and milk is a grave offense, an act
that is pervaded altogether with the oppression of life, an

---

*As a reminder of God and of the divine law ordained in Numbers 15:38.
**The priestly vestments were to be made of "blue, purple and scarlet" yarn, which is of
wool and twined linen.

320

oppression of a living being—and of property. Milk, which serves so naturally to feed the tender child, that he might enjoy the mother's breast, was not created so as to stuff with it the stomach, when you are so hard and cruel as to eat meat. The tender child has a prior and more natural right than you.

Just as the rule to cover the blood extends the sway of "You shall not murder" to the domain of the animal, and the prohibition of mixing meat and milk and the banning of linen and wool in a garment extends the injunctions, "You shall not rob" and "You shall not oppress," so does the rule against eating the meat of an animal killed by another animal or one that died by itself extend the duty to offer help and visit the sick to the animal kingdom: be compassionate at least on the unfortunate ones, if your heart is insensitive to the healthy and the strong.

When this seed is planted in the thick earth of the field blessed by the Lord, it will bear its fruit. It is necessary for its cultivation to join all these sensibilities into a national center so that the echo released by the moral voice shall not be the voice of weaklings, of ascetics and timid spirits, but the firm and joyous voice of life.

I entered here a limited analysis, but the road is long and wide. We must express not only a submerged feeling. Our concern is not only the need of defending Judaism in the diaspora where it is suffering decline. Ours must be "the voice of God with might," the voice "that hews out flames of fire" (Ps. 29:4, 7), the embodiment of the four spiritual dimensions that bring the goal to its fullest expression. "And the spirit of the Lord will rest on him, the spirit of wisdom and understanding, the spirit of counsel and might, the spirit of knowledge and of the fear of the Lord" (Isa. 11:2).

To sum it all up, the unification of our thought through joining its various trends and expressions is what effects the unification and integration of the substantive manifestations of life. All that we suffer from defective thinking embodied in life and in literature comes about only from an ideational fragmentation, in which partisans of one ideal refuse to countenance the perfection of the other, failing to rise to the level of seeking the amplification of their own view by integration with all views, seemingly different from their own, in an organic unity that bears within itself the light of life and peace.

The area that is more likely to embrace the influence of all the levels of values—the divine, the moral, the religious and the national—in the formative purpose of life, whose effect will soon be recognized in our own time, while its roots go deep and will offer nourishment for future generations—this is the almost neglected domain of the reasons for the commandments. This is due to be an enlightening influence on the scientific study of Judaism, to fructify its dimensions.

It is true that these tendencies have long been immanent in the soul of our people, but the circumstances of exile narrowed them, and the three other levels of value were included in a strategy of transition within the national component alone. But the spirit disturbed our peace. From time to time one or another component emerged in some dramatic way, the yearning for the divine, for instance, through the movements of philosophy and Hasidism; the moral through the various expressions of humanism; the national through the agitation* going on in our own time. But these disturbed the religious dimension of Judaism when they emerged from it, adding to its troubles. They diminished its vitality by sucking up its fructifying power. It is for this reason that we note to our astonishment the decline of religious Judaism precisely in a period of the national renaissance. But this is simple: It is its belated crisis, which has sucked up the vitality immanent in it until recent times.

These developments cannot go on in their chaotic form. We must mend with courage and with knowledge past abuses.

---

*The reference is, no doubt, to the Zionist movement.

•

We must gather up all spiritual trends that have been dispersed to their center, to ingather the spiritual fugitives of Israel and the dispersed of Judah. Through this spiritual ingathering of the exiles there will be released the physical potency for the ingathering upon the holy soil, the place suited for the realization of all ideals in their different aspects from potentiality to actuality. This will be effected not through individuals or parties, but through the *nation*, through the aggregate of the community of Israel, that will blossom in the beloved land, the fairest heritage of any nation.

Letters

A Note on the Text

Rabbi Kook was also a prolific letter writer. Some of his letters consist of but a few lines; others are extended discussions of various themes of mutual interest between him and his correspondent. They roam over the entire range of his many concerns in theology, law and practical affairs, but some are purely personal and offer a precious insight into the private world of his own life.

The sense of crisis in Jewish life pervades these letters. He reacts to the decadence of Jewish piety, to the wide defections from Jewish belief and practice, and to the alienation of youth, many of whom had chosen various secular ideologies ranging from Marxism to Zionism. His response to this crisis is a call for inner renewal, for focusing Jewish religious life not on the formalism of habituated practices, but on its moralistic and spiritual dimension. This he maintains is at the heart of the true meaning of Judaism, but it has been neglected. It is the sterility of the conventional way that has engendered the alienation, and through inner renewal and revitalization there will be a reconciliation.

Many of his letters are defensive. They answer critics who charged him with deviating from tradition in his doctrinal position as in his legal decisions. His decision that circumvented the traditional requirement that all agricultural labor be suspended every seventh year (as *shemitah*) came under special attack by conventional pietists. He argued that reality made this mandatory, and that there is ample precedent in Jewish law for reckoning with the claim of reality. Some of his letters refer to his attempt to launch a new party in Zionism that would transcend the separatism between the religious and the nonreligious.

Many of his letters are addressed to his son and there are a number of letters to his parents. These show deep love and tenderness. Some of his letters bemoan his involvement in the world of practical affairs, while all his being craved solitude and the opportunity to think and write. In one of his letters, which is included here, he sought a position outside the rabbinate, which imposed on him duties that were contrary to his nature. All his letters show him as a person of modesty and compassion, of breadth of vision, and of rare courage to stand behind his commitments no matter how unpopular. Every aspect of Jewish life concerned him, but his vision embraced the world, and he assessed the significance of Judaism by its role as a channel of world liberation.

The letters were published in a one-volume edition under the title *Igrot Rayah* in Jerusalem in 1923. A three-volume edition under the title *Igrot Ha-Rayah* appeared in Jerusalem in 1946 under the auspices of a special organization that concerns itself with the publication of Rabbi Kook's writings, with the cooperation of the Mosad Harav Kook.

The letters included here in translation are taken from the three-volume collection, but in one instance the text in the old edition was followed because it seemed more authentic. The published letters cover only a relatively short period of his active life, from 1888 to 1919. What was undoubtedly the most active period of his life, the years of his tenure as Chief Rabbi, is not reflected in these volumes.

By the grace of God, the holy city of Jaffa,
may it be rebuilt and established,
Mar-Heshvan 13, 5667 (1907)

*To my beloved son, the delight of my heart and soul, may he live to a
long and good life, Amen.*

You made me happy with your lovely and enlightening letter. How I would like to write you at length, but you
know, without my telling you, the usual distractions. But
please do not stint with your precious letters, and ease our
spirit, which is anxious to know almost daily about your
well-being, and everything that pertains to your condition.
Please write us how you have arranged your affairs, and
details about your studies. Please accustom yourself, my dear,
also to study and to read the writings of the later masters in
pilpul[1] so that, with the help of God, you may be satisfactorily
familiar with the style of the creative analysis of the law,
logically and with good sense. As to your study of moralistic
and speculative works, it seems to me that I need not exhort
you. You are already used to this. I hope that you will not
abandon this habit, which leads to every good, but you must
arrange this in a proper schedule, that you do not waste too
much energy in studying *halakhic* [legal] material beyond what
is necessary. And may the Lord lead you in the ways of
uprightness and equity.
Convey loving regards to Rabbi Uri Michelson, long may
he live; similarly convey loving regards to Rabbi Israel
Porath, long may he live.

---

1. Talmudic dialectics.

As to Rabbi Orenstein, judge him mercifully, as I judge him. From his point of view, he surely thinks that there is some benefit or, God forbid, the fulfillment of a command- ment in disparaging my worth. If he is in error concerning this, in my humble opinion, it is not appropriate to be exact- ing concerning an offense committed unintentionally. I hope that he will not hurt me in any way, neither materially nor spiritually. Maimonides in one of his letters put it thus: "Whoever wishes to suppress what has been disclosed will only add greater publicity to it."[2] Thank God, I have received letters from important rabbis concerning *Ikve ha-Zon*[3] accord- ing it the highest praise. May the Lord, praised be He, grant me, for His name's sake, to enhance the Torah and to glorify it, and to contribute to the appreciation of the study of the inner dimension of the Torah, in its authenticity, thereby to raise the dignity of the people of Israel and of the Holy Land generally. This will also enhance the esteem for Jerusalem, the city that is a source of strength to us. "Let Mount Zion be glad, let the cities of Judah rejoice" (Ps. 48:12).

If you should happen to see Rabbi Yakov Moshe Harlap, convey to him my loving regards, and congratulate him in my name for having arranged the publication of the holy manu- script of the Gaon and Zaddik, Rabbi Zevi Michal, his mem- ory be for a blessing. But caution him to be very careful about his health, and not endanger himself even for the publication of the above Torah study. It is possible to contribute new Torah studies at any time, but one can never retrieve a lost soul in Israel.[4]

As to the tales in *Avkat Rokhel*, for the most part there is

---

2. The footnote to Rabbi Kook's letter refers to the letter of Maimonides to Joseph ben Gabor. Those sentiments are expressed in the letter, but the quotation is not there. Cf. *Igrot ha-Rambam*, Mekize Nirdamim, Jerusalem, 1946, pp. 88-89.

3. One of Rabbi Kook's writings.

4. The last phrase, "one can never retrieve. . ." is found verbatim in Maimonides, *Mishne Torah*, Hilkhot Milah, ch. 1, end.

contained in them a systematic and forceful criticism of all the evil, the vulgarity and the absurdity of idolatry. It is only when these are brought out from the very narrow framework of a most puzzling tale that it takes on proper meaning. This is the nature of the study of mystical themes, but such matters were never written for a tendentious purpose, to achieve thereby some premeditated goal. It is similar to emotionally stirring poetry, which is not written for an ulterior purpose. This is the nature of the soul. Poems written for an ulterior purpose lack the genuine spirit of poetry. Parables written with such motivation are meaningless tales. The entire content of the genuine and holy parables is a faithful translation of the soul's vision in its realm of inwardness. This is its natural language. The practical truth is distilled from it according to its natural style of expression, assigning to wisdom its task to embrace and link the two worlds in full unity.

Be strong my son, be strong in the study of Torah, of morals and of good manners and, above all, in the true fear of God. Through the genuine love for Him will you grow and succeed in the mastery of His Torah, may His name be praised, as befits your own precious self and your father who is attached to you in love with all his heart and soul.

Igrot, I, Letter 40

By the grace of God, the holy city of Jaffa,
may it be rebuilt and established,
Shevat 12, 5667 (1907)

*I send greetings and good wishes to my precious friend, the renowned
scholar, in whom is everything delightful, our master Rabbi Avigdor
Rivlin, may he live to a long and good life, Amen.*

I have received from you several letters, and I have not
had the opportunity to answer you, as befits the love and
respect I feel toward you. Please forgive me and judge me
charitably.

I am most grateful to you, my friend, for your sincere
advice and for your indication that you wish to help me in the
sacred endeavor of printing my work through the Orthodox
community[1] in Germany. But it is not in accordance with my
nature to seek special favors. I only wish what the Lord,
praised be He, in His great mercy, will provide through such
circumstances as offer themselves as the spiritual effort moves
toward its climactic development. Thus I long to write and to
publish to the extent of my abilities. Perhaps as a result of
this, God will grant that some people of means will realize
that I am worthy of assistance so that I might publish material
that I have hidden in the heart or in manuscript form in my
home. But to present myself as a warring partisan, when I
love peace and seek it with all my heart and soul, especially
when I realize that particularly in Eretz Yisrael it is wrong to
accentuate differences, even for the sake of heaven—how is it
possible for me to adopt a style that is contrary to my spirit
and nature?

---

1. The Hebrew is *yereim*, lit. "the pious".

On the contrary, it is my hope that the Orthodox leaders in Germany will also recognize that they need to add to their way the broader and more enlightened approach. This consists in finding the dimension of light and holiness hidden deep in every individual Jew, and to bring it forth from all defilements that have attached themselves to him through alien influences. Then will hearts draw closer, and the house of Israel will be built progressively toward a united people dedicated to God on the Holy Land.

As to your condition, my advice is that if memebers of your family should write you that there is a way of holding on to the store by having your son join you, then it certainly would not be advisable to leave your business. But if there is a possiblity to transfer it to another city, it would be best. However, this is somewhat unrealistic. In my humble opinion it is therefore advisable to remain in the city of Boisk, as heretofore.

I ask you once again not to be angry that I sometimes delay answering you. You should know that my friendship for you is as genuine as it ever was, and perhaps even more so. But my distractions impede me. And do not deal with me measure for measure, but send us your precious letters, full of delight, which bring joy to my soul that is linked with you in love.

I will close with greeting and best wishes, as befits your great spirit and your friend who seeks your well-being, with great love.

Igrot, I, Letter 53

ABRAHAM ISAAC KOOK

By the grace of God, the holy city of Jaffa,
may it be rebuilt and established,
Menahem Av 14, 5667 (1907)

*To my dear friend, the honorable Rabbi Jehiel Mikhal Tikazinski,
may he live to a long and good life, peace and blessing.*

I find it necessary to share with you my proposal. As
you are aware, to our great sorrow, our revered Rabbi Isaac
Blaser has been taken from us, may the memory of the righteous be for a blessing. Under the cirumstances it appears that
it will be necessary to appoint an appropriate person to attend
to his work in the affairs of the *kolel*.[1] The work of the rabbinate is contrary to my disposition and my strength, and I am
most anxious to live in the Holy Land without the burden of
having to serve as a dispenser of legal decisions. Perhaps your
honor can transmit my proposal to those competent to act that
if they should see fit to choose humble me for the work of the
kolel, I would, in my humble opinion, be qualified for this,
with God's help. It seems to me that thus I would be able to
attain my goal to live in the holy city of Jerusalem, may it be
rebuilt and restored, without the yoke of the rabbinate and
involvement in legal matters.

If your honor has any suggestion to make, I hope you will
not delay honoring me with your reply. If there be any impediment, let it be as though I never mentioned it. And my
reward and my blessing, my help and consolation, will be

---

1. The kolel was a community of families that immigrated to the Holy Land from the
same country, before the Zionist movement, and devoted themselves to prayer and study,
depending for their maintenance on a charity fund to which the pious in the old country
contributed.

when God delivers His people, and shows compassion to His poor, and Zion and Jerusalem are comforted by the light of His deliverance.

Igrot, I, Letter 84

By the grace of God, the holy city of Jaffa,
I Adar II, 5678 (1908)

To my dear friend, the wondrous and brilliant sage, master of mystical wisdom, Rabbi Pinhas Ha-Kohen, may he live to a long and good life, chief of the Bet Din of the city Birz, may God watch over his coming and going, peace, peace, and blessing.

The precious pamphlet "The Building of the Nation" came to my attention. I read it with inner joy. I thank God who privileged me to reach this time, when the great rabbis have begun to concern themselves with the problems of our people on the basis of the Torah, in a scientific manner, one that will not prove embarrasing to us in any public discussion with friend or foe. But I cannot deny, my friend, that there is need to improve the style in subsequent printings, especially to be more careful as much as possible to avoid glaring errors in grammar, which inspire small-minded people, who are the majority, to belittle the general importance of the subjects treated.

I trust that you will take my advice in this respect, which is very simple, to give every issue before printing to someone who is familiar with Hebrew grammar to correct the most glaring matters. I also dare to ask your honor to beware of all homiletical and similar tendencies when dealing with subjects of great gravity. It is always important to preserve the demarcation line between one world and another, and the low-level type of homiletics must not be allowed to intrude on serious expositions. In any case, these deficiencies are like spots on the bright sun in the sky, in comparison with the great enlightenment that your honor will disseminate through his wonderful books, when they will make their appearance in the world, with God's help.

Truthfully, I must tell you my friend that I find nothing to criticize in your position. It is forged of pure gold of the old and the new under the holy influence of the inner dimension of the Torah, consistent with what I have long known you to be and your way of thinking. But you have recently added much learning and thought through the holy sparks you have raised from the multitude of shells of the new literature. Congratulations. This way is becoming for us, this is the approach that is obligatory for us.

On my part I am prepeared to support you in any way I can, for all are obligated to assist in a work for the sake of God. My brother Samuel, who arranged for the publication of my writings, is now in Jerusalem on business, but I do not know if he will attend to the matter of publishing. In any case I hope that my brothers will be among the friends who will assist you. Though material help will obviously not be able to come from the Holy Land, under present conditions, there is, however, hope for moral support of commendation and publicity, which are also important in a general undertaking.

I would have wanted to write your honor at greater length, but I am under many pressures, and there are many letters I must write and things I must do. But I cannot omit mentioning that we must be actively involved in the restoration of our people in the Holy Land, and that we dare not reject anything. We must be critical of the people of little faith who narrow God's role only to the way they envision it in their imagination. As the Baal Shem Tov[1] said, We must serve the Lord in all ways, so must we also anticipate the redemption in all ways. It is one of the fundamental principles in the service of God, concerning which we are examined on the day of Judgment (Shabbat 31a). One way does not negate the other

---

1. Israel ben Eliezer, the founder of Hasidism.

at all. What we must do is clear the paths, remove with all our strength the thorns and weeds and stumbling blocks that come up on them. But in their essence all paths lead toward the goal and the value of a path does not diminish because it is more immediately and plausibly directed toward the goal. On the contrary, "The Lord created the earth with wisdom" (Prov. 3:19), on which the Zohar (III 256b) comments that it was particularly the *sefira* "wisdom"[2] that engendered the *sefira* "sovereignty."[3] The final point I cite is: "The stone which the builders rejected" will serve as the most important building block for the shelter.[4]

From the published letter that was sent to him, your honor is certainly familiar with my objective in establishing a new type of Yeshivah to serve the needs of the new Yishuv generally. It is to revitalize it with the dew of Torah and to establish a regular and publicized study of the subjects of belief, in which the mystical aspect of the Torah, according to the system of the Cabbalah, in all its dimensions, will have a prominent part. Let us work, let us work, let us do what we can. The truth will sprout from the earth, and equity will look down upon us from heaven.[5] Undoubtedly, it is the spirit of God that bestirs us to act, and His light and His truth will support us to strengthen weak hands and make firm feeble knees.

Concerning the other religions I will state to your honor my opinion, that it is not the aim of the enlightenment that emanates from Israel to absorb or destroy them, just as it is not our aim to destroy the world's different nationalities. Our aim is rather to perfect them and to elevate them, to purge them of their dross. Then they will automatically be joined to the root

---

2. The first of the proliferating divine potencies, wholly immaterial and transcendent.

3. Where the material order begins.

4. In Ps. 118:22 the text reads: "The stone which the builders rejected has become the chief foundation stone."

5. A paraphrase of Ps. 85:12

of Israel, which will exert on them an enlightening influence. "I will purge the blood[6] from his mouth and the abominations from between his teeth, and he, too, shall remain for our God" (Zech. 9:7). This applies even to idolatrous cults, and certainly so to faiths that are partly based on the light of Israel's Torah. Noteworthy in this respect is the statement of Rabbi Elijah Gaon on the verse, "But Esau I hated" (Mal. 1:3): This refers to the peripheral part of Esau, but the essential part of him, his head, was interred with the patriarchs. It is for this reason that the man of truth, Jacob, the man of integrity said [on his reunion with Esau]: "I have seen you, it is like seeing the face of God" (Gen. 33:10). His word shall not go down as a vain utterance. The brotherly love of Esau and Jacob, of Isaac and Ishmael,[7] will assert itself above all the confusion that the evil brought on by our bodily nature has engendered. It will overcome them and transform them to eternal light and compassion. This broad concept, sweetened by the enlightenment of the true teaching of the Torah, must be our guide on all our ways in the end of days, to seal our understanding of the Torah with the imprint of the Messiah by turning the bitter to sweet, and darkness to light.

It is particularly at this time that we are ready to move from one branch of study to another and to be liberated from the curse alluded to in the statement that there is no peace for one who leaves one branch of study for another (Hagigah 10a). The basic reason for the lack of harmony[8] in the world and in Judaism is that a multiplicity of forces are exerting their influence simultaneously. The old way of choosing one path and

---

6. An allusion to violence or the idolatrous practice of eating the flesh of the sacrificial animal with the blood.

7. Traditionally the feud between Jacob and Esau was seen as a prototype for the hostility between Jews and Christians, and the feud between Isaac and Ishmael as a prototype for the hostility between Jews and Moslems. Elijah Gaon's discussions of Esau's internment is in *Saarat Eliahu*, ed. Warsaw, 1877, p. 50.

8. I follow here the text in the earlier edition of Rabbi Kook's letters (*Igrot Rayah*, Jerusalem, 1923) which is clearly superior to the later edition.

following it patiently can no longer prevail. We have developed far beyind this. To embrace all paths and to integrate them into a full and secure harmony—this is the beginning of the process to which Rabbi Meir alluded when by a change of the Hebrew letter *ayin* to the letter *aleph* in the word *or* he turned the sentence in Genesis 3:21 from: "And the Lord God made for Adam and his wife garments of skin and robed them" into: "And the Lord God made for Adam and his wife garments of light and robed them" (Genesis Rabbah 20:12 on Gen. 3:21).[9] It is this that made it difficult for Rabbi Meir's colleague to comprehend the full thrust of his thinking (Erubin 13b). He also refused to retreat from his practice of studying Torah under Aher[10] when the latter rode on his horse on the Sabbath (Hagigah 15a), and he did not hesitate to intercede after Aher's death that the heavenly tribunal that had rejected Aher without a trial reverse itself and try him, so that after submitting to the judgment he might be granted a share in the life of the world to come.[11] There was only one Aher in that generation, and there was one great spirit among them, Rabbi Johanan, who interceded with the heavenly tribunal and stopped the purging fires of hell that worked on him. We shall purge the many Ahers in our midst in order to bring them to the life of the world to come, to mend their defects and to bring the best among them into the fellowship of life; not one among them shall be rejected. It seems to me that in a previous conversation we touched on the concept that the righteous of the past had as their task to mend the tortured and rejected souls of former generations. This sacred responsibility must not be neglected in these latter days.[12] The souls of the

---

9. The Hebrew word *or* may have as the initial letter *ayin* which means "skin" or *aleph* which means "light."

10. Elisha ben Avuah, a Talmudic sage who lost his faith and became a heretic when his name was changed to *aher*, "another"; he had become a different person.

11. The Talmudic legend of the efforts by Rabbi Meir and Rabbi Johanan to win for Aher a share in the world to come is found in the tractate Hagigah 15b.

12. I follow here also the text in the earlier edition of the letters. The term used is *abrit ba-yamin*, which generally refers to the messianic age. Rabbi Kook believed that we were living in this stage of history.

wicked damage the world but when they are mended the world progresses again toward nobility.

With all my heart I look forward to the time when your honor will enlighten us with your wonderful books. May it be God's will that many join with us in fellowship, to labor in the vineyard of the house of Israel in wisdom, according to the truth.

May peace and God's blessing be on His people, as is the wish of your precious self and your friend who longs to see the enhancement of your teaching, with great love.

Igrot, I, Letter 112

ABRAHAM ISAAC KOOK

The holy city of Jaffa,
may it be rebuilt and established,
Nisan 22, 5668 (1908)

Greetings of peace to the renowned scholar, celebrated for wisdom and piety, our master, Rabbi H. Elazar Hakohen Bihovsky, may he live to a long and good life, Amen.

Your precious letter, written with the zeal of a sensitivie Jew, reached me, and though I am always ready to associate myself with the God-fearing people in any measure they project to strengthen the Torah, especially here in Eretz Yisrael, I am compelled to remind those engaged in work for the sake of heaven to be knowledgeable in what they do. As our sages said (Ber. 33a), Knowledge is important, for the Bible in one sentence mentions God twice as the God of knowledge [I Sam. 2:3, "For the Lord is a God of knowledge"].

Your honor must know that only a minor phase of the problem can be corrected through the method you suggest, through help from the government. The fundamental problem derives from more basic causes. The decline has come about not because the sages failed to protest against the heretics, who are undermining our Holy Land spiritually and materially, but because all they did was to protest, and no more . . .

As I see it, the reason that everything done to strengthen Judaism and the position of the Jewish community in all its aspects is unsuccessful is because of the neglect of the spiritual dimension, a total neglect in heart and mind. Everyone is trying to improve the "unenlightened piety," as though it

342

were possible to keep alive the body without the soul. I am prepared to say that even Hasidism whose entire raison d'être was to illumine every heart and mind with the divine light in its richness and splendor has changed its character. It now follows the way of conventional piety so that there is no difference between it and the non-Hasidic community. For this reason has love gone from the heart and all faces are stern, and reveal anger and depression. It is for this reason that all is in a state of decline.

P.S. Because of my preoccupation I cannot write at greater length at this time. I will close with many blessings, as befits your precious self and your friend who extends to you from the Holy Land best wishes for success in your endeavors in behalf of Torah.

Igrot, Vol. I, Letter 132

By the grace of God, the holy city of Jaffa,
may it be rebuilt and established,
Iyar 19, 5668 (1908)

Greetings of peace and blessing from the Holy Land to my beloved
friend, the sage honored for his knowledge of Torah and his true piety,
our master Rabbi Duber Milstein, may he live to a long and good life,
Amen.

It is some time since to my joy your honor's letter
reached me. I was happy to read your communication, which
is dear to me as is usual among faithful friends. But I was also
greatly saddened about your grief concerning your children. I
have wanted to write you before, as you requested, but my
distractions hindered me. I have only now been freed for a
little while, to write you briefly.

Yes, my friend, I understand well your sorrowing heart.
But if you should think as many of our Torah scholars do,
that it is in order at this time to reject those children who have
strayed from the ways of the Torah and religious faith, having
been carried away by the raging currents of the times—I say
unhesitatingly that this is not the way God wants. It is written in Tosefot, Sanhedrin 26b. s.v. "he-Hashud," that one
suspected of a sexual transgression is not to be disqualified as
a witness, because he is regarded as though he acted under
duress, that he was overpowered by his passion. It is written
similarly in Tosefot, Gittin 41b, s.v. "Kofin," that a person
who was aroused by a maid to commit an unchaste act is
regarded as having acted under duress. The same applies to
the "bad maid," the trend of the times, who has been permitted by the will of heaven to exercise sway prior to being
totally vanquished, and who has seduced many of our young

children with all her many charms to whore after her. They were fully under duress, and God forbid that we judge them as having acted voluntarily.

There is therefore hope for all of them. The inner essence of Jewish holiness remains hidden in their hearts under many good attributes that are to be found among them. The fact that evil was able to trap them was also due to their inner inclination toward good and kindness. When all the iniquity that prevails in the social order, according to their perspective, was portrayed before them, they became warriors for the improvement of society. Though they err in this in every respect, we cannot, however, compare them to the wicked who are only drawn after their animal passions, without any equitable motivation. If we should not throw stones on these fallen ones, but try to befriend them, as far as possible, then, when the current of the times will change and they realize the error in their basic philosophy, because of which they abandoned their moorings, they will be ready to repent and to change for the better. As a result of this, future generations will be influenced to rise to a very high level, holding firmly to the glory of Israel and to the light of God that shines in them so brightly.

Therefore, according to my opinion, my advice to your honor is that while you cannot take on yourself more than what is possible, still to the extent that you can, befriend them with assistance toward their livelihood and their pressing needs. This will give you the opportunity to express in your letters some admonition with good sense. It is in the nature of words that come from the heart to have an effect, whether much or little. Even the little is very important.

The way to admonish these young people basically is for the time being to exhort them not to give up their love for their people, from which they derive, and not to imagine that they will find an honorable way of life through fellowship with those of an alien people. They befriend them only when it is to their advantage, but in times of trouble they will rejoice

345

in their downfall. Through stimulating them to a love for their people, there will be aroused in them the feeling for religious faith and inclination to holiness that remain hidden in the Jewish soul. This may also result in a mending of behavior, which can result finally in the therapy of full penitence. But we must not despair of any of our holy children, and "a myrtle that stands among reeds is still a myrtle and is called a myrtle" (Sanhedrin 44a).

The penitence that will be inspired by reason and the aspiration for equity after the great and widespread crisis of the present need not be envisioned as accompanied by a fearful melancholy and shattering anxiety as we characterize ordinary penitence. It will be a simple expression of good sense, as a person who corrects an error in arithmetic that has been made clear to him through a clarification of the numbers. It is understandable, however, that one cannot avoid altogether being troubled by noting the crooked path we followed in our straying, each in his own way. And it is well for your honor to know that since all who joined the fighting armies of the time, in whatever cause they embraced, were inspired by a rational goal, according to their own opinion, their return will also be inspired by reason. Penitence inspired by reason is truly penitence out of love, which is very firm and honorable, and it is to such as these that the liturgy alludes when it promises that a redeemer will come "to those in Jacob who have turned from transgression."

The transgressors and rebels who are not prisoners of lust but of mistaken views will come back in a very high state of virtue. There is hope, therefore, for all our children, for most of them as for all of them, and let us hold on to them and not abandon them. "Instead of telling them, You are not My people, let them be called the children of the living God" (Hos. 2:1).

I close with best wishes and with great love, as befits your precious self and your friend who wishes you success in your endeavors in Torah, and who hopes that you will be privileged to witness God's blessings in the Holy Land, and in the happiness of His people on it, speedily, in our time, Amen.

Igrot, Vol. I, Letter 138

By the grace of God, the holy city, Jaffa,
may it be rebuilt and established,
Shevat 7, 5669 (1909)

Peace and blessing to my dear friend, the renowned sage, who seeks
after mystical knowledge and brings up pearls of wisdom from the
depths, our master Rabbi Pinhas ha-Kohen. May he prosper in his
studies, in body and soul, and in all that pertains to him.

A long time has passed, and I have been altogether
unable to discharge my obligation to you, my friend, by replying to your precious letters, to a point that I feel embarrassed to discharge it now, after so long a lapse of time. I feel
especially so because I cannot, under any circumstances, meet
what is needed to reply at length to every detail of your
communication, which is so rich in feeling and thought. The
gap between the trend of my thinking and yours, my honored
friend, is so great that it would require not letters and not
books, but a whole library. On its highest conceptual level it
is all clearly defined in the soul, but how much labor is needed
and how much analysis to express each point in its own way
so as to bring out all its richness. It is only then, by noting
their basic differences, that the varying concepts will be
clarified. But I am a slave committed to the public, to work
and to bear burdens for the people of God that has begun to
take root on its ancestral soil, in the hope of redemption and a
new blossoming of life. The practical tasks incidental to the
transformation in the conditions of our people are so immense
that they impede our spiritual work, even that essential for its
very life, not to speak of what is needed for its edification and
the enhancement of its character.

I stand in the midst of all this. Thank God He endowed me with a disposition that I feel all these movements and agitations, with all their pangs, but also with all their vitality and with faith in their efficacy. All these forces converge in my experience, and I must cope with them in action, suffering their incidental crises and listening to the open and hidden voice that speaks through them. I imagine that the noble soul of my honorable friend can feel my anguish even at a distance, and judge me with full charity for my long delay in answering, and that even now I must content myself with only brief comments.

The hopes your honor cherishes about conferences of rabbis have always seemed to me dreams that, at the present time, lack even the charm that adorns a beautiful imagination. The shepherds of our people are sunk in a deep sleep, not because of an evil disposition, but because of a weakness of soul, which for days and years and even epochs has not tasted truly nourishing food. This can come only from the illumination that emanates from the inwardness of the divine light of the Torah. If they should gather at a conference they will not ascribe to themselves any lack of knowledge or weakness of spirit, and they will not heed the call of the few who are girded with the might of the Lord. The agenda of the conference they will surely crown with some *halakhic* research on the most trivial subject, as far as its inner significance is concerned, but which will perhaps be extended in length and depth from the point of view of the subtleties needed to resolve it, like one who creates a machine at the cost of many thousands of talents of gold in order to produce one iron needle. Or they may put on the agenda some homiletical theme that they will embroider with moralistic thoughts detached from life, with some insipid Cabbalistic citation or antiquated philosophy. This will only aggravate the oppressive atmosphere surrounding the rabbinate, and a new pain will be added to the immense pangs of suffering of the community of Israel that is writhing in her anguish.

It is not so, my brother. This is not the way. We shall not seek conferences at this time, but we shall launch a literature. With a sharp knife, a double-edged sword, whose body and handle and two edges shall be the four letters of the name of God [YHWH], we shall cut the living tissue, which has not lost its sensitivity to be shaken and frightened and full of feeling. The medication that will heal their wounds will be the influence of the holy spirit and the river of delight whose source is the divine wisdom. With the foliage steeped in fragment of divine light we shall stop their hemorrhaging. And a new stream of life, emanating from Him who is the life of the universe, will be infused into the life-blood. It will come to birth thanks to the fresh health-endowing food that we shall offer them from the fields of true wisdom, which are tilled by the faithful workmen, the brave spirits, the lovers of the Lord and His people, the benefactors of His creatures and His world.

This is what we tried to accomplish in modest measures when we started publishing the journal Hanir [The Ploughing]. We must begin to plough, to root out the thorns from all sides, and prepare the household of Israel for the seeding of a new light, which will give us its produce as in ancient days, and with impressive purity.

It is not in vain that we were refined and scourged in the refining and cleansing furnace of such a long and fiery exile. Though we suffered much for the sake of enlightening the world, we must not deny that we, too, needed scourging, which had a beneficent effect on us, and, having dwelt in darkness, God has become a light unto us.

With fragments of light emanating from the river of delight, our beloved land, our center of life and the place that reveals our dignity and where our might lies hidden, we shall revive everything. We shall lose nothing, from our smallest possessions to the majesty of heaven and earth—we shall join everything in one entity and everything will again blossom. The simple, innocent and natural love for the people is bound to be engendered as an active and enlightening force among all those who deserve truly to be crowned with the title "great sages of Israel." On the lofty precipice will be built all our defenses, and the shields of our heroes will be placed on them. Might in abundance will come streaming from the vitalizing source, the land that is the center of our life, whose majestic splendor we feel as we return to it, confident in our hopes for redemption and eternal deliverance increasingly stirring in us. In its mighty arms it will embrace all the distant flock that were "dispersed from mountain to valley, without forgetting their home ground"[1] and their shepherds with them.

Wake up, wake up, dear brother, and from the illumination of our souls, which we will draw from the source of might and light, flashes of light will shine on the world, and the righteous ones of Eretz Yisrael and those of the diaspora will unite, to enhance the glory of our beautiful land and its majestic treasures, and they will no longer be of divided heart. The mystical meanings will be disclosed, the intimations will be clarified, the homiletical pronouncements will be made explicit, and the obvious will be raised to a higher significance. They will all together fill the world with abundance, which will be invigorating and add mightily to the cause of God.

My dear friend must get the thought out of his mind that only through his writings, on which he has invested much labor, will the people of Israel be nourished. His writings are much appreciated and precious to us, but they are *one* of the important manifestations coming to light in the spirit of the people, all of which have their roots in the Torah. Let him try to disseminate his thoughts as much as possible, but without undue exaggeration, which begets inner weakness and disillu-

---

1. Lit. "Their fences," the line appears in a poem by Yehudah ha-Levi.

sionment and nodding of the head and mockery from the outside. Let us merge our lights in unity, light will be added to light, and our paths will be increasingly brightened.

It is not for us to quarrel with the sages of the past, but to add to their light. Then, automatically, the creases will be smoothened out, and the good and living substance they embodied, drawn from the source of Israel, will be disclosed in all its majestic beauty. If we at times diverge from their views, "each generation has its own sages, each generation has its own leaders" (Avodah Zarah 5a). Every illumination is from God. We must always cherish the good that was serviceable in its time in any thought that was relevant for its day, even if it cannot always be sustained in its efficacy—"All the Torah which a person studies in this world is preparatory to the Torah of the Messiah" (Kohelet Rabbah 11:12).

Little by little, at times by jumping over or breaking through roadblocks, we shall prepare the hearts of our people for a healthy life. Then there will return the desire to be involved in the restoration of our people to normalcy, not that one may thereby be called "Rabbi" or to gain fame, nor so as to earn a goodly portion of reward in the Garden of Eden, nor that through the merits of such work to be spared pangs of retributive judgment in the hereafter. An element of permanent meaning is hidden in such thoughts, but they are small and petty in comparison with the mighty thought fed by the true riches of the Torah, whose ingredients have been compared to fine flour, oil, and honey and whose majesty is commensurate with its simplicity. The welfare of the people and the splendor of its might, its rescue from destruction and the raising of its dignity—this is the Eden ["the delight"] and the Garden, whose trees and branches and fruit are endless and whose foliage and flowers are an incomparable feast for the eyes. We are preparing the tools so that a community of Rabbis may come to birth. Then and only then will we be able to speak seriously about a conference; and God will be with us.

I must be brief. Your friend whose hand will join with yours in labor and the bearing of burdens, for the sake of the people of God and their inheritance.

Igrot, Vol. I, Letter 184

ABRAHAM ISAAC KOOK

By the grace of God, the holy city of Jaffa,
may it be rebuilt and established,
Tevet 25, 5673 (1913)

Abundant peace and continued blessing to my devoted friend, the
brilliant scholar and thinker, who is filled with the pure knowledge and
fear of God, our master Rabbi Judah Leib Seltzer, may he live to a long
and good life, Amen.

I received your precious article and I read it in the
midst of my many pressing distractions. I enjoyed your literary style, which reflects good taste, and your position, which
is sound in the major thrust of your essay. Such articles and
books are surely one of the best therapies for the grievous
affliction in our generation. But we must never lose sight of
the general therapy that addresses itself to our overall problem
and the neglect of which has brought about our downfall.
This is what I, in my sorrow and bitterness, am in the habit of
calling attention to, repeating it hundreds and thousands of
times: We have abandoned the soul of the Torah. This is the
great outcry that has been sounded mightily over many generations, from the days of the prophets, the teachers and the
sages, the great spirits of the early and later generations.

Our most talented people concentrated for the most part on
the practical aspects of the Torah, and even there only on
specialized subjects. This they cultivated and made it the
habituated subject of education. The emotional aspect, and
more than this, the philosophical, and that which is beyond it
and follows it automatically, the illumination of holiness,
which bears within itself the mystery of the redemption —
this they abandoned altogether. Anyone who challenges the

shepherds of our people about this shameful neglect is regarded as mad and presumptuous. The earnest call of those
who concern themselves with divine matters, the men of
higher piety, the pure Cabbalists who attained to the mystical
knowledge of God, the men of holy vision and mighty will,
those who sought intimations of redemption—theirs was a
voice calling in the wilderness. Thus far, after all our reproof,
after heresy assaults us from the sides, with its despicable
crudeness, apostasy ravages us like a pestilence, to seize from
us thousands of souls each year, while in the camp that represents the cause of Torah and religious faith there is consterna-
tion and disorder, no clarity of purpose and no well-defined
ideal. The dominant thought still is that we shall be able to
heal our affliction with nostrums, nostrums that will not
satisfy the soul, as long as we do not nourish it with that
which is most essential to sustain its life.

Under no circumstances will a strategy prevail that runs
counter to the voice of God, which calls to us from the souls of
the highest saints, from ancient times to the present. We are
summoned to a mighty penitence, a penitence stirred by love
in all its dimensions. It is precisely when the crisis is great and
the peril immense that we must choose the best of therapies.
We must be radical. With compromise on the basis of a half, a
third and a fourth we will accomplish nothing. Religious faith
has declined, it continues to lose its vitality, because its
ideological basis has been voided; no one studies it, no one
seeks it. Orthodoxy in its present battle of negativism contents itself with illusions that are destroyed by life and reality,
destroying those who entertain them together with them. We
cannot find comfort in the fact that the element of our people
that has yielded to heresy is even more vulnerable to destruction. The traditional statement that trouble shared by many
people is half a consolation does not apply here; it is rather a
double affliction. The invitation to look at the inadequacy of
the thinkers among the nations will not lend us strength and

life, when this is only an approach of negativism.

Why should we choose distant paths when the smooth road is open before us? There must be a rise of interest among us in the entire Torah with its spiritually, focused interpretations. Whoever is firm of heart, whoever wields a vigorous pen and whose soul is stirred by the spirit of God, is summoned to go forth into the battleground and cry out: Give us light. We would see a different picture, an altogether different picture in our generation if an appreciable part of our talented people, those who are knowledgeable in Torah and endowed with good sense, chose to toil in the vineyard of the Lord, in its inner dimension; to concern themselves with authenticating the concepts of religious faith and divine service, in clarifying the beliefs concerning divine matters, prophecy, the holy spirit, the redemption, the anticipation of deliverance, deliverance for our people and for the world, the perfection of the souls of individuals and of society, the evaluation of the spiritual state of past, future and present generations. A different courage would be engendered in the scattered flock of the Lord. A wondrous beauty would embrace the multitude of Torah scholars and higher illumination would emanate from them to our entire people and to the whole world. The recent tendencies in Jewish and world literature, which are steadily declining toward vulgarity, would experience a revival and liberation through us, through our profound thoughts, through our clear pronouncements that could become the life-giving principles for many nations, to bring them out of darkness toward the light. Evil and folly, the vanities of false beliefs, would be purged away, and we would be commencing the great heavenly work of clearing away the spirit of impurity from the land, and of launching the perfection of the world under the kingdom of the God of the universe.

This is what is expected of us, for this we were created. As long as we continue in our wandering, subject to slaughter like the deer because we fail to recognize our mission, small-minded people come to heal us with all sorts of ineffectual therapies, while the basic life-restoring medication is ignored. Some are moved by a lack of sensitivity and little faith, and others by pride and lack of knowledge, but again they think that the spread of Torah in its narrow and dry conception will serve as a general therapy for our afflictions. This has proven ineffectual in sustaining our position ever since various cultural forces and spiritual challenges have confronted us.

Your honor, my beloved, will not accuse me, and I hope that no one else will accuse me, of insufficient love for the practical aspect of the Torah, for the need of studying it diligently, with the fine points of textual and rational analysis, with acuteness and erudition. But matters have come to a point where the true meaning of the Torah, the higher level of the Torah, has been made void, where the deepest aspect of the soul has been crushed, where the capacity to think has been weakened, where our spiritual state and that of the world that is dependent on us has been brought to a state of fearful decline. If one should come and state that our help is to be found in the soul of the Torah, by enhancing the higher and true meaning of the Torah, the contrary-minded will come from all sides and bombard one with arguments: Are you advocating Cabbalah, moralistic writings, research, philosophy, homiletics, literature, poetry? All these are bankrupt, they have not delivered to us what they promised since the inception of their ferment. Such arguments are enough to choke the voice of God calling within us in the depths of our souls and penetrating to all worlds: Seek Me and live.

At a time such as this we must address ourselves to the most serious of our defects. I am not now concerned with detailed programs, how to arrange systems of study, systems of thought, a schedule of books, of schools, that by focusing primarily on the development of the simple meaning of the Torah will serve as a stronghold for the spirit of God, from

357

which will come forth champions of God, as in the past. All the particular strategies will emerge, once the main principle is recognized, once the only question to deal with will be concerning the means and the strategies.

I regret very much that I cannot at this time write more extensively, particularly that I am unable to write a critique about your honor's book, which I look upon with hope as an important contribution. I have only voiced some of my anxiety before a person of pure heart and sound mind, like my honored friend. May it be the will of our heavenly Father to encourage those who labor with the public for the sake of heaven and to strengthen the spirit of all in whose hearts there burns a spark of divine light, that they may join in one fellowship to illumine His people with the light of God. The mission of Eretz Yisrael as the land of vision will emerge only in such context from the many obscurities that surround it.

I sign with many good wishes to your honor and to all that are his. May God enhance his powers and bestow favor upon the work of his hands, as befits his noble self and his friend who hopes for the success of his teaching and honors him with heart and soul.

As to our friend the Ridvaz [Rabbi Yakov David ben Zeev], I have not seen his book but there is no basis for any anger among people who love truth as we do, thank God.

Igrot, Vol. II, Letter 483

By the grace of God, the holy city of Jaffa,
Adar 13, 5673 (1913)

To my friend, the great luminary, scholar, author and pietist, our
master Rabbi Abraham Resnik, may he live to a long and good life,
the head of the rabbinic court in Ashabad, may God watch over his
going and coming.

Peace and blessings from the Holy Land.

I received your pamphlet "For the sake of my Brethren and
Friends." I am understandably grateful to every colleague
who wields a pen, who pursues the way of integrity and is
zealous for truth and justice. One finds evidence of these
virtues at many points in your writing. But, in my true love
for you, I must not desist from indicating to you that we have
an obligation to be careful not to stumble on errors that seem
strange. Thus, the anecdote about Rabbi Raphael of Hamburg with Naphtali Weisel does not correspond to the historical information of so recent a past. Hamburg was never at that
time subject to Berlin. There never existed in Germany an
office of Chief Rabbi, certainly none with the title "grand
rabin," which is French. Naphtali Weisel never held a public
office and in general never enjoyed such public esteem. Similar stories are told about R. Moses ben Menahem [Moses
Mendelsohn] and J. L. Margolit, author of *Peri Tevuah* and *Tal*
Orot, but this was not because of a public office. It was rather
because of the esteem for Moses of Dessau [Mendelsohn] before King Frederick.

In any case, one must be careful in using satire. It may be
used only within limits.

May your hands be strengthened to bring blessings and

peace to Israel, with the fruits of your pen, and may you be blessed, as is becoming for your precious self, and as is the wish of your friend, who esteems you highly, and honors you with love.

Igrot, Vol. II, Letter 510

By the grace of God, Tishre 13, 5676 (1916),
with best wishes for a happy New Year,
and for the joy of the festivals, and
joy in God and His might.

To my beloved friend, the wise and the noble David Ha-Kohen, may he live to a long and good life, Amen.

You will forgive me, my dear, that I delayed responding to your precious thoughts. To the extent that I am able, I will express to you some thoughts concerning the subject that is at the summit of moral attributes, the subject of humility, that you touched on in your communication.

You were correct in linking the attribute of humility with the principle of novelty in the order of creation. But this refers to the core element of the principle, that is to say, to the very fact that the phenomenon of novelty exists as it does in its operative character. We know intuitively that true novelty derives from the substantive content of everything preceding it, that it emerges from its energizing essence. The fruit derives from the whole nature of the tree, from the depths of its trunk and roots, from the source whence it absorbs its juices, to its outer bark and the spread of its branches and foliage. In truth, every new expression does not derive from the one paragraph nearest it, the entity that is apparent to logic, but from the whole rational and vital, active and thinking essence of the one who innovated it. "When it is ordered from all, it is preserved" (II Sam. 23:1; Erubin 54a). Every new contribution that is forged from some aspect of the self, leaving aspects without spiritual involvement, is not a new creation but a mechanical rearrangement in the hierarchy of thought.

When we touch on this attribute we at once encounter the principle of constant creativity, the originality idealized as "an ever renewing spring and a never failing river" (Abot 6:1). This is the highest aspiration of the study of Torah for its own sake, which is related to linking oneself with God in an outreach of soul. It is an attachment of soul to that which is the all and the source of all and greater than all. And this most noble desire grows ever more potent, and does not leave any part of the self without absorbing its highest vitalizing essence. Thus the basis of the life of all, and the source of all in its comprehensiveness, touches in its spreading beneficence the channels of the soul, which is ever seeking the new that emanates with strength and purity and assertive potency.

The recognition that one draws from all and not from fragments alone assumed the narrow philosophy by exerting an impact at all times on one's outlook on the world and on life, on the conception of the moral good and on the disposition of the will in the depths of one's being. The nature of being then becomes manifest in its clearest form, and that is the concept of universality. Then the person recognizes that he is not an isolated phenomenon, that he is not an essence that exists independently, but a tiny spark that shines at all times from the illumination of the sun in its might, and that all living beings are so many sparks kindled from this source of light, that their existence can be comprehended only when traced to this source of light. This perception is the basis of morality, even of societal morality. It is the basis of science, even the materialistic and rational. It is the basis of humility, even on the practical level.

Obviously the concept of the "all" continues to expand. After we rise to a more enlightened perception, the vision of "allness" entertained previously is revealed to us as but a very tiny part, and we are embarrassed that we had focused on it and thought that here we had the basis of novelty and the basis of humility. This process is the graded movement of penitence out of love, which serves like a pillar of fire for those who are constant in their longing for the divine light. "They will go from strength to strength, each of them will appear before God in Zion" (Ps. 84:8, Berakhot 64a). It thus turns out that the higher humility is based on two principles. One is the perception that our private ego and all its being is rendered of relative insignificance when seen in the perspective of the aspiration for novelty, that is channeled to us from the substantive essence of the universal reality. The second is the fact that even this triviality, which has at least some semblance of humility, that might be able to leave some imprint on the soul, is at once nullified by the force of a higher negation. This derives from a positive thrust, higher and more abundant, released by the grandeur of the emergent new reality that shines so brightly, so that the previous reality that seemed so satisfying becomes dark and small in comparison with it. Thus is established the basis of humility and lowliness, which raises the soul with illumination after illumination, with flash after flash. The pauses between them serve only to assimilate the impressions, until they are turned into a spiritual enthusiasm that releases vitality and new life.

From what was said before we may infer that the unity of novelty and humility is so firm that they became one concept. It is only in the fullest unity that is adorned with holiness that we find sufficiency in all respects, without any deficiency. This is the basis for the demand that novelty, on its higher level, be seen as engendered from the preceding all. Without unity there is no novelty but only some shallow change of gradation. When novelty emerges from the universal whole, then it emerges from its source with unceasing assertiveness, with addition after addition, with one addition improving on the previous addition. The new phenomenon is thus always an improvement on what precedes it. "Your works are new each morning, great is Your faithfulness" (Lam. 3:23). When it is realized that this is the nature of existence as a whole, on the practical and the moral plane, one recognizes at once that the natural state, the happiest condition of any being, is humility. "You are the smallest among the nations" (Deut. 7:7)—to which is to be added the rabbinic comment that God declared: "I love you, because even when I bestow greatness on you, you humble yourselves before Me" (Hullin 89a). This greatness that inspires humility is the hereditary trait of Israel, which is destined to extend its influence to the entire world. Thus will man and every creature recognize their great worth and the firm security of their being, and they will be filled with vitality and bliss over the great future that awaits them. It will become apparent to all that every fellow-being who exists with us adds to our happiness because we share in the light of life that shines in him, with all the great unfolding of his future, even as we enjoy the light that shines in us. This is the spiritual bliss at the heart of the holiness of peace.

May the Rock of Israel soon spread His canopy of peace over His people and His world, and "the loftiness of man shall be bowed down, and the haughtiness of man shall be brought low, and the Lord alone shall be exalted in that day" (Isa. 2:17-18).

Time does not permit me now to elaborate on a favorite theme, and I conclude with greetings on the occasion of the holy festival, and the privilege of keeping all its precepts joyously, and with the hope that we be enabled to celebrate festivals resplendent with light and inspiration for all who seek God and His might.

I close with greetings of peace as befits your precious self and your friend who desires your success in all your endeavors.

Igrot, III, Letter 741

By the grace of God, II Adar 17, 5676 (1916)

To my darling son, may he live to a long and good life, Amen.

Thank God, the days of Purim have passed peacefully in our new "exile." We are thankful that many sincere people have been drawn to attach themselves to us, out of their love for the Torah and the fear of God. May the Lord be gracious to me and grant me the purity and firmness of spirit to pursue the sacred labor, on the level of inwardness as well as in its worldly demands.

Thus far we have not yet found a place to live in. The residence assigned to us has not yet been vacated by its previous tenant, and we have been forced to stay several weeks with our friend Haykin, may all be well with him. When I told them that under no circumstances could I bear living with a private individual, for all we had was night lodging in one of the hotels, they rented for us a temporary residence in the northern part of the city. The air here is better than in the eastern part of the city, but this is not the center of my work, and for this reason I have been unable to carry out any project for the improvement of either the affairs of the Mahzike Hadat,[1] or in the larger community. Though the Chief Rabbi and the Beth Din and other important rabbis are anxious to join with me in common endeavors, I cannot find the suitable conditions for practical work, because of the lack of a permanent residence while living here. However, God must have intended all for the good.

Understandably, the distraction, because of the many vis-

---

1. This is the name of the congregation in London where he served during this period.

itors, was initially very great. Even now I have not been relieved, and there are still many more waiting for the time when, with God's help, we shall move into our assigned quarters. It is difficult for me, son, to reflect and communicate with you about matters of the book, which have to do with the truth, as it is in my heart. The burdensome necessity to involve myself with people impedes me greatly from concentrating on inner concerns. My soul yearns and is thirsty for inner reflection, while the stream of distractions drags it to endless conversations, discourses [*pilpul*], expositions and thinking about finite matters, set in their narrow framework to which the simple masses, in their imitation-based piety, are accustomed. It is only with great difficulty that I can probe for the grain of truth and the pearls of equity that may be found in this stream of drudgery. Even before any spurt of thought matures in my heart a new stream of visitors comes, engendering ideas and concerns from the pressure of their habits and their weaknesses. I must begin my inner reflection all over again, between one interval and another, to turn my attention to the east where my mind and my heart are drawn, and to search for wells of inspiration from the sources of my own independent soul, for which I yearn. For Your help, O God, I hope and I shall always trust, to add to Your praise.

[Here he lists a number of people to whom he asks his son to convey regards.]

P.S. Please, son, write us all the details about yourself, about your work in the fields of the holy and the secular, and about anything that you judge will interest us. Be strong, and may God be with you and may the work of your hands be pleasing to Him. And may we be privileged to rejoice in your happiness, with every good. Amen.

Igrot, Vol. III, Letter 764

Poems

A Note on the Text

Abraham Isaac Kook, revered first Chief Rabbi of Palestine, has earned widespread recognition as the author of many volumes on *halakhah*, philosophy and Cabbalah. He is less well known as a poet, and only a small collection of his verse has appeared in print. A. M. Habermann edited a number of his poems and published them in the 1945 issue of the Hebrew periodical *Sinai*, where they reveal him as a poet of singular depth and style.

Rabbi Kook's poems are reminiscent of the religious poetry included under the general category of *piyyut*, but they are more lyrical and, unrestrained by the fetters of rigid stylistic forms, give direct and uninhibited utterance to thought and feeling. Rabbi Kook, declared Habermann, was a great poet "whose soul sang with a unique melody." The themes embraced in his poetry are those dealt with in all his writings: longing for God, the oneness of existence, love for all God's creatures, yearning for Zion's renewal. In the latter category he leans more often on conventional poetic form, and these poems are the weakest in this collection.

Rabbi Kook's poems are pervaded by a touch of melancholy. He seeks God but the vision that comes to him is only a faint intimation of the reality; he would like to share with others what he has seen, but he cannot find words to convey his vision. He is aware of a rich treasure of rites and customs and laws that his heritage offers those who seek nearness of God, but these are for him too confining. He is a Jew, steeped in his heritage, in his people's way of life and faith, but he belongs to the world, and his heart pulsates with love for all existence. He is moved to pray but the conventional liturgy does not fully express his yearning, and he composes his own prayer. Rabbi Kook was truly a rare spirit in whom the divine sensibility vibrated with unusual potency. He lived in two worlds, the world of traditional piety, of which he was an acknowledged master, and the world of mystical experience, which invested him with creative originality.

MY SOUL ASPIRES

My soul aspires
For the mysteries,
For the hidden secrets of the universe.
It cannot be content
With much knowledge
That probes
The trivialities of life.

FOR YOUR OWN SAKE, SERPENT

For your own sake, serpent,
Do not come to bite me.
I am not a crab;
I am a red hot pair of tongs.
And there on the hill
Silently sits the hunter, my God,
And He will arise.

ABRAHAM ISAAC KOOK

MY HEART RAGES

My heart rages
Like a boiling pot,
Like a stormy sea.
I aspire for the heights,
For lofty visions
Fed by divine lights,
By souls hidden in the realms above.
I will not be bound in chains,
But I will bear a yoke;
I am a servant of God
But not a slave of slaves.

I AM FILLED WITH LOVE FOR GOD

I am filled with love for God,
I know that what I seek, what I love,
Cannot be called by a name.
How can one designate by a name
That which is greater than all,
Greater than the good,
Greater than reality,
Greater than existence?
I love, I say, I love God.
Light infinite abides
In the utterance of the name,
In the invocation of God,
And in all the names and designations
The human heart has conceived and spoken,
When the soul soars upward.
I cannot satisfy my soul
With the love sustained by the web of logic,
Through the quest for light
Revealed by the world, by existence,
As it parades itself before our eyes.
Divine lights are born in our souls,
Many gods according to our perception —
Before we know Him
In the fullness of His mystery
God reveals
Intimations of Himself.
He commands all our being,
The life of the universe.
Wherever there is thought, feeling, will,
Wherever there is refined, spiritual life,
A light divine reigns,
It reigns and dies,
For it is a finite sovereignty —

As long as it is an inference
From the world, from existence,
The light eternal at times overpowers,
We seek a purer light, more inward,
More of the truth as it is in itself.
The light outruns the vessel,
Thought soars beyond existence,
The ordered world breaks down,
The vessels are broken,
The kings are dead,
The gods are dead.
The world stands naked, lonely, broken,
Stirred by a hidden longing
For higher light.
In His eternal mercy
God left in the broken vessels residues of His light.
In every life pulse,
In all existence,
There is a spark, a spark of a spark,
Faint and fainter than faint.
The inner light,
The light of God supreme,
Builds and establishes,
Assembles what is scattered,
Perfects worlds without end,
Orders and binds together;
God's eternal realm is disclosed
Through the light unbounded within the soul,
From God to the world
A new light is born,
A light emanating from the splendor of God's face.

WHEN I WANT TO SPEAK

When I want to speak a word
The spirit has already descended
From its hiding place.
Before it came to strum the strings of my will
The roots of many souls,
The highest mysteries,
Were already reduced to finite forms
And became letters pressing
At the lower region of my soul
Close to the concerns of my worldly self
And linked to its essence,
And I am forced to speak.
I speak out of all treasures that live in me.
The words flow on,
The thoughts flourish,
The sounds reach out,
Sound meets sound.
The ascending stream from my mortal self
Joins the descending stream from the source of my soul,
And seeds of light
Fill the world, my whole being.

RADIANT IS THE WORLD SOUL

Radiant is the world soul,
Full of splendor and beauty,
Full of life,
Of souls hidden,
Of treasures of the holy spirit,
Of fountains of strength,
Of greatness and beauty.
Proudly I ascend
Toward the heights of the world soul
That gives life to the universe.
How majestic the vision,
Come, enjoy,
Come, find peace,
Embrace delight,
Taste and see that God is good.
Why spend your substance on what does not nourish
And your labor on what cannot satisfy?
Listen to me, and you will enjoy what is good,
And find delight in what is truly precious.

HOW GREAT IS MY INNER STRUGGLE

How great is my inner struggle,
My heart is filled with an upward longing,
I crave that the divine delight
Spread through my being,
Not because I seek its delights,
But because this is as it should be.
Because this is the true state of existence,
Because this is the true content of life.
And I am continually astir,
I cry in my inwardness with a loud voice,
Give me the light of God,
The delight of the living God,
The grandeur of visiting
The palace of the eternal King,
The God of my fathers,
To whose love I am committed
With my whole being,
By whose awe I am uplifted.
And my soul continues to soar,
To rise above lowliness, smallness,
Above boundaries
With which nature, the body,
The environment, conformity,
Surround it, confine it in bonds.
A stream of duties comes,
Studies and inferences without end,
Complicated thoughts and deductive dialectics
Derived from letters and words —
It comes and surrounds my soul,
Which is pure, free, light as a cherub
That is immersed in a sea of light.
But I have not yet come to the point
Of staying in my shelter from beginning to end,

To conceive the delight of tradition,
To feel the line of every inference,
To perceive light in the world's dark.
I am filled with anguish
And hope for deliverance and for light,
For higher exaltation,
For the dawn of knowledge and illumination,
And for the inpouring of the dew of life.
Even through these narrow channels
Whence I am nourished
And find delight in the pleasantness of the Lord,
I shall discern the purity of the ideal will,
The hidden grandeur, the strength supreme,
Which fills every letter and dot,
Every chain of dialectic.
And I shall play with Your commandments
I have loved,
And I shall expound Your precepts.

EXPANSES, EXPANSES

Expanses, expanses,
Expanses divine my soul craves.
Confine me not in cages,
Of substance or of spirit.
My soul soars the expanses of the heavens,
Walls of heart and walls of deed
Will not contain it.
Morality, logic, custom —
My soul soars above these,
Above all that bears a name,
Above delight,
Above every delight and beauty,
Above all that is exalted and ethereal.
I am love-sick —
I thirst, I thirst for God,
As a deer for water brooks.
Alas, who can describe my pain,
Who will be a violin to express the songs of my grief,
Who will voice my bitterness,
The pain of seeking utterance?
I thirst for truth, not for a conception of truth,
For I ride on its heights,
I am wholly absorbed by truth,
I am wholly pained by the anguish of expression.
How can I utter the great truth
That fills my whole heart?
Who will disclose to the multitude,
To the world, to all creatures,
To nations and individuals alike,
The sparks abounding in treasures
Of light and warmth
Stored within my soul?
I see the flames rise upward

Piercing the heavens,
But who feels, who can express their might?
I am not like one of those heroes
Who have found whole worlds in their inwardness.
Whether the world knew of their wealth or not,
It was all the same to them.
These herds of sheep walking on two feet—
Of what use was it if they knew
Man's true height,
And what loss in their not knowing?
I am bound to the world,
All creatures, all people are my friends,
Many parts of my soul
Are intertwined with them,
But how can I share with them my light?
Whatever I say
Only covers my vision,
Dulls my light.
Great is my pain and great my anguish,
O, my God, my God, be a help in my trouble,
Find for me the graces of expression,
Grant me language and the gift of utterance,
I shall declare before the multitudes
My fragments of Your truth, O my God.

THE WHISPERS OF EXISTENCE

All existence whispers to me a secret:
I have life to offer, take it, take it—
If you have a heart and in the heart red blood courses,
Which despair has not soiled.

But if your heart is dulled
And beauty holds no spell to you—existence whispers—
Leave me, leave,
I am forbidden to you.
If every gentle sound,
Every living beauty,
Stir you not to a holy song,
But to some alien thought,
Then leave me, leave, I am forbidden to you.

And a generation will yet arise
And sing to beauty and to life
And draw delight unending
From the dew of heaven.

And a people returned to life will hear
The wealth of life's secrets
From the vistas of the Carmel and the Sharon,
And from the delight of song and life's beauty
A holy light will abound.
And all existence will whisper,
My beloved, I am permitted to you.

REMOVE MY SHAME

Remove my shame,
Lift my anxiety,
Absolve me of my sin
And enable me to pray before You
With gladness of heart,
To pursue Your commandments and Your Torah
In the joy of holiness.
Grant me
To bring happiness to all Your children,
To exalt and ennoble Your faithful,
Enable me to spread goodness and mercy
And blessing in the world.
Humble the arrogant
Who have tried to pervert me with falsehood
While I sought my happiness in serving You.
Save me from weakness
And from faltering
And from every evil trait,
Illumine my eyes
With the light of Your deliverance.
Help Your people,
Imbue the heart of Your people with reverence
And with awe before Your majesty.
Strengthen them with Your love,
Guide them to walk in the path of Your righteousness;
Kindle in their hearts
The light of the holiness of this Sabbath day
And return them to possess the inheritance
You have set for them,
Speedily, speedily, in our time, soon.
Amen.

SHALL I ABANDON THE SOURCE OF LOVE

Shall I abandon the source of love
For an endless craving after pleasures?
Shall I leave that reservoir
That is above all that is and is not,
Above the void and above the chaos,
Above its own beauty and strength?
And I am so thirsty for its light—
Its delights always still my thirst
By adding to my pining,
By increasing my thirst.
It uplifts and delights
While gently distressing my inner being.
I have my secret and my secret is my light,
And my light is my people,
The treasure of my life.
Exalted One who abides in eternity,
I am ever filled with strength
In proudly fulfilling Your will,
With joy and peace and unfailing help,
With a compassionate eye for the oppressed—
You will surely help a people in need,
With the grandeur of penitence
And the secret of serving You,
And the hidden wisdom
That opens its channels
Sending many streams,
Many streams of water
Into the broad places of the world.

THE FIRST ONE DREW ME

The first one drew me with his rope
Into his palatial abode,
And I listened to his song
From the strings of his violin.

The sea of knowledge rages,
Its waves beat in me,
Thought mounts upon thought, like a wall,
And God stands above it.

One silent thought floats lightly
Like a cloud in the sky,
If I ask here below
Of the bewildered ones in the gates,
Whither floats this
Prisoner of the skies?
None can disclose the tale
Or even explain it in part.

I PINE

I pine
For the supernal light,
For the light infinite,
For the light of the God of truth.
The God of my life,
The living God,
Who sustains the universe.
My longing consumes my strength
Of body and spirit,
I am not endowed with the knowledge

Nor have I been prepared
To still this great longing.
I prostrate myself profusely
Before the Sovereign of all worlds
Whose hand is open
To satisfy every living thing with favor.
Grant my desire,
Grant me the light of Your revelation,
Satisfy my thirst for Your light,
Illumine me with Your light
And I shall be helped.

WHO IMPEDES ME?

Who impedes me,
Why can't I disclose in writing all my thoughts,
The most hidden musings of my soul?
Who prevents me,
Who has imprisoned my thought in its shell,
And does not allow it to emerge into the world?
Who chokes the flights of the soul
And does not allow them to be revealed
In all the splendor of their radiance?
My inner powers cry out in weariness,
They feel imprisoned, as in a jail,
They complain
They are imprisoned without justice and without law,
They are right, equity and justice are on their side.
They threaten to break out with might,
To topple walls that hem in,
To go forth to freedom, to sing aloud
Their great song, holy and joyful,

385

Full of life's vigor,
The life of holiness and purity,
The life of beauty,
The life jubilant pulsating in all realms of being,
The life of glory divine,
In which they will find delights abounding.
O when, when, will come your liberation?
When, when will I speak and write
All my heart conceives?
Then shall I speak and find relief,
I shall declare the praise of God.
And the lips will express all the heart meditates,
And the pen will expound all that is hidden in thought,
And out of darkness will go forth light, light, light.
The Lord is my light and my deliverance.
Whom need I fear?
The Lord is light for me.

Bibliographies

WRITINGS ABOUT RABBI KOOK

Agus, J. B., *Banner of Jerusalem*, Bloch, N.Y., 1946, reprinted in 1972 under the title *High Priest of Rebirth*.

Agus, Jacob, "Rabbi Kook" in *Great Jewish Thinkers of the Twentieth Century*, ed. by Simon Noveck, B'nai B'rith, Clinton, Mass., 1963.

Bergman, S. H., *Faith and Reason: An Introduction to Modern Jewish Thought*, tr. and ed. by Alfred Jospe, B'nai B'rith Hillel Foundation, Washington, D.C., 1961, pp. 121-141.

Bokser, B. Z., "A Commentary on Rabbi Kook," *Conservative Judaism*, Vol. 29, No. 1, Fall 1974, pp. 72-80.

Bokser, B. Z., "Jewish Universalism: An Aspect of the Thought of Harav Kook", *Judaism*, Vol. 8, No. 3, Summer 1959, pp. 214-220.

Bokser, B. Z., "The Poetry of Rabbi Kook," *Conservative Judaism*, Vol. XXV, No. 3, Spring 1971, pp. 56-64.

Bokser, B. Z., "Rabbi Kook as a Mystic," *Judaism*, Vol. 24, No. 1, Winter 1975, pp. 117-124.

Bokser, B. Z., "Rabbi Kook, Builder and Dreamer of Zion," *Conservative Judaism*, Vol. XIV, No. 2, Winter 1965, pp. 67-78.

Bokser, B. Z., "Rav Kook" The Road to Renewal", *Tradition*, Vol. 13, No. 3, Winter 1973, pp. 137-154.

Buber, Martin, *Israel and Palestine*, East and West Library, London, 1952, pp. 147-154.

Epstein, I., *Abraham Yizhak Hacohen Kook: His Life and Times*, 1951.

Hertzberg, Arthur, *The Zionist Idea*, Doubleday and Herzl Press, New York 1959, pp. 416-427.

Jung, L., *Guardians of Our Heritage*, 1958, pp. 489-509.

Metzger, Alter B. Z., *Rabbi Kook's Philosophy of Repentence: A Translation of "Orot Hateshuvah*," Yeshivah University Press, 1968.

Rosenstreich, Nathan, *Jewish Philosophy in Modern Times*, Holt, Rinehart & Winston, New York 1968, pp. 219-238.

Wiener, Herbert, *9½ Mystics*, Collier Books, New York, 1971, ch. 10.

WRITINGS BY RABBI KOOK REFERRED TO IN THIS VOLUME

Arple Tohar, "Clouds of Purity," is a collection of Rabbi Kook's meditations that began to be published in Jaffa in 1914, but was never finished. Eighty unbound pages of this volume have been circulated unofficially. Parts of this collection have been incorporated in other published works of Rabbi Kook.

"Derekh Hathiah," "The Road to Renewal," an essay that appeared under the Hebrew title "Derekh Hathiah," in the periodical *Hanir* in 1904.

Eder Hayakar, "The Precious Mantle," is a collection of two major works, a tribute to his father-in-law Rabbi Elijah David Rabinowitz, whose name is abbreviated in the term *Eder* (in Hebrew EDR), and a collection of short essays under the name *Ikve Hatzon*. The tribute to his father-in-law includes the texts of twenty letters, which the latter wrote to various correspondents. This volume was published by the Mosad Harav Kook in Jerusalem in 1967.

Hazon Hageulah, "The Vision of Redemption," is a collection of statements by Rabbi Kook on the restoration of the Jewish people and the rebuilding of Eretz Yisrael. It was published by the Agudah Lehotzoat Sifre Harayah Kook in Jerusalem in 1941.

Igrot Harayah, "The Letters of Rabbi Abraham Isaac Ha-Kohen Kook," is a three-volume work covering Rabbi Kook's correspondence from the years 1888 to 1919. The first volume was published by the Agudah Lehotzoat Sifre Harayah Kook in Jerusalem in 1943; the second volume was published by the same organization with the assistance of the Mosad Harav Kook in Jerusalem in 1946; the third volume was published by the Mosad Harav Kook in Jerusalem in 1965.

Midot Harayah, "The Moral Principles of Rabbi Abraham Isaac Ha-Kohen Kook," printed together with *Musar Avikha*, "The Admonitions of A Father," Mosad Harav Kook, Jerusalem, 1971.

Orot Hakodesh, "The Lights of Holiness," is Rabbi Kook's most significant work. It consists of three volumes of short meditations on the mystery of God and man's life in a God-dominated universe. These were written originally in the form of a spiritual diary. The selections and construction of the three volumes was the work of his disciple David Ha-Kohen. The first two volumes were published by the Agudah Lehotzoat Sifre Harayah Kook, in Jerusalem, 1938; the third volume was published under the auspices of the same organization in Jerusalem in 1950.

Orot Hateshuvah, "The Lights of Penitence," is Rabbi Kook's most popular work. It consists of seventeen chapters on the role of penitence in the life of the individual and the world. The first edition appeared in Jerusalem in 1925. The most complete edition was published in 1966 in Jerusalem by the Yeshivot Bnei Akiva "Or Etzion" and Merkaz Shapiro.

Orot, "Lights," is a collection of essays, some of which appeared separately in journals or in booklet form. The earliest edition appeared in Jerusalem in 1925 under the auspices of *Degel Yerushalayim*, a movement Rabbi Kook launched to further his own philosophy of Judaism. It included *Orot Meofel* and *Orot*

Hathiah. A larger edition of this work was published by the Mosad Harav Kook in 1963, and it included an expanded version of the *Orot Meofel*, a group of essays entitled "Lemaalekh Hadeot Beyisrael," which appeared originally in 1912; a group of essays called "Zironim," which appeared earlier in 1914; and another group of essays entitled "Orot Yisrael," which was published in 1943. All our references to *Orot* are to the 1963 edition.

Olot Rayah, "The Offering of Rabbi Abraham Isaac Ha-Kohen Kook," a two-volume work that includes the full text of the Daily, Sabbath and Festival Prayer Book, the Passover Haggadah and the Ethics of the Fathers, with a running commentary by Rabbi Kook. The first volume, which has an introductory section on the significance of prayer in the life of piety, was published by the Mosad Harav Kook and the Agudah Lehotzoat Sifre Harayah Kook in Jerusalem in 1939; the second volume was published under the same auspices in Jerusalem in 1949.

"Talele Orot," "Fragments of Light," an essay that appeared originally in Hebrew under the title "Talele Orot" in the journal *Tahkemoni* in Berne, Switzerland, in 1910.

Shirat Harav, "The Poetry of the Rabbi," is a collection of the most significant poems of Rabbi Kook. The poems were edited by A. M. Habermann, with an introductory essay, and published in the journal *Sinai* in 1945.

Index to Foreword, Preface and Introductions

Gnosticism, xii.
God, cf. Unity; alienation from 25, 26; creation of, 2, 27; as Creator, 8, 22; essence of, 3, 9; existence of, 3, 133; help of, 31, 32; immediacy of, 3; knowledge of, xviii, 3, 6, 10, 246; light of, 16, 30, 32; is Love, 190; names of, xx, 11; nature of, 3, 11; nearness of xii; people of, 31; presence of, xv, xviii, 243; providence of, 244; quest for, 8, 12, 369; return to xiii, 18, 25, 31, 39; reverence for, xxiii, 27; service to, 28; thirst for, 1, 248; transcendence of, 27; ways of, xxiii; will of, 32; word of, 12.
Gordon, A.D., xxiv.
Grace, xii, xiv.
Greek philosophy, 2.
Grieve, 2.
Guide of the Perplexed, 243.

Habermann, A.M., 369.
Ha-kohen, David, 189. cf. also Cohen, David.
Halakhah, 5, 244, 368.
Halevi, Judah, xii, xiii, 2.
Hanir, 246, 390.
Harayah, 32.
Harmony, xiv, 6, 7, 8, 24.
Hasidism, xii, xiii, xxiii, 14, 131, 132, 247.
Hatarbut Hayisraelit, 247.
Hazon Hagewah, 10, 12, 17, 18, 28, 390.
Hebrew, xxi, 15, 17, 19.
Hebrew University, 17.
Heresy, xxiii.
Holiness, call to, 18; commitment to, 17; and enlightenment, 9; of existence, 26; goal of, 21; of God, 32; higher, xxiii, 8, 132; and Israel, 11, 15; and life, 11,

189; light of, xiii, xiv, 3, 8; and silence, 4, 5; sparks of, xiv, 16; and Torah, 13.
Holy Land, xi, 247.
Holy sparks, xiii, 7, 9, 13, 132.
Holy Spirit, xii.

Ibn Gabirol, xii.
Idealism, 23.
Idolatry, 3, 247.
Igrot Harayah, xxvii, 10-12, 17-19, 29, 31, 327-328, 390.
Ikve Hatzon, 13, 17, 25, 27-29, 390.
Illumination, xv, divine, 4, 191, 246; grasped, 247; and Jews, xix, 247; and Messiah, 23; and prophets, 243; and reason, 190; and sage, 244; source of, 189, 246.
Individualism, 6, 7.
Isaac, 12.
Isaiah, 11:9, 23; 62:2, xxii.
Ishmael, 12.
Islam, 2, 12.
Israel, xiii, xxv, 22, 29, 32; cf. Jews, Judaism.

Jacob, 12.
Jaffa, xviii, xxi, 2, 18, 32, 189.
Japanese, 19.
Jews, cf. Israel, Judaism Love; exile of, 27, 247; faith of, 2; and ghetto, xxi, 2; history of, xx; identity, 11, 12, 13, 245, 248; liberalism of, 20; monotheism of, 26, 191; and mysticism, xi, xii, xiii, xxii, 3, 4, 132; and nationalism, xviii, xxi, 10, 20, 247, 248; and parochialism, 12, 13; persecution of, xx, 13, 27; religion of, xi, 247; renewal of, xvii, xviii, 15; settlements, 10; spiritual state of, 14;

godliness, 10; growth in 4; hidden, 9, 25; of holiness, xiii, xiv, 3, 8; infinite, 8; of Israel, 29; of knowledge, 13; of life, xxiii; new, 4, 249; source of, xiii, 4, 10, 243, 247; of truth, 13.
Lights of Holiness, xxvii, 189-191, 391; cf. also *Orot Hakodesh*.
Lights of Penitence, xxvii, 39, 391; cf. also *Orot Hateshuvah*.
Loew, Rabbi Judah, 3.
London, 2, 189.
Love, for freedom, 21; for God, 8, 16, 28, 31, 190; of God, xiv; for Jews, 16, 17, 20, 30; universal, 7, 8, 16, 30, 131, 369.

Maimonides, xii, 2, 245.
Man, anguish of, xix, 5; ascent of, 26, 28, 29; destiny of, 24, 190; happiness of, 11, 246; heroism of, 10; nature of, 23, 24, 25, 131, 190; original state of, 22, 23; perfection of, 8, 9, 14, 22, 39; vision of, 189.
Marxism, 244, 327.
Mercy, 24, 31, 32.
Messiah, xi, xii, xiii, xviii, xx, xxiv, 11, 23; false, 247.
Middle Ages, xii, xix.
Midot Harayah, xxvii, 131-132, 391.
Mitzvot, 13.
Mizrahi, 17, 18, 19.
Moral Principles, xxvii, 131-132, 391.
Morality, and animals, 249; categories, 131, 132; concern for, 10; and holiness, 5; perfection of, 23, 246; and religion, 131; source of, 7; state of, 22.
Musar Avikha, 131, 391.
Mysticism, xi, xii, 3, 4, 19, 132,

189, 245, 246, 248, 369.

Nahman, Rabbi of Bratzlav, 131.
Neoplatonism, xii.
Noah, 22.

Old Settlement, 17.
Olat Rayah, 6, 21, 23, 392.
Orot, 3, 10, 12, 17, 20, 24, 26, 243, 391-392.
Orot Hakodesh, xxvii, 5, 7, 8, 9, 13, 21-25, 33, 189-191, 391.
Orot Hateshuvah, xxvii, 25, 26, 39, 391.
Orot Meofel, 17, 20, 391.
Orot Yisrael, 17, 24, 26, 391-392.
Orthodoxy, xiii, xxi, xxii, 14, 20.

Palestine, 2, 10, 16, 17, 18, 189, 245, 369.
"Pangs of Cleansing", 245-246.
Particularity, 6, 7, 24, 39, 248.
Penitence, act of, 14, 25; and healing of world, 26; and perfection, 39; source of, 25; way of, 12.
Perfection, growth in, 9, 22, 24; higher, 8, 22; of life, 8, 13, 23, 247; of man, xiv, 8, 9, 14, 22, 39; and religion, 3; striving for, 21, 24, 25, 244; of world, 6, 14, 24.
Philo, xii, 2.
Pietists, 10, 18, 327.
Piety, 370.
Piyyut, 369.
Pleroma, xii.
Plotinus, xii.
Poems, 369-370, 392.
Prague, 3.
Prophecy, xi, xv, 11, 14, 243.

Rabbinate, 2, 18, 19, 189, 369.
Rabinowitz, xxi.
Rafael, Yitzak, xxviii.

Redemption, xxii, xxiii; of Jews,
xi, 10, 14; of man, xi, 9;
messianic, xiii; of world, xxiii,
14.
Religion, and ascent, xiv, 28, 29,
245; essence of, 2; hostility to,
10; other, 12, 28; and
perfection, 3, 131; place of, 28;
purging of, 10, 245; tolerance
of, 246; validity of, 246, 249;
viability of, 248.
Remorse, 25, 26.
Righteousness, 27, 244.
"Road to Renewal", 246-248, 390.
"A Row of Plants," 243.

"The Sage Is More Important
Than the Prophet", 243-244.
Soul, desires of, 9, 25; and
existence, 5; individuality of,
190; light in, 5, 243; perfection
of, 39; potency of, 245.
"Souls of Chaos", 244.
Sacrifices, animal, 23.
Secularism, 10, 11, 16, 17.
Sefer ha-Midot, 131.
Shabbatai, Zevi, xii, 247.
Shintoism, 19.
Shlesinger, 31.
Sin, source of, 7.
Socialism, xxi.
Song, 22.
Spirit, enlightened, 21; of
generation, 13; of God, 15;
holy, 14; maturing of, 28.
Stavsky, Abraham, 19, 20.
Switzerland, 189, 249.

Tahkemoni, 23, 29, 248, 392.
Takhemoni, 17.
Takkana, 5.
"Talele Orot", 23, 29, 392.
Talmud, xi, 13, 26, 132.
Teilhard de Chardin, xiv.
Tel Aviv, 17.

Temple, 23.
"A Thirst for the Living God",
243.
Torah, goal of, 13; knowledge of,
14; light of, 16, 29; and man's
perfection, 190, 247; and
mysticism, 245; precepts of, 32;
soul of, 14; study of, 13, 15,
248; wisdom of, xxviii; and
world, 28.
Tradition, xiii, xxii, 4, 5, 10, 12,
23, 243, 244, 245, 247, 327.
Truth, 8, 9, 13, 190, 246.

Unity, xiv, of existence, xviii, 7,
8, 9, 23, 26, 369; of God, xv,
11, 27; grace of, 29; of life, 24.
Universality, 6, 7, 12, 13, 21, 22,
29, 191, 248.

Voice of Prophecy, xiii.
Volozhin, xx.

Wisdom, xxviii, 6, 9, 24.
" Works of Creation", 244-245.
World, chaotic, 7, 8, 244; defects
of, 7, 21; and enlightenment,
22; fragmented, xiv; perfection
of, 6, 26, 39, 131, 246; service
to, 28, 29, 191; transformed,
27.

Yeshivah, 17, 18.
Yeshivah Shaarei Torah, 17.
Yoma 66a, 26.

Zaddikim, xii, 190.
"Zironim", 243, 391.
Zion, 28, 369.
Zionism, coalition, 18; endeavors,
27; Labor, 20; movement, xiii,
xvii, xx, xxi, 11, 19, 20, 244,
327; religious, xi, xxi, 18;
revisionists, 20; secular, xxi.
Zohar, xxii.
Zoimel, 2.

Index to Texts

voice, 222; word, 75; yearning for, 322.

Ecclesiastes, cf. also Kohelet; 7:27, 161.
Eden, Garden of, 60, 122, 148, 231, 352.
Egypt, 83, 149, 216, 286, 313, 316, 317.
Elijah, Gaon of Vilna, 298, 339.
Elisha ben Avuah, 340.
Elite, 223-224.
Elohim, 81.
Enlightenment, divine, 125; of existence, 230; external, 206, 301; and faith, 262; higher, 205, 225; inner, 206; and Israel, 295, 315, 338-339, 350; life of, 208; and messianiac age, 51; and penitence, 74, 114; progress in, 50, 77; public, 75; and religion, 180; of souls, 70, 71, 173, 220, 274; state of, 263, 305, 318.
En Sof, 88, 149, 208, 211, 221, 222.
Eretz Yisrael, 154, 260, 298, 316, 332, 342, 351, 358.
Erubin, 13b, 340; 54a, 361.
Esau, 339.
Eternalists, 305, 306.
Evil, absence of, 176; attributes of, 160; avoidance of, 70, 219; awareness of, 45; is evil, 85; and good, 71, 80, 133, 160, 237, 297, 345; grief for, 123; hatred for, 60, 136, 137; inclination to, 192, 231; layers of, 62; and melancholy, 64; overcoming of, 78, 177, 279, 339; and past, 58; protection from, 212; purging of, 53; realm of, 82, 94; source of, 97, 108, 167, 183, 339; weakened, 164, 167.
Evolution, 220-221, 231-232, 306, 313.

Exile, 78, 284, 289, 294, 295, 299, 301, 322, 323, 350.
Existence, cf. Unity; all of, 45, 47, 63, 69, 70, 86, 117, 156, 228, 230, 232, 282, 286, 292, 293, 308; continuity of, 315; and divine presence, 207; earthly, 59; and evolution, 221, 231, 313; of God, 162, 266, 267; and good, 69, 292, 293; happiness of, 69, 80, 221; and harmony, 63, 64, 65, 71; ideal form of, 49, 279; and knowledge, 192; love for, 227; mystery of, 257; nature of, 50, 58, 69, 136, 363; particular, 81, 87, 288; and psychic reality, 287, 289; purpose of, 121, 315; rhythm of, 284; as sinless, 87; source of, 263, 267, 289; stability of, 276; transcendent, 287; truth of, 218, 283; universal, 80, 288; unrefined, 219, 278; yearning of, 56.
Exodus, 313, 316, 317.
Exodus, 3:14, 267; 15:18, 146; 16:7, 233; 17:14, 137; 19:5-6, 210, 28:5,8, 319; 31:6, 207; 33:16, 315.
Exodus Rabbah, 7, 169; end, 119.
Ezekiel, 156, 309; 1:14, 215, 222; 1:22, 265; 1:24, 80; 16:63, 318; 33:11, 64; 33:19, 72; 36:24-29, 280; 37:13, 12, 265.

Faith, 140-149, 261-269; in divine, 287, 291; essence of, 262; fire of, 292; glory of, 215; in God, 140, 141, 143, 146, 203, 261, 264, 279, 299; and holiness, 121, 146, 265; and illumination, 143, 144; insufficiency of, 193, 280, 355, 357; of Israel, 89, 117, 274; levels of, 140, 148,

Heresy, 176, 261, 262, 271, 279, 286, 340, 342, 355.
High Holiday liturgy, 314.
High Priest, 108.
Holiness, 217-218; cf. also Light, Soul, Perfection; and action, 58, 59; basis of, 225; as builder, 217-218; degrees of, 53, 94, 100, 101, 117, 142, 159, 160, 213, 214, 237; desecration of, 90, 212; as destroyer, 217-218; emanation of, 192; and faith, 121, 146; growth in, 212, 232, 233; and holy sparks, 158, 219; and humility, 364; influence on, 304; joy of, 102, 382; life of, 83, 88, 283, 309, 386; and penitence, 48, 61, 121; and pride, 154, 155; pursuit of, 151, 219, 237; of reality, 208; recognition of, 68; revealed, 45, 206; and sanctification, 140; source of, 79; stirring of, 51; supernal, 77; and Torah, 52, 354; treasure of, 104; vessels of, 269; and will, 67, 69, 178, 192; and wisdom, 192; world of, 73, 74, 104; of zaddikim, 219, 220, 297.
Holy Land, 299, 333, 334, 337, 342, 343, 347.
Holy of holies, 88, 155, 214, 279.
Holy One, 203, 207; attributes of, 156; estimation of, 110; and Israel, 83, 89, 123; kindness of, 108; and new creation, 84; as sustainer, 160.
Holy sparks, 89, 101, 158-160, 337; ascent of, 230, 252, 274, 286; as beneficial, 160; descent of, 159; guarding of, 215; hidden, 274, 278; and light, 273, 274, 277, 294, 358, 362, 379; presence of, 89, 158, 273;

scattered, 219, 275, 279; and wisdom, 223.
Honor, 171-172; of God, 50, 51; of man, 174, 175.
Hosea, 2:1, 350; 14:2, 113.
Hoshen Mishpat, 93.
Hullin, 60a, 121, 89a, 364.
Humility, 177-179, 209; basis of, 362; cultivation of, 99, 155; degrees of, 202; depth of, 75; and enlightenment, 264, 301; and esteem, 114; and fear of God, 167, 175; and honor of God, 171; joy of, 153, 233, 364; and perfection, 177, 361; and pride, 154, 174, 178; and union with God, 74.

Ibn Ezra, 236.
Ideals, 276, 277, 304, 307, 316, 322, 323.
Idolatry, 88, 89, 113, 115, 156, 171, 179, 236, 253, 255, 261, 265, 270, 271, 281, 289, 294, 295, 296, 304, 331, 339.
Igrot ha-Rambam, 330.
Igrot Rayah, 339.
Ikve ha-Zon, 330.
Illumination, divine, 116, 117, 140, 173, 195, 203, 232, 309, 343; of fear, 165, 166; from God, 352, 385; and nation, 279, 293, 312; and penitence, 45, 53, 60, 61, 74, 85, 126; and prayer, 116; psychic, 290, 295; of reason, 48, 144; of righteous, 124, 125, 182, 208; of soul, 45, 97, 100, 109, 116, 122, 153, 176, 197, 214-215, 226, 230, 257, 261, 268, 293, 295, 296, 306, 351, 363; spiritual, 225, 231, 290-295, 317; of Torah, 77, 142, 220, 349, 354; of will, 70, 126; of wisdom, 71, 194; of

world, 65, 142, 144, 208, 213, 309, 356.

Improvement, 186; and evolution, 220, 221; of existence, 273; of man, 201; of society, 345.

Imsoni, Rabbi Simeon, 296.

Individualism, 307-308, 315.

Intention, 211-212, 237, 276.

Isaac, 142, 162, 177, 339.

Isaiah, 2:3, 210; 2:17-18, 364; 2:18, 220; 11:2, 91, 320; 11:9, 196; 11:10, 175; 14:27, 80; 25:8, 52, 175; 26:2, 83; 26:4, 121; 27:13, 285; 29:9, 123; 29:13, 172; 29:18, 114, 220, 258; 30:18, 89; 30:24, 319, 33:14, 257; 35:5, 196; 35:7, 66; 35:10, 180; 40:4, 115; 40:12, 119; 40:31, 178; 51:3, 148; 51:16, 192; 55:3-5, 89; 57:19, 193; 58:2, 113; 58:12, 97; 64:3, 136; 66:2, 170; 66:13, 48, 62.

Ishmael, 339.

Israel, cf. Community, Jews, Judaism; children of, 210, 236; chosen, 280; deliverence of, 53; eternity of, 260; faith of, 283, 339; fugitives of, 323; glory of, 345; God of, 89, 283, 286, 299; God's inheritance, 143; history of, 253, 289-302; house of, 264, 301, 333, 341, 350; and humility, 364; land of, 265; light of, 274, 279, 285, 293, 298, 312, 317, 350; love for, 228, 323, 350; nation of, 91, 276-286, 287-302; and penitence, 56, 99; people of, 50, 55-57, 83, 92, 127, 211, 259, 290, 291, 293, 330, 351; princes of, 300; return to God, 113; song of, 229; soul of, 294, 296, 299, 301; wisdom of, 118.

Israel ben Elizer, 298, 337.

Jacob, 57, 111, 142, 143, 162, 176, 210, 339, 346.

Jeremiah, 2:6, 216; 3:12, 113; 5:12, 170; 10:16, 143; 10:25, 143; 23:27, 163; 31:17, 298; 31:34, 317.

Jerusalem, 78, 118, 119, 210, 236, 260, 286, 290, 299, 334, 335, 337.

Jesse, 175.

Jews, cf. Community, Israel, Judaism; chosen, 289; cleansing of, 92, 254, 350; deliverance of, 193, 356; destiny of, 135, 137, 289, 290, 317; and divine sensitivity, 289; faithfulness of, 90, 142; heritage of, 310; history of, 305, 313, 314, 316; and holiness, 86, 146, 280, 290, 333, 345; illumination of, 356, 358; and integration, 311; lost, 169; love for, 135, 345, 346, 350, 351; and messiah, 136; as nation, 271, 276-286, 287-302; and nature, 57, 127, 151; penitence of, 126, 266; pride of, 304; religion of, 267-268, 279; renewal of, 296, 303-323; restoration of, 57, 117, 128, 337, 352; soul of, 50, 92, 107, 141, 199, 271, 280, 285, 289, 293, 322; and study, 291-292; and study of texts, 294-301; survival of, 89; and Torah, 77, 86, 146, 199, 336, 351; and universality, 310; and world, 143.

Job, 11:6, 200; 20:15, 89; 22:28, 142, 184; 28:7, 216; 36:3, 236.

Joel, 3:1, 254.

Johanan, Rabbi, 340.

Joseph, 83.

Joseph ben Gator, 330.

Judah, 323, 330.

Judaism, cf. Jews, Israel;

affirmation of, 305; concepts of, 270, 305, 306, 311; continuity of, 284; defending of, 305, 321; disharmony in, 339; interpretation of, 304; realm of, 296; as religions, 322; renewal, 303-323; strengthening of, 342; study of, 322.

Judges, 4:2,3, 236; 5:3, 151; 5:31, 174.

Judgment, Day of, 337.

Justice, abandoned, 88; absolute, 77, 86, 93; acts of, 211; ascending of, 78, 137, 233; demanded, 54, 317; desire for, 91, 309, 346; divine, 93, 94; on earth, 93; of God, 89, 91, 106, 290; of holy king, 71; impediments to, 76; and providence, 81; sense of, 320; striving for, 50, 60, 86, 121, 141, 338, 346; ways of, 329.

King, 71, 90, 229, 285, 377.

1 Kings, 14:9, 160.

᳹ 2 Kings, 21:1-18, 115.

Kohelet, cf. also Ecclesiastes; 7:20, 55; 12:1-2, 88.

Kohelet Rabbah, 11:12, 346.

Kolel, 334.

Kook, Rabbi, 111, 119, 137, 156, 175, 230, 330, 339.

Kook, Samuel, 337.

Lamentations, 3:23, 214, 363.

Law, cf. also *halakha*; abandoned, 58; branches of, 94; civil, 93; decisions of, 334; divine, 58, 320; and divine word, 75; of God, 58, 281, 283; of the good, 293; of life, 43; and Lord, 63, 120; of morals, 43, 86, 212; of nature, 43; and sages, 254; and

slaughter, 319; study of, 329; superficial, 238; and world of order, 256.

Lebanon, 273, 285.

Letters of Kook, to his son, 329-331, 365-366; to David Ha-kohen, 361-364; to Rabbi Abraham Resnik, 359-360; to Rabbi Avigdor Rivlin, 332-333; to Rabbi Duber Milstein, 344-347; to Rabbi H. Elazar Hakohen Bihovsky, 342-343; to Rabbi Jehiel Mikhal Tikazinski, 334-335; to Rabbi Judah Leib Seltzer, 354-358; to Rabbi Pinhas Ha-kohen, 336-341.

Leviticus, 11:44, 140; 17:13, 318; 22:28, 318.

Liberalism, 278.

Liberation, through Jews, 356; joy of, 88; and Messiah, 264; and penitence, 61, 63, 78, 115, 116, 117; permanent, 91; of self, 205, 232, 291; from sin, 46, 63, 95, 126; of soul, 93, 212, 216, 233, 386; of word, 193.

Life, of all, 65, 261, 362; claims of, 212; collective, 278; creation of, 315; essence of, 163, 164, 201, 265, 287; eternal, 209, 340; force of, 56, 70, 73, 75, 79, 84, 128, 182, 251, 259, 306, 313, 314; fountain of, 305, 306; fragmented, 90, 272; glory of, 223; and God, 56, 156-157, 176, 250; goodness, 263; happiness of, 64, 74, 75, 122, 151, 159, 176, 211, 259, 286, 315; higher, 304; and ideals, 277, 284, 315; inner, 47, 58, 147, 202, 209; laws of, 43; levels of, 312; light of, 65, 70, 75, 117, 120, 136, 147, 192, 237, 273, 277, 313, 315, 322, 364; meaning of, 136,

193; mending of, 45, 55, 167; mystery of, 82, 114, 223; nature of, 55, 63, 136, 316; new, 363; obstacles of, 202; oppression of, 320; perfection of, 51, 55, 145, 183, 224, 310; practical, 90, 93, 94, 199, 202, 300, 309; process of, 69, 70, 81, 87, 104, 136, 147; purpose of, 322; radiance of, 141, 207, 209; renewed, 88, 120; service to, 306; source of, 46, 49, 51, 52, 57, 86, 87, 163, 182, 192, 195, 207, 268; spirit of, 308; spiritual, 53, 54, 58, 68, 90, 93, 98, 120, 123, 186, 204, 207, 276, 287, 288, 296, 308, 309, 311, 312, 357, 373; state of, 214; transformed, 69, 165, 348; treasure of, 41, 104, 164, 209, 235, 314, 383; tree of, 114, 212, 215; true, 60, 283; values of, 141; vision of, 309, 310; way of, 86, 93, 224, 265, 271, 273, 284, 299, 308.

Light, cf. Life, Penitence, Soul; augmenting of, 287, 353; of compassion, 235; convulsion of, 268; degrees of, 53; descent of, 278; desire for, 251, 274, 373; dimmed, 276, 277, 317; divine, 47, 56, 61, 64, 70, 72, 79, 87, 92, 98, 141, 142, 145, 153, 155, 173, 179, 182, 203, 207, 215, 222, 238, 261, 265, 273; 283, 297, 299, 311, 313, 343, 349, 350, 358, 363, 373; of the dream, 218; emanation of, 216, 288; of En Sof, 88, 208, 212, 221-222; essence of, 269; and eternity, 209, 277, 286, 339, 374; exalted, 293, 378; of faith, 142, 144, 149, 180, 262, 265, 274; of God, 45, 58, 74, 80, 85, 91, 99, 103, 112, 114, 116, 117, 118, 135, 138, 144, 153, 193, 211-213, 230, 250, 265, 274, 283, 286, 335, 338, 345, 350, 358, 374, 377, 384, 385; of the good, 82, 92, 138, 235, 274, 293; hidden, 261; higher, 268, 374; of holiness, 65, 70, 79, 82, 85, 86, 103, 108, 125, 163, 176, 220, 238, 295, 312, 381, 382; of humanity, 278, 282; of the ideal, 201, 276, 277; of illumination, 317; infinite, 75, 256, 281, 373, 384; inner, 303, 304, 374; of Jews, 333, 351; obstructions to, 61, 67, 75, 76; of righteous, 173, 215; source of, 274, 285, 289, 311, 362; supernal, 76, 77, 194, 195, 274; of the Torah, 52, 93, 94, 97, 120, 141, 198, 220, 238, 339, 349; treasure of, 315, 379; universal, 206; of universe, 314.

London, 365.

Lord, cf. Divine, God; courage in, 202; courts of, 251; deliverance through, 116, 289, 386; denied, 170; fear of, 89, 166, 175; forgiveness of, 46; goodness of, 64, 85, 289; help of, 116; of hosts, 290; joy in, 123, 180, 214, 233; kindness of, 46, 47; knowledge of, 196, 254, 265, 318; law of, 63, 120; light of, 386; love for, 350; mercy of, 135, 289, 332; name of, 89, 121, 136, 143, 209, 275, 330; nearness of, 113; peace of, 193; presence of, 110; return to, 117, 127; serving of, 286, 316, 337, 356; strength of, 232; teaching of, 93; Temple of, 80; trust in, 121, 178; and universality, 273; vision of, 218; word of, 210; works of, 136, 260.

Love, 135-139, 226-227; cf.
Penitence; for all, 135, 136,
137, 138, 139, 140, 155, 209,
219, 238, 277, 279; descent of,
227; divine, 62, 251, 300; and
faith, 140; for God, 78, 103,
111, 135, 136, 139, 151, 152,
165, 166, 172, 174, 177, 203,
226, 280, 331, 373, 377; for
good, 60, 226, 238; and
Hasidism, 298; for Jews, 135,
345, 346, 350, 351; as joy of
life, 315; for life, 166, 207, 315;
pattern of, 59; in penitent, 48;
and repentence, 77; source of,
227, 238, 383; sufferings of,
218; and transgressions, 71; for
truth, 112, 299; virtue of, 181;
for world, 226.

Mahzike Hadat, 365.
Maimonides, 98, 303-306, 330.
Malachi, 1:3, 339; 3:7, 127.
Man, cf. Soul; alienation of, 46,
152, 155, 170, 237; anguish of,
64, 67, 170, 204, 214, 250, 263;
ascent of, 86, 148, 152, 170,
174, 183, 206, 208, 209, 214,
222, 223, 231, 232; deliverance
of, 114, 193, 201, 356; as divine
image, 136, 137; fall of, 318; as
fragmented, 316; freedom of,
64, 65, 78, 119, 131, 161; future
of, 195; and harmony, 63;
healing of, 46, 61, 63; as image
of God, 85, 280; integrity of,
75; joy of, 70, 159, 161, 170,
203, 204, 209, 226, 232, 233,
261, 265, 277, 300, 302, 311,
364; liberation of, 264; nature
of, 44, 75, 155, 167, 183, 319,
339; newness of, 192;
obligations of, 93, 99; original
state of, 87; peace of, 46, 54,

60, 63, 68, 70, 202, 203, 250;
perfection of, 152, 199-203,
206, 226, 311, 313; primitive,
282, 314, 317; purging of, 97,
289; sin of, 100, 278; as Son of
man, 94; song of, 228; as spark,
362; transformation of, 45, 48,
49, 159, 288; value of, 82, 172;
vitalization of, 314; weakened,
167.
Manasseh of Judah, 115.
Margolit, J.L., 359.
Meir, Rabbi, 340.
Melancholy, and evil, 64, 100; and
penitence, 102, 346; and sin,
66, 67.
Mendelsohn, Moses, 359.
Mercy, 101, 125; divine, 46, 70,
102, 147; of God, 65, 102, 103,
106, 112, 119, 121, 150, 160,
185, 236, 290; of holy king, 71;
light of, 95, 280; of Lord, 135,
289, 332; of shekinah, 157;
supernal, 81; for world, 158.
Messiah, age of, 51, 84, 229, 255,
292; coming of, 52, 125, 147;
false, 297; and liberation, 264;
light of, 53, 97, 117, 175; and
penance, 100; spirit of, 136; and
Torah, 339, 352.
Micah, 2:12, 176; 5:6, 64.
Michal, Rabbi Zevi, 330.
Michelson, Rabbi Uri, 329.
Midrash, 60, 119, 121, 169.
Milstein, Rabbi Duber, 344.
Mishneh Torah, 98, 304, 330.
Mitzvot, 292.
Modesty, 181.
Morality, absolute, 307, 308;
attributes of, 143, 158, 186,
361; claims of, 72, 95, 96;
commitment to, 150, 151;
concern for, 264, 285;
correction of, 45, 105, 133, 186,

290; course of, 47, 140; deeds of, 211; defects of, 92, 106, 152, 156, 231, 253, 266; duty of, 318; and faith, 198; and humility, 178; impulse of, 87, 93, 283, 317; of Jewish people, 57, 118; laws of, 43, 86; light of, 96; norm of, 58, 212; pattern of, 75, 138, 181, 238, 283, 307; perfection of, 54, 151, 231, 290, 318; principles of, 163; recognition of, 68, 266; refinement of, 291, 293; sense of, 54, 58, 65, 68, 94, 95, 143, 150, 164, 199, 224, 231, 232, 288, 307, 317, 318, 319, 320; severance of, 65; source of, 315, 318; state of, 73, 91, 136, 150; virtues of, 50, 164; and will, 70.

Moses, 143, 210, 217, 218, 233, 254, 255, 267.

Moses ben Menahem, 359.

Moses of Dessau, 359, cf. Mendelsohn, Moses.

Moslems, 339.

Mysticism, of commandments, 259; devotees of, 199; dimension of, 194, 279; and knowledge, 77, 209, 268, 351, 355; summons to, 192, 194; and tales, 331; and Torah, 52, 77, 193, 194, 199, 338; vision of, 194, 199, 219; of world, 193.

Nature, cf. Man, World; of being, 362; concept of, 127; and education, 140; of existence, 50, 58, 69, 136, 363; human, 44, 57, 58, 75, 122, 167, 179, 319, 339; laws of, 43; of life, 55, 63, 136, 316; and penitence, 43, 44, 47, 60; purging of, 133; of reality, 196; of soul, 69, 107, 113, 331; of spiritual reality,

287; and wisdom, 192; workings of, 55.

Nazarite vows, 55.

Nedarim, 10a, 55.

Nehemiah, 8:10, 180.

Niddah, 73a, 254.

Numbers, 6:11, 55; 12:8, 218, 254; 15:38, 319; 23:27, 118.

Offerings, of sacrifice, 89, 110, 316; sin, 105.

Orenstein, Rabbi, 330.

Orthodox, 332, 333, 355.

Passover, 108.

Penitence, cf. Creation, Illumination, Will; acts of, 76, 77, 94, 103, 123; aids to, 92; and contemplation, 73, 78, 98; concern for, 68, 69, 71, 76; cosmic, 82; delay in, 108; delight of, 44, 48, 53, 58, 60, 70, 73, 79, 100, 109, 121, 122; desire for, 50, 56, 61, 65, 76, 78, 97-99, 109, 116, 117; emergence of, 50, 51, 74, 119, 214; and faith, 43, 44, 61, 149; forms of, 84, 103, 113, 115, 123, 150, 154, 266, 346; and future, 61; general, 47-49, 53, 82; higher, 53, 88, 91, 98, 102, 107, 114, 118, 119, 123, 124, 125, 150, 154, 159, 215, 276; as honoring God, 50, 51; levels of, 67, 70, 87, 105, 107, 110, 111, 114, 117, 123, 124, 159; light of, 54, 56, 60, 61, 63, 67, 69, 71, 80, 96, 100, 107, 115, 127; from love, 46, 61, 84, 85, 93, 101, 107, 100, 112, 122, 123, 150, 169, 346, 355, 363; lower, 124, 154; masters of, 69; mystery of, 81; and nature, 43, 44, 47, 60; need for, 85, 92,

1 Samuel, 2:3, 352; 15:29, 260; 24:13, 64.
2 Samuel, 7:23, 149; 23:1, 361.
Sanctuary, 108, 309.
Sanhed, cf. Sanhedrin.
Sanhedrin, 37a, 142; 44a, 350; 59b, 316.
Sefer Yezirah, 195.
Sefira, 79, 80, 194, 313, 338.
Self, anxiety of, 68; assessment, 173; deliverance of, 68; and evil, 62; and good, 123; and harmony, 65; higher, 243; liberation of, 205; love, 168; newness of, 192, 361; perfection of, 68, 205; song of, 228; spiritual, 80, 155; weakened, 72.
Shabbat, 31a, 337; 88b, 151, 174; 118a, 314; 137a, 105.
Shabbetai Zevi, 297.
Sharon, 381.
Shekinah, anguish of, 65; and penitence, 99, 107; ways of, 157.
Shir Hashirim Rabbah, 1:11, 229.
Shofar, 110.
Simhat Torah, 73.
Sin, against another, 62, 67, 76, 95; and anxiety, 66, 67, 106, 123, 382; atonement for, 55; avoidance of, 73, 80; awareness of, 45, 115; burden of, 46, 85, 88, 120; of community, 44, 85, 100; fear of, 57, 103, 168, 169, 197; forgiveness of, 44, 46-50, 56, 62, 78, 106, 300; and good, 83, 273; healing of, 46; of individual, 44, 46, 47, 100; inevitability of, 55; as obstruction, 61, 67, 72, 74, 76, 77, 85, 91-92; and pain, 96; of past, 45, 106, 122, 170; penance for, 100; removal of, 54, 80,

119, 302; repentance of, 44, 48, 50, 56, 57, 59, 62, 67, 68, 77, 95, 107, 108, 110, 120, 345; state of, 116; transformed, 45, 60, 63, 71, 72, 79, 83, 84, 86, 100, 101, 109, 152.
Singer, Zvi, 308.
Singularity, 272, 273.
Sisera, 236.
Society, cf. also Community; good of, 85, 234; happiness of, 161, 166; harm to, 291; illumination of, 293; improvement of, 345; and morality, 307; perfection of, 205, 211, 227, 290, 310, 315, 316, 356; redemption of, 128; reformation of, 50, 266; sin of, 85.
Song, 228-229, 299, 305.
Song of Songs, 229.
Solomon, 229.
Sotah, 49b, 255.
Soul, cf. Freedom, Illumination, Israel, Jews; of all souls, 117; anguish of, 46, 49, 63, 65, 66, 98, 102, 113, 122, 123, 150, 159, 204, 282, 285, 299, 340, 355; ascent of, 87, 91, 94, 113, 159, 164, 202, 212, 214, 216, 227, 230, 231, 250, 252, 267, 373, 377; and body, 193, 222, 225; and chaos, 256-258; cleansing of, 66, 67, 77, 76, 91, 92, 118; of a creator, 216; desires of, 261, 371; discernment of, 79; divine, 92, 146, 302; essence of, 141, 215, 306; and evil, 64; glory in, 264; and good, 69, 85, 282, 283; and harmony, 71; health of, 53; heroism of, 61, 85, 114, 139, 258, 280, 286, 288; hidden, 376; higher, 206, 215, 234, 278; holiness of, 51, 58, 70, 115,

and penitence, 41, 43, 47, 61, 92; practical, 102, 110, 354, 357; principles of, 48, 53, 57, 77, 86, 108, 127, 137, 146, 158, 166, 170, 171, 262, 339; promises forgiveness, 44; revelation of, 199, 200, 260, 314; as resurrection, 313; riches of, 352; soul of, 357; source of, 183, 209; study of, 52, 57, 61, 62, 73, 74, 99, 103, 106, 108, 110, 138, 139, 154, 164, 169, 170, 182, 197, 198, 206, 213, 222, 231, 259, 301, 302, 330, 331, 338, 352, 357, 362, 382; sweetness of, 107, 339; and truth, 112; violation of, 57; way of, 95, 96, 146, 344; as word, 75, 154.

Tosefot, Gittin, 41b, 344.

Tosefot, Sanhedrin, 26b, 344.

Tradition, delight of, 378; improvement of, 288, 290; of Israel, 298; of religion, 47, 141, 145, 165; and study, 295.

Transgressions, erased, 48; and faith, 146; and love, 71; of the tribes, 83; turned from, 346.

Truth, abandoned, 88; ascent to, 73, 173, 233; and faith, 179; and fear of God, 168; about God, 147; life of, 237; light of, 112, 192; and penitence, 112; prophets of, 217; search for, 217, 273, 338, 379; source of, 112.

Unity, of all existence, 194, 225, 226, 227, 314; disrupted, 71; divine, 49; of God, 211, 225, 264, 272, 289, 311; of humanity, 272, 317; of life, 250, 321; and light, 85, 251, 352; of man with all existence, 63, 64, 65; of man with divine, 313; of mysticism, 195; of novelty and humility, 363; obscured, 195; of particular with universal, 52; spiritual, 196; vision of, 312; of soul and creation, 380; of world, 86, 225, 227.

Universality, 272, 273, 276, 362.

Weisel, Naphtali, 359.

Will, cf. Good; ascent of, 67, 94, 113, 183; and delight, 221; divine, 135; exalted, 70; of existence, 86; freedom of, 64, 65, 72, 119, 120, 174, 213; of God, 135, 146, 150, 341, 383; and holiness, 67, 69, 183, 214; of holy king, 71; light of, 183, 184; of man, 180; mending of, 45, 86; nature of, 210; and penitence, 59, 61, 69, 70, 72, 84, 88, 96, 113, 126; perfection of, 177, 206; and pride, 153; purification of, 67, 77, 96, 112, 183; strengthened, 71, 72, 84, 88, 108, 112, 166, 183; transforming of, 49; universal, 56; value of, 211; weakening of, 71-73, 75, 77, 79, 87, 94, 105, 164, 251.

Wisdom, cf. Illumination; of being, 88; degrees of, 53; divine, 73, 350; emanation of, 79, 80; eternal, 316; and fear of God, 162, 166; hidden, 383; of the holy, 192, 224; and intention, 211; light of, 109, 147; of Lord, 338; and mysticism, 194; pursuit of, 62, 99, 114, 151, 169, 204, 213, 224; revelation of, 292; of sages, 255; spirit of, 293, 321; source of, 120, 166, 224; and will, 67, 192; worldly, 192; and understanding, 207.

World, all, 193, 229, 231, 252; of chaos, 256-258; creation of, 55, 57-59, 81, 86, 200, 338; decline of, 219, 220; deliverence of, 114, 193, 356; disharmony in, 339; elevation of, 210; as emanation, 112, 124; evil of, 83, 125; and evolution, 220, 229; existential, 252; forgiven, 48, 50, 56; fullness of, 310; good to, 200; grandeur of, 251; happiness of, 60, 65, 69, 80; healed by penitence, 48, 54, 55, 56, 57, 61, 65, 67, 69, 70, 78, 82, 84, 99, 103, 109, 124, 126, 127, 341; illumination of, 65, 142, 144, 208, 213, 309, 356; light in, 56, 125, 149, 175, 208, 209, 218, 268, 350, 351, 375; mystical dimensions of, 73, 74, 77; nature of, 125, 183, 220, 229; of order, 256; perfection of, 49, 52, 56, 57, 69, 125, 135, 137, 148, 158, 201, 202, 212, 218, 226, 258, 266, 290, 356; purging of, 218; redemption of, 266; reforming of, 51, 143, 163, 165, 211, 218; service to, 97, 124, 186; spiritual, 82, 194-196, 250, 252, 304, 312; stability of, 208; suffering of, 171, 263; transformed, 48, 53, 82, 277; unity of, 86, 225, 227.

Worship, 103, 115.

Yakor, David ben Zeev, 358.
Yakum of Zerorot, 142.
Yeshivah, 338.
Yoma, 75a, 186, 86a, 48, 56, 100.
Yose of Shuta, 142.
YHWH, 350.

Zaddikim, 149, 182, 219, 220, 232, 268, 297, 300.
Zechariah, 8:22-23, 289; 9:7, 274, 339.
Zephaniah, 3:9, 89.
Zion, 91, 126, 210, 218, 260, 286, 299, 330, 335, 363.
Zionist Movement, 322, 334.
Zohar, I, 103a, 267; I, 146a, 162; II, 85a, 262; II, 162b, 50; II, 227b, 64; III, 27b, 229; III, 110a, 262; III, 256b, 338; Tikkune Zohar, 10, 13, 229; 60, 147.